DIAMOND HEART

Book Four

Books by A. H. Almaas

Essence with *The Elixir of Enlightenment: The Diamond Approach to Inner Realization*

Facets of Unity: The Enneagram of Holy Ideas

The Inner Journey Home: Soul's Realization of the Unity of Reality

Luminous Night's Journey: An Autobiographical Fragment

Diamond Mind Series

Volume 1. *The Void: Inner Spaciousness and Ego Structure*

Volume 2. *The Pearl Beyond Price: Integration of Personality into Being: An Object Relations Approach*

Volume 3. *The Point of Existence: Transformations of Narcissism in Self-Realization*

Diamond Heart Series

Book One. *Elements of the Real in Man*

Book Two. *The Freedom to Be*

Book Three. *Being and the Meaning of Life*

Book Four. *Indestructible Innocence*

Diamond Body Series

Spacecruiser Inquiry: True Guidance for the Inner Journey

Brilliancy: The Essence of Intelligence

The Unfolding Now: Realizing Your True Nature through the Practice of Presence

For more information on A. H. Almaas and all of his publications, please go to: www.ahalmaas.com.

DIAMOND HEART

Book Four

Indestructible Innocence

A. H. Almaas

Shambhala
Boston & London
2001

Shambhala Publications, Inc.
Horticultural Hall
300 Massachusetts Avenue
Boston, Massachusetts 02115
www.shambhala.com

9 8 7 6 5 4 3 2

Printed in the United States of America

⊗ This edition is printed on acid-free paper that meets
the American National Standards Institute Z39.48 Standard.
♻This book was printed on 30% postconsumer recycled paper.
For more information please visit www.shambhala.com.
Distributed in the United States by Random House, Inc.,
and in Canada by Random House of Canada Ltd

For permission to reprint excerpts, the author is grateful to: Dharma
Publishing for *Knowledge of Freedom, Time to Change,* Chapter 28
"Limits on Meaning," pp. 287–300, Tarthang Tulku, 1984.

Library of Congress Cataloging-in-Publication Data
Almaas, A. H.
Indestructible innocence / A.H. Almaas—1st Shambhala ed.
p. cm.—(Diamond heart; bk.4)
Originally published: Berkeley, CA: Diamond Books, 1997.
ISBN 978-0-936713-11-3 (alk. paper)
1. Self-realization.   2. Self   3. Awareness I. Title
BJ1470 .A465 2000
158.1—dc21   00-040025

TABLE OF CONTENTS

PREFACE

We live in a world of mystery, wonder, and beauty. But most of us seldom participate in this real world, being aware rather of a world that is mostly strife, suffering, or meaninglessness. This situation is basically due to our not realizing and living our full human potential. This potential can be actualized by the realization and development of the human Essence. The human Essence is the part of us that is innate and real, and can participate in the real world.

This series of books, Diamond Heart, is a transcription of talks I have given to inner work groups in both California and Colorado, for several years, as part of the work of these groups. The purpose of the talks is to guide and orient individuals who are intensely engaged in doing the difficult work of essential realization.

The talks are organized in a manner that shows the various states and stages of realization in the order that occurs for the typical student, at least in our teaching method: the Diamond Approach. They begin with the states, knowledge, and questions most needed for starting the work on oneself, proceeding to stages of increasing depth and subtlety, and culminating in detailed understanding of the most mature states and conditions of realization.

Each talk elucidates a certain state of Essence or Being. The relevant psychological issues and barriers are discussed precisely and specifically, using modern psychological understanding in relation to the state of Being, and in relation to one's mind, life and process of inner unfoldment.

Hence, this series is not only a detailed and specific guidance for the student, but also an expression and manifestation of the unfoldment of the human Essence as it reveals the mystery, wonder, exquisiteness, and richness of the real world, our true inheritance. Each talk is actually the expression of a certain aspect or dimension of Being as it descends into the consciousness of the teacher in response to the present needs of the students. The teacher acts both as an embodiment of such reality and as a channel for the living knowledge that is part of this embodiment.

It is my wish that more of my fellow human beings participate in our real world, and taste the incredible beauty and integrity of being a human being, a full manifestation of the love of the truth.

Richmond, California 1986

INTRODUCTION
to Book Four

This fourth in the Diamond Heart series of books, containing talks by A.H. Almaas to groups of his students, has three main themes. The first, conveyed in Chapters One through Eleven, is the realization and development of the Personal Essence on the level of unity—the understanding and embodiment of the person as part of a larger whole, part of the unity of Being. In these talks Almaas conveys the need for the balanced human being to integrate the understanding of oneness in order to develop a level of maturity beyond self-centered living.

This teaching is invaluable to the student on a spiritual path who seeks to actualize the full potential of inner and outer life. Almaas explores the various issues that confront the student working through egoic delusion toward a living understanding of oneness, and describes the qualities and characteristics required for integration of spiritual truth into human life.

Realization of Being is not simply realization of the true self, but also realization of reality—of primordial true nature, more fundamental than the realms of form and mind. The second theme in *Indestructible Innocence* is the movement to and exploration of this nonconceptual realm. This is the dimension of Being "beyond form," in which there is pure awareness with no conceptual content. This dimension is a radical departure from the perspective of egoic reality, and even from the view of manifest Being as fundamental ground, which arises as various essential qualities. Almaas conveys vividly the quality of awareness that Krishnamurti called "freedom from the known"—awareness unfiltered by concepts. It is this "empty" awareness that is most often associated with Buddhism, particularly Zen. This part of *Indestructible Innocence* clarifies the similarity between the Diamond Approach and other spiritual traditions in relation to the basic dimensions of reality that are experienced on this path.

When we encounter and appreciate the significance of fresh, nonconceptual awareness as our true nature and the nature of everything, we know our nature as intrinsically free from the beliefs and identities that bring us so much suffering and frustration. We see too how all the work supporting maturation and clarification of the soul, the development of objectivity, and the understanding of the oneness of reality—the work Almaas teaches in the first part of this book—contribute to this freedom. We see clearly as delusion the notion that seekers in all paths entertain at some point—the idea that freedom is freedom of the self *from* mundane or constructed reality. We come to know, instead, that the more the human soul is oriented toward truth and living in accord with that truth, the less need there is to defend the false structures and attachments that keep us imprisoned in egoic identity.

Almaas's talks on the nonconceptual dimension can be be difficult for some to comprehend intellectually, but our hope is that the reader might taste some flavor of the freedom of awareness beyond personal mind. And for those engaged in meditation or other spiritual practices that penetrate the nonconceptual dimensions, these talks may offer useful understanding. In particular, Almaas discriminates two types of barriers to realization of the nonconceptual.

One type of barrier is epistemological, involving issues related to one's conceptual construction of self- and world-views, a construction determined by one's personal history, one's cultural context, and also by one's relation to the physical world. Chapter Twelve conveys this process of the construction of the world of concepts in the developing child's mind. This constructed world becomes not only the world that we live in, but actually the world that *is lived* by the human soul, in the sense that our thoughts, perceptions, emotions, images of ourselves, even many aspects of the flow of bodily energy, are governed by the conceptual world we construct as we develop.

Here the first barrier to realization, the epistemological, connects with the second, the psychodynamic. This is the level of issues related to personal defensiveness and attachment. To put it simply, there are many things we do not see the truth about, regarding ourselves, others, or the world, because we don't want to. For example, we might be frightened of losing our idea of ourselves as good (or as bad!), or we might be dependent on our idealized notion of a lover or a friend. These factors are barriers to the soul's openness to the complete truth of our experience, inner and outer. In the way he and other Ridhwan teachers work with students, Almaas utilizes a profound understanding of self psychology, recognizing the depth and unconsciousness of many levels of ego structure and identity which, without specific psychodynamic work, are very difficult to see through, even with repeated transcendent experiences. In this area Almaas makes an original contribution to the understanding of the difficulties of realizing and integrating the dimension of nonconceptual awareness—a realm that is actually rather accessible to practitioners of various paths, particularly those involving meditation.

In Chapter Sixteen, the present volume goes on from the exploration of the nonconceptual dimension to the third theme: an overview of the dimensions of Being as discovered through the process of realization. It describes the relationship between the boundless or formless dimensions and the dimensions of objective or noetic forms in which manifestation arises. Here the discussion particularly connects with Western philosophy, especially the neoplatonic tradition most clearly elucidated by Plotinus.

One of the greatest puzzles for the serious student of spiritual disciplines arises from the encounter with the realm of pure awareness, usually accompanied by a perception of emptiness of the self or of the world previously seen as solid. Here there is great wonderment, and sometimes concern. What does this insight mean about the world of forms? What does it mean about the spiritual world, and about the realm of Essence? Almaas begins in Chapter Sixteen to clarify the ontological status of the essential qualities of Being and of the human soul which he has discussed in his previous work. These qualities are universal concepts or noetic forms which can be known as objective forms not constructed by the personal mind, just as the forms of the physical world are not determined by the individual mind, although they are recognized through the construction of concepts. Until the realm of these forms is understood, the experience of many practitioners seems to present a dichotomy or dualism between mental structures (which are seen as unreal) and basic nature, which is seen as the real and also as completely nonconceptual.

The perspective Almaas teaches in the later chapters of *Indestructible Innocence* can free the understanding of essential qualities from the tendency toward reification of these qualities, revealing how the Diamond Approach is a teaching truly grounded in a nondual perspective. Just as realization of unity frees the soul from the delusion that separating boundaries are ultimately real, so the realization of the nonconceptual dimensions frees the perception from the duality of emptiness and existence, and from the related notion that manifestation of forms constitutes an actual separation from the ground of Being. This perspective is more than a philosophical understanding; as is clear in Almaas's teaching, it has human and practical implications for the realization and integration of Being while living a human life in the world.

The present discussion of these dimensions of Being is an introduction to this material presented in talks to students exploring the various dimensions of Being addressed by the Diamond Approach. Consequently, it is not a complete presentation of Almaas's teaching on these realms. The full teaching includes work with many more subtleties and implications involved in the realization of the boundless and formless dimensions and in the further work on Universal Mind, or Nous.

DIAMOND HEART
Book Four
Indestructible Innocence

ONE

Clarification of Personality

M any spiritual teachers describe their experience of realization as if they suddenly became realized and the personality just died, or fell away. So it is understandable that you might fantasize that one day you will finish your meditation and there will be no personality left. This idea of enlightenment or self-realization is misguided, although it is true that you can experience sudden revelations or insights that can change the rest of your life. My perception of what happens with people who claim to have lost their personality totally and spontaneously is that there often remains a split-off or suppressed part which will manifest as a distortion or a lack of integration. This means that there has been an essential realization, but the realization has not clarified the personality. It is, rather, a state of transcendence of the ego personality. If the personality is abandoned rather than integrated, the totality of life cannot be lived.

We can look at the process of realization from the perspective of transcendence or from the perspective of embodiment. When people talk about getting rid of the ego, they're talking about a transcendent experience. It is possible to transcend the personality or the ego, or even physical existence. However, there is a more difficult process which leads to the state of embodiment of reality. Rather than simply transcending the personality or physical existence, this state involves actually embodying essential existence in one's life.

Of course, some systems do encompass both transcendence and embodiment. If you look at your experience here in terms of essential realization, what you will see in the approach to our Work is transcendence followed by embodiment. This is what is sometimes called death and rebirth; death is transcendence and the rebirth is embodiment. In embodiment, the personality itself becomes permeable, and thus it is influenced by the essential realization. True essential personal life becomes possible only when essential realization permeates the personality so that you are living according to your realization. You have a personal, practical life—relationships, career, interests, things you enjoy doing, things you don't want to do. You're still a person, not just a disembodied spirit.

This process of embodiment is very intriguing and exciting. It is fulfilling and satisfying in such a way that you realize how having a human life makes sense. It makes sense to all of you—to the mind, to the heart, to the personality, to your body. Human life is not complete until the realization can be integrated into every aspect of you, so that all elements of you are in harmony and have an understanding of the situation. If one part of you is alienated, rejected or split away, the integration is not yet complete.

Embodiment becomes possible as the personality is clarified. The idea of clarifying the personality can be confusing because we often experience the personality as the source of our trouble. As we work on ourselves, we are constantly seeing the problems and suffering of the ego—ignorance, hatred, rage, fear, jealousy. So how, we wonder, can the personality be spiritual? It seems that the best thing we could do would be to obliterate it, to wage spiritual warfare, inner guerrilla warfare. In fact, many stages of the Work do feel like a kind of warfare. But successful warfare doesn't mean destruction of the enemy; it leads, rather, to the annexation of the territory. This is often the original reason for warfare; it is actually a movement towards expansion rather than destruction.

It's a strange thing, this struggle we go through between our beingness and the personality. It is like warfare—one side triumphs over the other—but even though there is an annexation of the territory, inner turmoil continues. The counterrevolutionary action inside doesn't end just because one side annexes the other and takes it over. As long as one side is dominating the other, there cannot be peace. In order to resolve this conflict, we need to understand the actual nature of the personality. If we look at it objectively with no preconceived ideas, what is this creature? Why does it cause so much trouble? Why does everyone blame everything on the ego? Many spiritual books call personality the devil, the animal or the monster, judging and rejecting it. At the same time, everyone talks about love. People say you must submit or surrender your personality.

It is true that sometimes the personality appears as a monster or a devil. If you look with an inner eye, it might even look like such a thing. But what *is* this personality that sometimes appears as a devil, sometimes a child, sometimes a man, sometimes a woman, sometimes a frustrator, sometimes a saboteur, sometimes a doer, sometimes an observer, sometimes a rebel, and so on? The personality must have some kind of intelligence, some amazing power, to manifest in all these ways. One minute it appears as an innocent child; the next, it's a monster. One moment it's vulnerable and defenseless, the next moment it's a gladiator.

At some point we can perceive that the inner child, the ego, the ego identity, the emotional self, the mind, the false personality, the observer, the doer, the actor, the one who resists, and the one who hates, are actually all one. They're just different faces of the same thing that we call personality, appearing in different forms depending on the situation. We have seen that Essence is a substantial presence, but we are surprised when we realize that it is not only Essence that is substantial; the personality itself is a substantial existence. You can observe that even your personality itself is a material. It has an inner substance.

It is true that there are thoughts and feelings and sensations connected to it, but at some point you feel your personality as a kind of presence. It doesn't have the sense of immediate reality and freshness, the sense of truthfulness, brilliance and luminosity of Essence; in fact, it is usually felt as a thickness, a dullness, a heaviness. But personality is not just a collection of thoughts; it exists as its own kind of material or medium.

Many systems claim that the personality does not exist, that ego does not exist. It is true that from a certain perspective one can see that it does not exist. But at the level where personality does not exist, neither does anything else. Your body does not exist on that level, nor does physical reality for that matter. As long as there is conceptualization, your personality exists just like anything else, just as Essence exists. When we can see this substantial existence of the personality, it is possible for us to comprehend what it would mean for the personality to be purified and clarified.

For most people, the personality manifests at the beginning as a kind of resistance, a leadenness, a cloudiness in the mind. When the personality is unclear, the personality exists as an unclarified, impure substance. We call it "impure" not in a judgmental or moralistic sense, but because it doesn't exist as its own pure nature. What are the impurities of the personality? What will be clarified from the personality? The answer is simple: the past. The thickness, the dullness, the suffering that you experience as the personality are there because the personality does not exist in its pure form. It carries the past with it, and the past exists as conflicts, memories, undischarged feelings, misunderstandings, ignorance, and all the reactions, associations, and fantasies corresponding to all the ignorance from the past.

The personality is like dirty water that has been used many times to clean things but it has not been cleaned or purified itself. The personality needs to be filtered. The past needs to be discharged, eliminated. The substantial state of the personality—what I call false pearl—creates a certain contraction in the spleen and pancreas area. I believe the connection to the spleen and the pancreas is that the physiological job of the spleen is to eliminate dead white corpuscles. The white blood cells exist for defense and protection, which is what the personality is trying to do. Once these cells have done their job, they are cleared from the blood.

The personality, however, does not usually discard old defenses that are no longer needed, and these old defenses constitute much of the unclarity and dullness of the personality. At different points in your work you experience different aspects of this unclarity, depending on what area you are working on, and the previous level of clarification of your personality. For example, you might be working for some time on material in the personality that has to do with security and the essential aspect of Will, and another time you might be working on defenses regarding Strength.

Also, the deeper you go into your work, the more the subtle structures in the personality are experienced as false. We call this unclarity the "false pearl," contrasting it to the true person, which we call the Pearl.

So perhaps we are beginning to understand something about the unclarity, the opaqueness of the personality: It contains elements that were supposed to have been discharged, but have not yet been eliminated. A major part of what needs to be eliminated is conditioning that was once useful for protection and defense, even for physical survival. Many of our patterns, conflicts, and ignorance remain as part of the struggle for survival, for protection. We are now stuck with those patterns and mechanisms that we developed in our past to protect us from too much pain or from annihilation. We have not been able to let them go, and they have determined the content of our personality.

This is the process of the clarification of the personality: Each time you understand an issue or an identification with a past conflict or a now-unnecessary defense, you discharge feelings associated with the issue and work through the feelings and the beliefs about it. As you have seen many times, working through an issue—which involves ceasing to be identified with it—typically allows the arising of an essential state. In this process of working through an issue related to any essential quality, the personality confronts the part of its structure that substitutes and compensates for the lack of that true quality. For example, issues around essential strength will uncover the false strength of the personality. When this compensation is seen through and the essential strength is freed, there is no more need for the personality structure of the false strength.

Thus, the arising of each essential aspect will shed light on a certain element of the ignorance in the personality. When you are inquiring, the presence of an essential state allows you to become very specific about your issues. In the process of inquiry, the personality becomes clearer and purer each time a quality of essence is realized and the issues around it are understood. You let go of some old beliefs, old self-images, and old tensions. If you feel the state of the personality when it is somewhat relaxed, you realize that although it's still dull and heavy, it is also comfortable or even warm and cozy. The felt sense of the personality is like the blankets that babies carry around with them. It reminds you of your blanket, your bed, of your mother when she took care of you when you were sick. It's a protective device that has been doing its job. Then, when the actual essential states are able to arise—states that the personality has been unsuccessfully trying to recreate through such devices—there is a potential for a clarifying impact on the personality. Of course, sometimes essential states arise without a connection to issues, for instance, as a result of meditation or some spiritual practice. But when a person experiences these states without looking at the issues, which is a common occurrence, there is no clarification of the personality. The personality stays the way it is.

It is this development that is often called spiritual realization: The person is in an essential state, and in some sense identified with it, but the personality remains as it is. In order for the person to embody the essential experience, Essence must impact the personality; it must transform the personality. We can integrate this influence only by working through the actual issues and understanding how they manifest in all areas of our lives, specific and general. When you are working on understanding a specific issue and an essential state manifests, you may notice that the experience doesn't end your struggle with the issue. There is still a duality between personality and Essence. Spiritual realizations or essential states may lighten and harmonize your daily life or make you feel more fulfilled, but the struggle of the duality continues. You might also notice that you are still engaged in the process of development but from the perspective of personality rather than from the perspective of Essence. This persistent lack of clarity is the hallmark of personality.

In your process, you might find that particular personal issues have become more clear and that issues from your personal history have become more clarified. But there must come a time when you begin to look at the personality itself, not in terms of its particular issues but as a whole. The issue then is not a matter of, "I don't have my will," or "Why can't I find a girlfriend?" or "I don't feel any self-worth." Each issue is real and needs to be resolved but there is something which underlies all the particular issues. When you explore this underlying something, an awareness will emerge that the duality itself is the source of the conflict. You will discover that the fact that you feel that there are two entities—Essence and personality—instead of one, is the problem.

This issue of perceived duality then becomes the focus of your work. The split in your experience has been there for as long as you can remember. You can remember that you have always labeled your experience as good or bad, pure or impure. Some of your experience has been luminous, full of love, intelligence, and clarity. But part of you remains somewhat opaque and stubbornly continues to reassert itself. Before your awareness of Essence, you identified with the opaque part and wanted the good stuff. But after experiencing these wonderful states, you realize that these experiences don't solve the problem. You might have many experiences of Essence—yummy, powerful, sweet experiences like Merging Love, Value, and Truth. But as long as your identification is primarily with personality, these experiences tend only to inflate the personality and you develop an inflated ego, believing yourself to be a personality that *has* Essence. So then you might feel proud that you are someone who knows God, who communes with God, right? You feel that you are important, that you have accomplished something. All this experience happens and you may become full of yourself, full of richness, power, clarity, and will. But eventually you begin to realize that this sense of "filling" the personality with Essence is a problem. You begin to become aware that the problem is you, yourself—your very identity, and the way you look at all things. The issue is not what you get or don't get. At this point in your process, the suffering doesn't come from the content of your experience or from any object of your perception. It comes from the operator in you, the one who perceives, acts, and experiences. That's the problem: you as the doer, the actor, the observer. You begin to perceive that something needs to happen to "me." You begin to see that you suffer because of the split, the duality.

This understanding becomes accessible only when you have experienced Essence in a very deep and integrated way. When you first begin to work on yourself, the personality is all you experience and so of course you want to make it better. Then you begin to perceive the more real part of you—Essence—perhaps in the form of Value or Truth. It's not that it wasn't there before, but you had just never seen it, or at least it had been hidden for years and years. So the next stage is that there is a struggle in which the development of Essence increasingly exposes the personality.

Now you have an opportunity to develop a new understanding of the duality between Essence and personality. You see that despite your essential experiences, the personality continues to act, thus maintaining its identity. This perpetuates the duality; this very activity of doing something is the problem. The personality is operating, working on itself, becoming realized, achieving this and that, and all this activity is what creates your suffering. The mere fact that you do, that you hope, that you desire, is the problem.

So you turn towards the issue of identity, and see that your very identity is an inner activity. The past exists in us as activity, and the content of personality is an activity, a movement. Ego activity is the substance of suffering; it is contraction itself. You can see this more specifically if you look at the activity in each center of the body. If you look at the activity in the head, you'll see concern and worry. In the heart, it's a sense of guilt and frustration. Looking at activity in the belly, you'll see it as attachment and desire. But it is all the same thing: ego activity. And ego activity is always connected with issues from your past. It is what is called personal karma, or the wheel of life and death. It is the movement of your mind, your personality, your choices, preferences, judgments, resistances—anything you do actively. The moment you choose to do something or to reject something, you are acting, and that inner activity is the content of personality that makes the personality unclear. It muddies the water and separates the personality from the clear stillness of Essence.

Essence is Being, and Being is complete stillness, with no action. When you act, the movement of your thoughts or desires separates you from Essence. You're not Being. But a very interesting thing happens when you become aware of the movement of your personality and you don't go along with it. What happens is you realize that when you don't go along with it, there is no one to go along or not go along.

There are actually two ways of working on the personality: one of them is seeing the personality, thus becoming separate from it, which is called disidentification. The other method involves complete immersion in the personality. In the state of self-realization, based on disidentification and separation from the ego, the personality is not matured and integrated with Essence; it is not clarified completely. The personality has merely been set aside, not worked through and transformed.

In using the second method, we need to understand more thoroughly what is meant by immersion in the personality. There is a willingness to clearly and completely experience the personality itself without resistance, without the attempt to escape from or "transcend" it. In this process you have to *be* the personality itself, to completely embody it. You see, conceive, and experience yourself in action as the personality. You have to experience for yourself that, "I am the personality completely, I am that and my very movement is suffering." This must happen completely, not by disidentifying—by looking from above and witnessing—but by *being* it. The experience must be sensual, physical, and intuitive. It is not a reflection or a thought. This is direct perception, beyond the discursive mind.

At this point we can see the importance of clarifying your personal issues. It is difficult to see the ego activity as a whole when you are identified with one part of the personality which is engaged in unconscious conflicts. In this condition you are controlled by an unconscious issue that keeps you stuck in ego activity without realizing it. When the issues are clarified, it is easier to become aware of the movement itself, of the wheels in motion—not of what is being churned but of the actual churning itself. When you become aware that you are the machine in action and you are completely convinced that the activity itself is what is churning up problems, only then is it possible for the wheels to stop. When the wheels stop and there is no activity, there is also no defensiveness. You're not defending yourself in any way because, as we have seen, the very basis of personality activity is defense. When the activity stops, you recognize that most of your thoughts and desires and efforts are resistance and what you have been resisting is the present moment, the now.

You realize that the "nowness" and presence are your Beingness. And you begin to experience the presence of the

Supreme Being as you, as yourself, in this moment. This experience enables you to see that the activity of resisting the present moment is exactly what has been separating you from Being. When there is ego activity, you might be aware of your being, but you are somewhere else. When the wheels are turning, they are pushing away who you are, separating you from Being. This separation is also what makes personality feel perpetually deficient.

The moment you become aware of the vicious cycle of the activity of defensiveness, you will see clearly that what you have been rejecting is yourself, and that the rejection is useless and unnecessary. Then you will relax and stop. The complete perception of this cycle *is* the stopping of the wheels. Then the personality is dissolved by clarity. There is clarity because there is no movement in the personality separating it from Being.

As you can see, this insight comes only with a great deal of work. It takes a long time to get to the point of seeing the totality of ego activity. To see it experientially and directly rather than from a disidentified or transcendent perspective is made possible by a deep exploration of the territory of personality from within. This experience of Being relies on many kinds of realizations, understanding unconscious issues, and expansion into Being. When you are working on one particular issue you will see a part of this supreme reality, but working on all your issues makes it more possible to see the whole.

You must see the totality of your personality in the present—all the thoughts, desires, feelings, and dreams, which are continuous with your past. You may also see your personality, at all times continuous with the social structure around you, in all your relationships, the influence of your society on your personality, and so on. You will see that your ego activity is what connects you to the social network of personality, making you vulnerable to the various external influences that obscure the truth of who you are, and what reality is. When you see this completely, it is possible for the movement in you—that connects you with the rest of society—to stop. When it stops, you become pure, clarified personality, soul with no ego structure. This clarifies and heals the split from Being. The split simply is not there. In that instant you see that you and the supreme reality are one. For the first time, you can perceive the actual substance of the personality without the past. The basis of the personality, the underlying principle that makes it possible for you to be a person, the thing that you have rejected all this time, is nothing but the supreme reality as a person. The very substance of the personality is ultimately a substance which I call the Supreme Pearl, or the supreme person: pure personal presence with no qualities. It is just Being, pure and simple, but manifesting as a human person. So when the personality is completely clarified, and yet you feel you are a person, the personality doesn't disappear; it is now the supreme person, the truest person. This is a sublime reality existing as you, the human individual.

Here, the supreme reality is seen as a personal reality, not only as the objective, impersonal Supreme, which also exists. After the realization of Supreme Being, there is a further process which is this unification, the final merging of the personality with the supreme reality. This is the same thing as the complete understanding and clarification of the personality. You recognize that you are the most real a person can be, the supreme person. Some people call this state of being the Son of God, because it is related to what Christ stated when he said, "I and the father are one."

This process of clarification—which is the clarification of the soul—is the development of the Personal Essence, what we call the Pearl Beyond Price. The development of the Pearl is a process which keeps moving towards further clarification until it becomes the Supreme Personal Essence.

Each essential state has become personalized as the personality has become clarified, as each essential aspect has become you. You yourself become the personal essential reality, and thus, this reality can be integrated at the level of the Pearl. When you experience Compassion, that Compassion becomes you. "I, personally, am Compassion. I am Value, I am Truth." When you own it, it is no longer you experiencing it, but you know you *are* it. The personality becomes so permeable that it is completely merged with the aspect. This is what I call the personalization of the essential state. As the essential aspects are personalized—Compassion, Merging Love, Will, Peace, Value, Identity, and so on—you will reach a further, a more boundless personalization, which is the personalization of the Supreme.

The surprise is that this is what you have been all the time. It's never been otherwise. You've always been the supreme person, all the time, in your very substance, including the substance of the personality. That's why you have always identified with it, that's why you cannot disidentify from it: It is you. How can you disidentify from that? How can you get rid of that? It is ultimately you. Here we see that to try to disidentify from the personality and live from a transcendent identity is to leave the very ground of the reality that was never truly separate from personality.

You come to realize, then, that the purified, clarified personality, which is what I call the supreme person, is just a clarity. You experience yourself as the clarity. It's not just that your mind is clear; all of you is a clarity, an absolute openness and clarity, completely light. When all the impurities go, you remain as a lightness, an openness. But this is a personal openness, a person who is freedom. You are not a free person, you are a person who is the freedom. It is complete personal freedom. As the past is digested and eliminated, that personal freedom remains as the freedom of the personal Supreme, or the eternal person. You are a transparent personal form of pure presence, a body of clear light.

The supreme person is eternal in that you can experience yourself, personally, as timeless. When you become One, when the personality is clarified and unified, you will feel that it is an eternal oneness outside of time. It has nothing to do with time. Some people say that the self doesn't really exist; and on this level, it feels like a kind of emptiness, a nothingness. This is because of its lightness. It's not just that there is no gravity; it feels like empty gravity. You just light up; you're full of joy. You are full of personal joy, personal happiness. Finally, you are You, completely; yet, who you are is the supreme reality itself, or the personalization of the supreme reality. It is not exactly nonexistence; it feels like nothing but it is a substantial nothing which is a qualityless essential presence.

When you become yourself, you are clarified and your action becomes love instead of frustrated ego activity. Action from your true personality is a flow of love, which has actually been the basis of the whole process all along. You realize that the flow of love doesn't begin with this new experience of integration; it has been present during the entire process. You understand that even the activity of the ego, which created resistance and suffering, was based at the beginning on love and compassion for yourself and others.

All that effort to be a person has been the result of the developmental thrust towards being the supreme person, whether you were conscious of this thrust or not. But most of the time you misunderstood this thrust. You thought it meant you needed to be this or that person. That is why you have been resisting and rejecting. You want to protect yourself, and this desire is motivated by love. Sometimes you've resisted in order to protect other people, like your parents; you've done this because you love them. But we forget this original love; the accumulations of the past have blinded us to our original motivation. This is why you need to understand all the accumulated layers of your reactions, until you get to what lies beneath. Only then can you understand the initial impulse of resistance, which is love. Only when you perceive the love under it all, will you realize you have not been eliminated or replaced by Essence, but that you and Essence are one. Duality was never really there. There has been only ignorance and an accumulation of undigested experience.

When you see this unity and understand that it has always been there, you will understand the meaning of Ridhwan, the name of our school. In Arabic, *ridhwan* means totally satisfied, satisfying, fulfilled, fulfilling, contented, contenting. You are personally and impersonally contented, objectively contented for yourself and all others. Your story and the story of each and every human being makes sense in the light of this unity underlying all of experience. Without this understanding of unity, your mind's questions are still unanswered. Many people say (and it is true for some states of realization) that the questions are not answered; the questions are simply not there any more. In this state of embodiment, however, all of the questions, including even your mental questions, are actually answered. They must be, for you to be completely satisfied and fulfilled. Your mind itself is full of *ridhwan*. All of you, not just one aspect of you, is satisfied. All of you is complete. There is no duality. All of you must become satisfied: your mind, your body, your personality—every aspect of you. All of it must be integrated, not discarded.

This is what I call then the integrated identity. Personality, Essence, Supreme, body, mind, are all one identity operating without a split. Then you are simply ordinary. You are not someone who is working on himself. You are someone who is just living. You do what you do without feeling that there is something wrong with you, that some part of you needs to be rejected.

It cannot be that there is one part of you that works on another part of you. That is artificial. Can you imagine a tiger working on himself? Really! A tiger is an integrated being. Integrated human beings don't work on themselves either. It would be just as ridiculous as thinking that your dog is meditating, trying to understand his personality. Doesn't it sound ridiculous? You don't exist as a package of different things. Your mind makes these separations, and sets up all situations so that this part is always struggling with that part. But when you are unified, you see that your system functions naturally—what needs to be digested will be digested; what needs to be eliminated will be eliminated. When this happens naturally, there is no disharmony. This is health. It is the normal, ordinary state for a human being. In a state of health you don't think about your health. You don't dwell on it. Everything is fine. It's the same when you are completely integrated—you don't think about yourself. You just live in a healthy way.

This understanding is a synthesis of all our work so far. Where has it been leading? What is the thread? We are trying to see the thread connecting all of it, the thread of the clarification of the personality. This is a good time to speak explicitly about this process, so that you realize that personality is not the culprit. Personality is not something to be eliminated. It is simply full of fear because it does not know its true nature. The personality needs to be completely and thoroughly understood and cherished. Only with that compassionate, accepting, objective love is it possible to understand the true reality of the personality.

With clarification comes this understanding, and then your heart becomes completely nourished. Because of the fullness in the heart, love can flow. The heart is completely contented—the ultimate "eating and drinking to your heart's content." The heart spills over, and it's no big deal. You don't think about it; it is spontaneous and natural. If you are a truly normal, ordinary person, living your life in a healthy way, you cannot help but be loving; that loving-ness is the source of, and the motivation for, your action.

You live in joy and you relate through love, because you are taking no action that is divisive. So what is seen at the beginning as opaque, dull, and heavy, becomes light, clear, and timeless. By accepting and understanding the person-ality, by going through this process of clarification, you learn that understanding yourself allows you to love yourself.

The thing that we experience as personality at the begin-ning, and for a long time on the path, is actually nothing but the soul. The personality is our soul, but our soul imprinted and shaped by past experience. Our past expe-rience shapes and forms our experience of ourselves and of our conscious and dynamic soul, and obscures its true nature by remaining as residual content in our true nature. These residues are the self-images, the internalized object relations, the reactions, the suppressed feelings, memories, and the many defenses we use to protect ourselves. The pro-cess of clarification is basically the dissolution of these residues through the light of understanding. This way, the personality reveals itself as the soul developing towards individuation. The soul develops into the Supreme Pearl Beyond Price, which is the individuation of Being. This is the embodiment of Being.

TWO

Being
and the Search

Today we will explore a question related to Christ's teaching. Christ taught about the relationship of love and compassion to peace. What we will discuss regarding this teaching is something practical: What is the most loving and compassionate thing one can do to create peace, both personally and universally? We can sum up this teaching by saying that the most loving and compassionate thing you can do for peace is to do absolutely nothing. When I say to do nothing, I do not mean what would ordinarily be thought of as doing nothing. We will try to understand a much more fundamental perception of what it means to not do, why that would be a loving and compassionate thing, and why it leads to peace.

Peace is the absence of suffering. One reason for suffering is that most people are not looking for peace; they are looking for pleasure. Peace is not a top priority for most people; pleasure usually comes first. Therefore, people seek pleasure. There is nothing wrong with wanting pleasure, nor with pleasure itself. But what leads to the absence of peace is seeking pleasure, for the simple reason that seeking pleasure assumes that pleasure is somewhere else, some other time, in a different situation, and not here and now. That is the basic premise of seeking, not only pleasure, but seeking anything, including peace. When we seek, we are moving away from the pleasure or peace and from the source of pleasure and peace. So when I say to not do absolutely anything, I mean not to seek—not to seek for pleasure, or peace, or security, or love, or anything at all—because implicit in the activity of seeking is that there is something to do, or to arrive at. Seeking assumes that there is something to be found, someplace to be reached, some goal to be arrived at.

It is amazing to see multitudes of people—almost everyone—searching for something that would be there if they merely stopped the search, and which cannot be there until they stop searching. People tend to believe that first they must find what they seek and then they will stop. The truth is that the finding can happen only when the search stops. This is the absurdity of most of our activities and preoccupations—we are seeking something and by this very act of seeking, we get farther away from that which we seek. This observation reflects a perspective most people do not share. From the conventional perspective, it sounds absurd. Even people who know this from their own experience do not remain convinced enough to actually change their behavior of seeking. They still don't believe that the pleasure, the peace, the love, the fulfillment, is right here, now.

All these qualities are in your very own being; they are not something or somewhere else. Who you actually are is the source, your very nature is the source of the pleasure, peace, love—all that you normally seek. Regardless of what you think you need, every second of your life, all the way through, it is only you who will satisfy that quest. If you seek pleasure, you will tend to produce only suffering, sooner or later.

This means that all the other things in our lives—accomplishment, success, riches, fame, getting this or that—are meaningless from the perspective of our true nature. It is all necessary; it is necessary for people to work, to make money, and so on. But these things are only necessary for survival; they will not bring fulfillment or peace, and often they don't bring pleasure. It is interesting that we can perceive this truth just by investigating the immediate world around us and then the next moment we behave as if we have seen nothing. Many people in the world have enough money, enough work and enough food; they have people who appreciate them, and so on, but probably ninety-nine percent of those people are unhappy. Yet we are still not convinced: We believe, "I will be in the one percent. If I get what I want, I will be happy."

Actually, the one percent who find fulfillment are the ones who do not care about those achievements; that's why they are fulfilled. It is not because they are successful or because they got something—wealth, position, a lover, whatever. Don't believe the people who appear on TV, telling their success stories, and saying how happy they are. It is not true. You can see it in their faces. They get an idea in their minds that they are happy: "I got what I want, so I must be happy since I have always believed that's how it works." Some people might be deceived by this but anyone who knows true fulfillment will see that is not true. We might be excited when we get what we wanted, which keeps our hopes up for a while. We believe that other things will follow which will complete our happiness; but usually we find out that isn't true. I am not saying that success or wealth or position are bad in themselves; I am saying that in themselves they are empty. All activities in life—all accomplishments, all situations, all relationships—are empty, if you are not there, if you are not present in them. This is a basic law of human nature.

Since we don't believe this law, however, we go about seeking. Even though all of you have experienced fulfillment and peace at times when you came to be fully present without striving, you continue to believe that seeking and getting what you seek will bring fulfillment. You need to see how persistent that belief is, even in the face of many experiences that reveal it to be false. If you look at your assumptions clearly when you are suffering, you can see how in that moment when you believe the delusion of seeking, you are believing that peace cannot be simply here and now. You will perceive that you really believe that if you get this or that, you will be happy. In a very deep place, every personality is absolutely convinced of this point of view.

It takes a human being a very long time, a tremendous amount of work, and recurrent, ever-increasing disappointments before he or she begins to consider, "Maybe I'm wrong, maybe there isn't anything in this world that will do it for me." You have to hit your head against the wall so many times. You have to suffer a great deal before you question your fundamental beliefs about reality. In working with people, it seems to me that my work is just helping to reveal that what they believe is not really true. Everyone suffers because they act according to certain beliefs or views of reality with such conviction that they will fight for these views to the end. Even if they come to group and want to investigate the truth or become self-realized, their motive is to continue their seeking more efficiently.

To the extent that we live from the perspective of trying to find fulfillment, or from trying to get better, we live in an empty world. However, if we just rest, forget all the searching and give up the seeking, the world becomes beautiful and full. When you are seeking, you separate your consciousness, your soul, from your being, from your source, so that your whole perception then is perception devoid of being. Regardless of what you acquire or achieve, you are poverty-stricken because you are operating from an impoverished perspective. In this situation, you can only perpetuate your impoverished point of view. That seeking, by its nature, is a movement away from the fullness of reality and the source of pleasure, peace, or whatever is so feverishly being sought. Reality can't be reached by seeking; you do not see it because you are seeking for something else. Whatever you are seeking, it could seem more and more refined, or closer to the truth, or closer to fulfillment, but none of this will make a difference. It is the activity of seeking that matters; no matter what you seek, this activity is the same. You might be seeking your father's approval, or a lover, or success in your work, or enlightenment. It is all seeking, so it is all the same.

In all seeking, and in the activity inherent in seeking, there is an assumption that you are deficient. This is one way the activity of seeking reinforces the sense of poverty. My observation is that regardless of how many times a person hears this, or even realizes it, he tends to continue behaving in a way that implies deficiency. This is a deep conviction: that we are fundamentally deficient, that we do not have anything good or real. From this ingrained perspective, the good stuff is always somewhere else; it can be found only somewhere else or sometime in the future or even the past.

Seeking is the basis, the very fabric, of suffering. The question might arise that if there is nothing to search for and seeking is the wrong thing to do, then how can you do this work? What is practice for? Our Work, as you know, is to understand yourself, to come to awareness of your true nature. What does it mean to understand yourself? What is the process of inquiry if I am not trying to look into all the nooks and crannies, finding all the yummy things and trying to get rid of the terrible things? To understand the practice of inquiry we need to come from the perspective of not seeking, from the perspective of pure being, from our own inner nature and source.

It seems that when someone has done the Work for some time, the normal ego activity of seeking pollutes the practice in the Work. So students tend to approach the practices of the Work from that perspective. If I say we have essence, you seek your essence. If I say you need to deal with your issues, you start to dig for your issues. Everyone becomes a hunter. This is the primary source of our suffering. We have talked about the sources of this perspective of seeking, of discontent, deficiency; we understand a lot about the patterns. Today, however, we are considering the activity itself.

You perpetuate your suffering by the very activity you think is going to release you from suffering. Many people assume that inquiry and understanding are a matter of figuring things out, a matter of searching for issues in your mind, or tensions in your body, or difficulties in your life, so that you can resolve the issues, relax the tensions, get rid of the difficulties. You hope that this activity will make you suffer less. If you are not trying to get rid of suffering, you are looking for some essential state or pleasurable condition, so you can grasp and hold on to some aspect of your essence. But this is a ridiculous thing to do, because you *are* the essence. How are you going to trap the essence if you are the essence? Who is going to trap your essence? Who is going to get it?

The consequence of this activity of trying to get something and trying to get rid of something else, is that you identify with the activity of searching. You are doing it, the activity is always present, and you take it to be you. Thus, you continue projecting outside the thing you are looking for. In the process of doing the Work, you merely continue the activity of seeking that you engaged in while pursuing personality goals and desires. You used to be looking for the right person, the right job, the right situation, and now you are looking inside yourself. Now you substitute looking for real confidence instead of looking for recognition. Instead of searching for success, you are searching for enlightenment. It is just different words for the same thing; it is the same activity whether it is directed inside or outside.

This seeking activity is not loving or compassionate for yourself or anyone else. The fact that it perpetuates your separation from yourself and continues to act out your most fundamental delusion, means that this activity is actually painful. From the point of view of personality, it would seem a good thing for a person to pursue what he thinks will make him happy, but we see that this activity can only bring about more frustration and suffering.

So what is inquiry, if not seeking and eliminating? How can we understand if we don't go hunting for states and eliminating old patterns of behavior? It is very simple. Understanding, itself, is very simple. Understanding is there when you are not searching. You do not need to look for understanding; it is not something to pursue. You do not have to make efforts to have insights. Your efforts are not rewarded with realizations. Understandings, realizations, and insights appear when you are relaxed, when for a moment you have stopped your seeking. Look at your own experience: When do you experience an expanded state, or have an insight and deep understanding? Is it when you are busy trying to figure things out? Or is it when you have forgotten about the struggle for a moment? You might see that your deep insights, the true and deeper understandings, arise when you are not doing anything in your mind, when you just are, simply present. Of course, you might be engaged in some kind of exercise, some activity in your mind, thinking, searching for this or wondering about that, when you have some insight, and you might think that is what brought about the insight. However, if you look carefully, you will notice that in the midst of searching or struggling, once in a while there is a gap—you get tired and give up for a moment. At that moment insight arises. However, you often don't see that gap because it is so short, so you think it is the activity of the mind that was responsible for the insight.

When I say you need to understand yourselves, I do not mean that you should all start thinking about yourselves and become hunters pursuing issues and insights. What I mean is that you need to be compassionate and loving towards yourself and let yourself be. If you let yourself be, there will be a spontaneous curiosity about what arises. To simply live and rest and let yourself be, allows this spontaneous inquiry. When you are just being, you are not busy thinking, worrying, trying to figure things out. Your mind is clearer and emptier, and whatever truth you need to understand about your situation is already there. It has always been there, actually; you do not see it because you are busy in your mind. You are not present enough to see. When you are present enough, when you are just being, you will see naturally and spontaneously.

So we see that true understanding is not a matter of searching; to seek understanding is the same thing as trying to seek wealth or love or anything external. It is just a different arena, a different place. The attitude that you are deficient, that you need to get something in order to have peace and fulfillment, reveals that you are not seeing yourself. You are not seeing that who you are is not someone who needs to get something. Your very nature, by itself, is pure pleasure, pure bliss, pure peace. Only the activity of searching cuts you off from this peace.

If you look within your mind or at your life, you notice that you are so busy. I don't mean busy doing physical things, but mentally and emotionally busy. Your mind never stops, never rests, except perhaps in deep sleep. There is always something going on; the mind keeps busy with whether this is the right thing or the wrong thing, whether I'm bad or I'm good, or it worries about what's going to happen, plans for the future, tells stories about the past, and so on. You do not let yourself simply rest. You do not stop arguing with yourself or entertaining yourself. Then you ask why you are not happy. This fuels a new flurry of mental activity: "Maybe I should do therapy, maybe join a group." You get involved with some new external activity that seems promising. When it does not work the way you had hoped, the activity or group or person seems wrong or bad. When things are frustrating, you might say: "They didn't love me or like me." Then you look elsewhere for someone or some group that loves you the right way. Always you seek more and more activity, never stopping and settling into your present experience without having judgments about it. The simplest thing is just to relax and be there, to live without ideas about it, to drop the judgments, the ambitions, the seeking. That is what most people do not do.

Of course, most of us have ideas about when we will be able to rest. Many of us have very elaborate and specific conditions that we feel must be satisfied before we can have peace. Even when those conditions are fulfilled, we rarely allow ourselves to rest anyway; usually we just set new conditions. Most of the time, the conditions cannot be fulfilled. But these conditions are actually redundant. Since our true nature is peace and love and full of pleasure, why are we putting conditions on it?

If we really engage in our work here, if we engage in the practice of inquiry we will see that the activity of seeking is actually the source of our pain and suffering. If we do not see that, but continue to believe that the seeking is what is going to take us to happiness, we will just get more frustrated. Even if you acquire or achieve something that you have believed will make you happy, you will not feel satisfied, you will not be fulfilled, because the activity of seeking is in itself pure suffering.

Understanding is actually a kind of meditation; it is not a seeking, not a figuring out, not an attempt to find information outside oneself. It is spontaneous, an effortless insight. To engage in the process of understanding does not involve doing anything. If there is anything to be done, it is a matter of attention—just being sure you are present. When you are present in your being, the insights will arise naturally and understanding will arise naturally.

Searching for understanding, trying to seek out or resolve issues, pursuing states and trying to grasp them—all these activities are built on a lack of clarity about what understanding is. We often think that understanding is information in our minds. You may have information in your mind, but that is not what I call understanding. True understanding has to do with transformation. If there is no transformation at the moment of understanding, then there is no real understanding. Without transformation, understanding is just a mental activity, part of the seeking activity.

True understanding that arises on its own is simply your own essence touching your mind, or being in contact with the situation. The actual contact of Being with any situation, or with any part of your mind, is understanding. Insight or understanding are nothing but your being eating your experience, metabolizing it, including your inner experience. This is the process of transformation itself. Being comes into contact with a part of your personality, or with an experience, and in that contact between Being and that part of the personality or the experience, the experience or part of personality is absorbed into Being. That absorption is not just a mental thing, it is a real experience of transformation, a metamorphosis. And this metamorphosis, which is itself understanding, never leads to weakness, deficiency, or impoverishment. It always leads to greater capacity, greater strength, and greater maturity. What is maturity, if not the complete absorption and metabolization of your experience?

Capacity and capable functioning come from absorption of whatever internal and external experiences you have. Absorption of experience leads to true growth and development. This growth, in which Being comes in contact with mind and experience, is an alchemical reaction or a synthesis which develops into the capacity for functioning in the world. This synthesis is actually what makes us grow as human beings. It is not something you have to search for; it is there all the time. The only thing that needs to happen for you to absorb, digest, metabolize, and assimilate your experience is to be there—simply to be. If you are searching, trying to figure things out, thinking, worrying, hoping, and desiring, you are cut off from your being. If you are cut off from your being, there is no contact between Being and experience and therefore no understanding. When there is no understanding there is no metamorphosis, and without that there is no growth and development in functioning.

Do you see what this Work is, from this perspective? Do you see what understanding is? From this perspective, the work of inquiry and understanding that we do is nothing but the metabolism of unmetabolized food in your mind. It is nothing more than that. You have had many experiences throughout your life that you still have not digested, that remain in your mind as the unconscious: memories, thoughts, identifications, feelings, actions, patterns, and the like. They are giving you trouble because you have indigestion—mental indigestion—because these reactions need to be digested and absorbed. Your mind is meant to be empty, not full of all your history and reactions and identifications.

Our work of inquiry can be understood as a process of metabolizing experience—past and present experience. By being fully present in your experience you metabolize it and grow. When it comes to the past, our Work can be seen as understanding or metabolizing your unconscious mind, your ego, or personality. True metabolism doesn't lead to deficiency or weakness, but to development, growth, and the functioning capacity of Being. Without experience Being cannot be in the world. Metabolism leads to the capacity to be in the world, and that is what it means to have a human life. However, if we fail to metabolize our experience—for example, by rejecting it and thus stopping the metabolic process—we retain undigested experience, which in time will become suffering. Because of the unmetabolized food in your mind, which is the influence of the past, your capacity to directly contact your experience in the present is severely reduced, so you cannot eat properly. There is already food in your system that has been rotting for years. First, you need to metabolize what is inside you to some degree, in order to have a greater capacity to metabolize your present experience. This has two results for our Work: One is the cleaning out of the past, and the other is that the more you have done that, the more capacity you have in the present. This allows events in the present to transform you. If you are really present and in present time, any impression or experience will lead to metamorphosis and maturity.

Usually this does not happen because of the barrier created by the unmetabolized past. It is unmetabolized because you do not want to experience it. What stops any person from digesting their experience (inner or outer) is the unwillingness or incapacity to be present in it or with it. When I say metabolism or digestion, I do not mean doing anything, I mean simply being there. Being, of its very nature, absorbs and metabolizes experience. When it comes across experience it absorbs it. It is awareness, it is understanding, it is attention, it is intelligence.

So as you see, we are not looking for states, nor trying to get rid of anything. The Work is nothing more than being present in your experience in an undefended way. When you are present in your experience without defenses, then there is contact between this beingness or presence and whatever happens in internal or external experience. When this contact happens, there is a process of transformation which we call metabolism or absorption. This process of transformation causes you to get bigger or more expanded. That is how you grow up. Just as your body grows up by eating food, your soul develops by eating experience. From this perspective, there is no bad experience since any experience can be metabolized if you are present in it. Some experiences are painful, some are pleasurable, but they all can lead to maturity. The only exceptions are experiences beyond your capacity for metabolism, whether painful or pleasurable.

We are seeing that understanding is not a matter of ending up with words and ideas in your mind about who you are or what reality is. Genuine understanding leads to greater maturity, to an enhanced capacity to live in this world harmoniously. So understanding is a very practical thing; it is the very process through which growth happens on all levels and in all dimensions.

Sometimes when people try to do this Work and believe it is not working, it is often the case that they have been searching for something, or trying to get rid of something, and it has not worked. They have been doing everything but working on understanding themselves and their situation. This activity of seeking and trying to change things is nothing but moving undigested food around; pushing it around doesn't help digestion, so it cannot lead to transformation. Understanding requires that you are deeply present, really there. You simply are, your beingness is in intimate contact with whatever arises, whether it be thoughts, perceptions, feelings, or contact with your situation. From this conjunction of life experience and Being arises the functional aspect of Being, the mature human individual, what we call the Personal Essence. Understanding is a process by which the human being, or Personal Essence, develops and matures. Of course, we could go into all kinds of details about the process of understanding—what stops it, and so on. But from the beginning, we need to see that understanding is not a matter of searching, hoping, desiring, or going after anything. It is a matter of being here, now, in your very experience, and coming in direct, undefended contact with your experience. It is a natural process of development and unfoldment if you don't resist it; it is what is supposed to happen to a human being anyway. That is our potential and our destiny.

Understanding arises spontaneously when you let yourself be. The food of experience is presented to you all the time; you don't have to look for it. It is not possible to be without experience. All that is left is the digestion. You just need to digest the experience, just like after eating your food you do not need to do anything in particular for digestion to happen. Your stomach is there and it is a natural process. You also do not need to do anything to digest your experience; simply allow the digestion of understanding to happen naturally. You do not need to think about it, or figure it out, or seek for a goal called digestion.

From this perspective, the Work is not something separate from life or from the world. Understanding is also not separate from the world. It is not something extra that we do, it is not special or additional. It is actually something everyone does, some people more efficiently than others. In the Work we just focus on it. We isolate the process of digestion so that in time we become more efficient. If we become more efficient, there is a chance of greater development and maturity. It is something that everyone is naturally engaged in since it is the living of life itself—the practical, everyday, every-second digestion and absorption of impressions and the learning and growth that result from that. There is no specific experience or state that you need to achieve. Understanding doesn't require that you have to hunt for certain issues or patterns in you, nor that you have to get rid of them. All experience is food, and if you are really present, you will digest more of that food, faster and more completely. At another time we will address in more detail the process of metabolism in terms of absorption and elimination, but for now we need to understand the basis of it. You can read about this process in the book on the Personal Essence. (See *The Pearl Beyond Price*, Almaas, 1988)

The development that arises out of understanding, the maturity that results from assimilation of experience, leads to what we call the personal sense of being: the part of you that you feel is you, and that is capable of functioning in the world while still being. Personal Essence is the aspect in which you feel most clearly that you personally are being. You feel, "I am here; I am a substantial sense of presence." There is fullness, beingness, thereness. In fact, every time you search, what you do more than anything else is push away that fullness of your being.

The less a human being is seeking, the more he is fulfilled. A miserable human being is one who is seeking intensely. I am talking about emotional suffering, not about someone who has a roof fall on his head or something like that. But even if a roof falls on your head, if you do not engage in the activity of searching, you have a better chance of recovery and well-being. Even if you have no money, you will be happy if you let yourself be. Even if you have millions, if you are seeking, you will be miserable. Of course, if you have no money and no food, there will be hunger and it will hurt. Even then, you might have another kind of contentment and fulfillment that is beyond that hurt.

There is nothing new in what I am saying. It has been said for thousands of years. But usually it goes in one ear and out the other because we continue to believe in our activity. "If I don't do such-and-such, I will never be happy." We are not talking about activity like driving a car or buying food; of course, you need to do these things. I am talking about inner activity, and the expression of that inner activity in external activity. You could be engaged in very intense outer activity while inside you are still, but most of the time external activity is an outer reflection of the activity of the mind. We are busy externally because our minds are busy. We are not being present in our activity. That is why many teachings say to slow down, to be a little quieter, to make your life simpler. You need to slow down, just to see the process and understand. This is so that you will see the difference. It is not because external activity is bad, it is more that you are too busy inside and outside to have the chance to see what is really here. When you are really being, it doesn't matter how fast you go outside. But if you are not being, no matter what speed you are going, you are still going farther away from yourself.

This world we live in, the world of appearance and everything that is in it, has nothing wrong with it. In a sense, it is neutral in that things are neither good nor bad. What makes it a place of suffering is that we are not present in it; what makes it a place of fulfillment is that we are present in it. For fulfillment is nothing but the fullness of our presence.

The world is like a magic show—you manifest whatever you have inside you. If you have suffering, you will manifest suffering, and if you have happiness, you will manifest that happiness and the world will be a happy place for you. If you have fear and hatred, you will manifest these things. The world is like your dream life; it is as simple as that. Your dream life is very dependent on your mind; it is not God who determines your dream life. No one else is coercing you to dream one way or another. Your dreams are an expression of who you are; there is a whole universe going on in your dreams.

We see the same thing in our collective world—all of us together are creating all kinds of things, but the major part of what we see in life and how we see it, has to do with mind and with what we take ourselves to be. You might complain for years about not having a boyfriend or a girlfriend. You might work hard until at some point there is a slight shift in some issue that releases as you understand a part of yourself. Then suddenly, a boyfriend or girlfriend seems to arise out of nowhere, as if by magic. It is as if there was a resistance inside you, a part that didn't want to have a boyfriend or girlfriend. It could be the same story with anything—a satisfying job, enough money—all the things most people are searching for. You might be looking for a meaningful job, you might work on lots of conflicts, self-images and issues about it but nothing happens; but when you are deeply ready inside, it happens as if by magic. I have had this phenomenon reported to me hundreds of times. It might be the least likely thing in the world, but if you wholeheartedly want it, it manifests as if by magic.

You might actually influence your reality much more than you think. Someone may want more clients for their business. I might help with the issues but nothing changes, until suddenly clients begin appearing out of nowhere for no apparent reason. How did this happen? Frequently it happens when the person has given up completely and stops doing everything he has been doing to get clients. The only thing that could be said to be the cause is nothing, doing nothing.

We do not trust the power and richness of our being. We always operate from the perspective of deficiency and poverty, and we are convinced that that is who we are and how we should go about our lives. That is fine for anyone who believes it is that way, but they can expect to suffer. If you do not believe me, we can talk about it in twenty years.

Of course, there are many forces that push us towards the attitude of seeking. We have a multitude of desires, a tremendous amount of hatred for ourselves and others, and an endless ignorance about who we are and what reality is. Part of my understanding is that we have to inquire into all of that so that the forces and energies that motivate the search will decrease and eventually disappear. But from the beginning, we need to see that searching is suffering, and that seeking, by its very nature, is abandoning ourselves, that the action of looking separates us from our natural unfoldment and pushes away Being. Searching is acting from a wrong premise, while understanding is a natural, ordinary process that requires no effort.

S: I find myself, especially lately, spending a lot of time trying to seek knowledge. I'm memorizing things and trying to learn things; because there is going to be a quiz on them. I guess what I am asking is how I can approach that in a way that . . .

AHA: Well, I will tell you how I do it. I read all kinds of psychological books. I read them very intensely. But I read them because I want to read them. It is a spontaneous thing. There is no effort. I am truly interested. Usually a lot of understanding arises from this, but it is a spontaneous activity to pick up a book and read it. From this perspective, a great deal can be absorbed, and the knowledge you get from it could create an understanding in you. You can see something about yourself or something about other people. There is curiosity about it and it is exciting, and because of that, when I read it I read it very slowly. I am not intent on finishing the book; I am interested in reading it and understanding what is there. There is pleasure in it, like when someone is really into a novel. Studying can be the same thing. It might look like there is an activity and I'm reading and I'm searching and looking through the references and all that, but there really isn't any search. It is a spontaneously arising activity that is very creative. I will have been looking at a book and there will be something I do not understand and I will go look in the dictionary and I will seem to be intense. Someone might think that I seem to be searching. But I am not searching. I am enjoying it.

S: So, it seems to depend on where you are coming from.

AHA: If there is something arising from within you that is natural and spontaneous and deep, *that* is not seeking. Your being can flow in a certain direction, and be acting, without it being ego activity. Ego activity is split from being. Being does not function according to what your mind says: "You shouldn't do this, you shouldn't do that. This is good or this is bad." That position of judging how things should be leads to seeking and searching. On the other hand, sometimes your energy, your own being, flows in a certain channel in a spontaneous, effortless flow. In this flow there is no seeking.

A great deal of knowledge and understanding can arise out of such authentic activity, and become integrated as true understanding. This is why two people can read a book and understand it at different levels of depth. The difference is not that one is smarter, but that he is really into it—the impulse towards the understanding comes from his heart. It is not because he is going to know more or become more successful. Most of what I have read, I read for no apparent purpose. I didn't know where it was going to lead; I was just interested. I learned a lot from books that way.

I am sure that everyone has had that experience of absorption. You absorb something so fully because you are enjoying it. You love it. Sometimes reading something is a big chore. You have to plod through. "When am I going to finish? I can't wait to get to the last page." But when I am reading a book, for instance a scientific book, I am not doing it because I am going to get knowledge. I do get knowledge, that is part of it; but it is entertaining me at the same time. I read object relations theory books the way some people read comics. I enjoy them the same way. Sometimes it is difficult to understand, but that is fine. It is worth it.

Also, why you love something is another factor. Usually, if your being is present while you do something you love, it does not have just to do with you; it has to do with something larger. The things that I read and study usually relate to my work. My reading is beneficial for the work I do and the people I work with. It is more beneficial for them than it is for me. But that usefulness translates into my loving reading these things. So it is a compassionate act, in a sense. However, the fact that I often learn things out of compassion and concern for others does not mean I am concerned and want to help others. The action doesn't come out that way. It manifests as being really interested and liking to do it. So it feels as if it is for me. It feels like it is completely for me but at the same time it is not just for me. And when this is happening I am not thinking whether it is for others or for me.

That is what Being does when it is present—if you let yourself be Being, its very nature is a source of Love, a source of Compassion, a source of Intelligence, Understanding, Will, Strength, and all of the essential aspects. When we go into the area of seeking, we cut ourselves off from these things and we feel deficient. If we really allow ourselves to be and we learn to digest our experiences, as I said, what will develop, what will emerge and mature is the Personal Essence. The Personal Essence is what is called the Son of

Man. Another phrase for it is the Son of God. Because we are that, we are the children of Being. We are the individual personal manifestations of absolute Being. We are Being. This is a fact; it is not something you are going to arrive at. It is always the true state of affairs; it cannot be any other way. If we were not this Being, we would have no awareness.

Christmas is not the celebration of the birth and life of one individual; it is the celebration of the birth and life of the human individual, the true essential person. Christ represents all of humanity. He was not just a special person. His specialness is that he recognized and embodied the true meaning of being a human individual. He let himself be open. He had the courage to do that, and gave us a model. When he says, "I am the Son of God," I understand him to mean that every human being is the Son of God, that every human being can know that he or she is the Son of God. When he talked about God as his father, he was saying what is true for all of us.

If God is our father why do we go about our lives as if we are deficient and poor? Seeking for something is an undignified action for the human being. In seeking, we are not respecting who we are. If we are the children of God, we are rich to begin with. Why go about looking for things as if we've got nothing?

We need to question that attitude of impoverishment, that attitude of seeking and searching. We need to look at it very objectively. We need to see how it is suffering and how it leads to suffering. We need to see how it is the source of suffering and how absolutely unnecessary and redundant it is. It is not a matter of resolving one issue or another. It is a matter of just letting yourself be, leaving yourself alone, settling into your nature.

THREE

Human Maturity

To live fulfilling and rewarding lives, we must live like human beings. Our problems, our conflicts, our suffering, our disappointments, and our lacks are not due to the causes we ordinarily ascribe them to; they are primarily the result of the fact that we are not living the way we are supposed to be living. If any being is not living the way it is meant to, the deviation from the inherent potential of that being will manifest as disharmony, conflict, problems, or perhaps physical or mental dysfunction.

Only living in a way that is natural to us will free us from unnecessary struggle and strife, only living in a way that is truly human. A natural way of life is not determined by what some authority says; rather it is a life lived in accordance with natural laws of functioning of our beingness, of who we are. To really consider this fact necessitates a radical shift in our way of looking at ourselves and in the way we conduct our lives. We must first accept that since there is unnecessary strife, struggle, and pain in our lives, this means that we really don't know what it's like to live as human beings. We need to see that we really don't know how a truly mature human being lives, or what kinds of values and principles govern the life of such a person.

The first thing we need to confront, then, is the ever-present, arrogant belief that we know what a human being is, what it's like to live as a human being, what a human being's life is about, and how a human being is supposed to conduct herself. Let's entertain the possibility that a person with the normal level of consciousness—composed of emotional reactions, ideas, and beliefs taken from the past and from other people—is not yet a human being. She is a reflection, an imitation, an unfinished attempt to become a human being. Her potential has not developed. Such a person is run by influences that are supposed to rule only children.

The forces that rule the life of the ordinary human being are not those that are meant to rule the life of someone who has grown into the full potential of an adult human being. If we continue to live according to these principles, values, and influences, we remain at a childish stage of development. I am not saying that this is morally bad, but rather, that it falls short of the potential of being a genuinely mature human being. If we do not allow ourselves to grow the way we are meant to, there is bound to be conflict, tension, suffering, misunderstanding, and problems in our lives.

To truly understand what it is to be a mature human being, we must begin by questioning our assumption that we know what a human being is, how a human being should conduct her life, what principles should govern the life of such a person, and what kind of things a mature person does. We are familiar with the principles and influences that govern the mind of the ordinary person: fear, desire, greed, insecurity, competition, jealousy, and elementary needs of all kinds. These influences are the traces left in us of our ancestors in the animal world, together with ideas, misunderstandings, and prejudices that we have acquired. These beliefs are appropriate for a certain stage of human life, but not for all stages. They are okay for a child, but an adult is supposed to have grown out of them. A genuine, mature human being is a human being who is not ruled by such influences.

Security needs such as the need for money, power, prestige, acceptance, and approval are actually the needs of a child. These needs express the part of the human being that remains undeveloped and unrefined. Even an idea that most people would take as obvious—the idea that a human being should be happy, and have pleasure instead of pain and suffering—is not a principle that should govern a mature human being. That principle governs all of the animal kingdom, but the mature human being can rise above it and live with higher, more refined, and more satisfying values.

So, as I have said, the first thing we need to do is to suspend our belief that we know what a human being is and what a human being's life is all about. We have to admit to ourselves that we don't know, or see that if we do know something about what it is to be human, what we know is very little. We need to acknowledge that there is a lot more to know about what it means to be a human being. Maybe you have not questioned yourself from this perspective. Maybe you have taken the ordinary things that happen in your life to be what a being human being is all about. Maybe you have assumed the correctness of the principles that govern your life and the lives of everyone else you know.

The majority of humanity lives at an infantile stage. It is necessary for us to pass through that stage, but we do not have to stop there. However, it is not part of generally accepted societal wisdom to understand what a true human being is, or what the function of a human being is. Because society at large does not have this knowledge and functions at an undeveloped level, we are given no guidance about how to grow up. Society is necessary for the basic security and social needs of human beings, but the human being needs more than that. The fulfillment of the true human potential requires meeting much deeper, finer needs.

Work like ours exposes the animalistic and childish influences and needs which govern our lives, and brings the more refined aspects of ourselves to bear on our lives. In this process, so convinced are we of our base and deficient nature, that often we will actually attempt to use the finer elements of who we are to satisfy our elementary needs. An example of this pattern is using essential or spiritual experience to feel superior to those around us. However, our beingness and its capacities are not there to satisfy the personality's needs, such as the need for approval, recognition, love, acceptance, security, power, or even pleasure. The finer elements of the human soul are there to transform your personality so that it grows out of those childish patterns. Contact with essential qualities is supposed to have an impact on who you are, so that you can become a mature human being and be what you are meant to be. These finer elements are not meant to be compartmentalized within us to provide us with a sense of accomplishment or to make us feel good in some other way. The need to feel good is the need of a child or teenager. You might think that when you feel happy and you have a lot of pleasure that you've made it. Well, yes, you have made it, as a teenager. That is still a far cry from being a mature adult.

The learning we do here, and the kind of experiences it generates in us, constitute a certain kind of nutrition, to help us to grow up. These experiences change us, and this change will manifest as a transformation of the values and principles that govern our lives. While this transformation will affect the rest of our lives, it will be most apparent in our relationships, in how we conduct ourselves as individuals with other human individuals.

If you have inner experiences of being Value and Compassion and Clarity and Peace, but you still relate to other people like a sniffling infant, your work has not done its job yet. Those qualities are not just there for your enjoyment. This is the way a child sees things. A mature human being can put these experiences to good use and actually live in a way that manifests these real human qualities.

The purpose of our having experiences of the refined elements of our nature is not so that we can accumulate them like money in a savings account, so that we can use them to give us a sense of having something. If you are acting according to such childish principles, something in you has not yet changed. It is not the objective of the Work to satisfy childish needs. The objective of the Work is to guide you to grow and mature so that you can live in accordance with your true nature.

Although the Work is not about gratifying childish needs, this does not mean that those needs have to be rejected or put down. They need to be acknowledged and understood so that you can see that you are not really a child and can let go of them, or go beyond them.

From this perspective, we see that the Work we do here is not a simple thing; it is not easy. It is not meant to be easy. It is not based on the values and principles that most people bring with them, but on quite different values. A large part of the work here involves the friction between these two value systems. The interaction between them produces a grinding, a honing that is supposed to expose the old beliefs and the infantile patterns so that we can drop them. This does not mean that people do not have a right to live their lives according to what we call infantile values and principles. Everyone has the right to do that. But a person who chooses to be in the Work is a person who already feels that she wants to grow up. She already has some inkling that childish values are not "it." The Work's function is to support the growth of mature human beings, not to feed and comfort babies.

The Work we do here is the kind of work that must be done by any human being in order to truly grow up. It is difficult, it takes a long time, it is complex, and it involves much more than you imagine at the beginning. When you come here initially, you arrive with many ideas and beliefs about what the Work is going to do for you. If you stay in it, you will realize that the Work will not do just the things you expected, but a thousand more things. You will also see that to be engaged in the Work in a genuine way, so that you can grow to be a mature human being, you have to do a lot more than you thought. This is because there is a lot more to a human being than you originally believed. The process of maturation takes a lot of work, a lot of effort, a lot of dedication, and a lot of patience.

Within a couple of months or years after starting the Work, you might be better able to feel and express your emotions and be more in touch with your body. For many people, this is all they want, but this is only the first, most elementary, step in the Work. This step is necessary and important, but we do not see it as an end. A human being is not ultimately supposed to be governed by her emotions or bodily sensations. As I have said, if your ideas about what you will get from the Work continue to be governed by your emotional and physical desires, you are in for a big disappointment. To be genuinely involved in this Work, you have to be willing to suspend your beliefs about what life is all about. You have to be courageous enough to say, "I don't know." And then you need even more courage to feel that you want to know.

So when we begin the Work, we have to work on the emotional parts of our personality, and then we work to expose our preconceptions, assumptions, and beliefs about reality and ourselves. Later, we might have experiences of Essence in its various stages and aspects, and the Work becomes the integration of these refined elements of ourselves. Then the whole personality itself needs to be transmuted and transformed in accordance with these deeper elements of ourselves. We must become more refined human beings, more mature human beings, more evolved human beings, more actual human beings. Then maybe we can live the life of a true human adult.

This process is long and complex, and of course it varies from one person to another. But for everyone it entails a great deal of work. You need to understand a lot about your mind, about your emotions, about what patterns constitute your character, and what causes you to behave as you do. This takes time and patience. The process involves a lot of pain and difficulty, although it is also exhilarating and joyful and exciting. A lot of perseverance is required to perceive your essential aspects and then to realize and integrate them. None of this is easy, and it will not be done for you. The teacher can only guide you by pointing to things; you have to do the work, and it is a lot of difficult work. And in the society we live in there is no support for this kind of process. Our social environment does not recognize, does not understand, and does not support such development. You were conditioned by that society, so the obstacles you have to free yourself from are many and powerful, and they pervade your mind and personality.

The kinds of understanding, the kinds of perceptions, the kinds of experiences, and the kinds of realizations you have to go through are many, and involve many levels and dimensions. You move from one stage to another, back and forth, and that takes patience, and compassion for yourself. It takes the generous, realistic, and mature attitude towards life that if you want something, you have to work for it. Nobody can do it for you and nobody can give it to you, because it *is* you.

We should consider ourselves lucky if we find someone who knows something about how to go about this process, and who is genuinely interested in the development of our human potential. Such a person is rare in human society, and should be looked upon with the utmost appreciation and gratitude. Any work that helps you with this process should be held with the deepest respect and value, because to do so is to respect and value your own potential and the potential of humanity in general. Such work should be held above everything else because it *is* ultimately above everything. It should first of all be put above one's childish values, principles, and influences. That is what it takes. This is not a moralistic point of view, but a practical one. The Work must be done this way because otherwise it will not work.

This kind of respect, valuing, and appreciation needs to manifest not just towards the Work or just towards me as a teacher, but it must also manifest towards each other. If we are learning to be genuine human beings, we should behave maturely towards each other instead of treating each other as rivals, enemies, or sources of gratification, which are the usual ways people relate to each other. If we are going to learn to be human, it will have to begin right here.

What I am saying is that it is not enough to simply understand what is happening inside yourself; your understanding must manifest in your actions and in your interactions with others. That is where the work of integration can happen, and that is where the impact of the refined elements of your nature will transform your personality. Without this integration, the Work will not be complete, and may, in fact, generate all kinds of abnormalities and distortions. We need to pay attention to how we behave and interact, from the perspective of the higher elements within us.

You cannot be a genuine human being if your outer life does not correspond to your inner life. If there is a contradiction between your inner experience and your behavior towards others, a big distortion is taking place. If you know certain things but behave according to other things, if you value certain parts of reality but when it comes to actual living you throw those values out the window, a very strange kind of split is occurring. This will lead to frustration for you and trouble for those around you. This Work is not about just realizing yourself, feeling wonderful and forgetting about everyone else. It is the very nature of being a mature human being to respect others as real human beings, too.

If you really want to experience what it is like to be a genuine human being, you need to put in the effort it takes to live like one, regardless of how difficult it is. As I said, a large part of the work here involves the friction between the principles, ideas and beliefs that you came with, and the principles of the Work. Through the process, you will understand and realize previously unknown parts of yourself. This will lead to modifications in your behavior which you must work towards consciously and continuously.

You should behave in a genuinely human way, not only with me or your teacher, but with everyone in your life. Otherwise, you are perpetuating the infantile part of you; you are still acting like an animal. So, with each other here and with all the people in your life, you should make a conscious effort to live according to those finer elements that you understand and realize, rather than indulging in the old patterns. Ideally, there will be mutual respect and appreciation, mutual kindness and understanding. Another human being is an expression of the most sublime thing there is, just as you are such an expression. If you don't relate to that human being with respect, appreciation, and recognition, you are not respecting or recognizing that sublime element in yourself.

We are not separate. Our sense of separateness is superficial and exists only in the physical dimension. In our human element, we are not separate; we are very much connected. Every other human being is just as precious as we are, and worthy of as much respect and love and consideration. This understanding needs to manifest in our conduct in each moment. This is the part of the Work that will transform you.

First, we have the work of essential realization. The next step, which is harder, is to learn how to manifest that realization in your life. You must face the question of how you are going to live that realization. How are you going to let it influence your life so that your life will become a truly mature human life? It takes great effort to remember yourself and those finer elements you are learning about, in order for their perspective to affect your life and your relationships with others and with your environment. The principles and the values you live by must change from acquisitiveness, competition, jealousy, and rejection, to an attitude of graciousness, generosity, respect, and gratitude. If you are really going to be a mature human being, you will behave according to those values even though others may not. You do not give yourself the excuse that because another person is acting like a jerk, you are not going to behave in a decent way. If you do that, you are betraying your human element. You are being disrespectful to who you are and what you can become.

If you are interested in becoming a truly mature human being, you must conduct yourself according to the highest values you know, all the time. It is part of being a mature human being to put in the effort of conducting yourself thusly. If you believe that the integration of your realization should just happen by itself, or that it should be easy, you are not understanding what life is all about and you are behaving like an infant. To become a gracious, generous, respectful, loving, kind, and clear human being, you have to work at it. It is not going to simply happen. God is not going to do it for you. You have to put effort into it, minute by minute; otherwise you will not transform.

Of course, no one is saying you have to do this; no one has to do the Work. It is your choice. If you want to do it, this is what is required. You might say, "It's too difficult. I'm angry about it and I don't like it." So it's difficult. If you want to become mature as a human being, you must see your anger, your hurt, and your frustration, and tolerate it and in spite of it live like a mature human being. If you say, "It's too difficult, so I'm going to hide or run away and forget about the whole thing," you are behaving like a little child who wants his mommy when things get difficult. If you want to grow up, you have to act in a grown-up way.

The refined values of love and compassion and truth are not going to become part of you and manifest in your life if you are just sitting on your ass and meditating, or trying to understand yourself. If you think it is enough for you to just sit in group or have a breathwork session and experience those finer elements of yourself, you are working with the wrong perspective. You have to work at living your life in accordance with those values until it becomes second nature. To do this you need to respect yourself. Otherwise, you are indulging yourself as you would a child, and disparaging your true potential, and thus betraying the deepest part of yourself. Our whole problem is that we keep betraying who we are by living in a way that does not befit our actual nature.

When you are being your true self, you are not looking for pleasure, you are not avoiding pain, you are not trying to get approval, nor trying to get someone to admire you. You are not out to criticize someone else, or to defeat someone else, and you are not out to gain fame or power. You are naturally and spontaneously living as a genuine human being who has respect and consideration for other human beings. You are not trying to love someone; you are just loving, without even thinking about it. If you are a mature person, it is second nature that you are loving, that you are giving, that you are respectful, and considerate, and that you behave and act in a refined and mature human manner.

To make these values and manifestations second nature, you have to put conscious effort into them. You have to make it your work. This does not mean that you have to be solemn and grim and serious; that is not the point. The point is to act with sincerity and to put conscious effort into being aware of yourself and others in order to treat yourself and others with respect. This also does not mean giving up pleasure; it means not seeking pleasure. It does not mean creating pain; it means not avoiding pain.

Life is to be lived with the integrity, dignity, and self-respect of a person who knows that the point is not whether something feels good or bad. The point is not to lose your self-respect, not to abandon your true reality, the highest and purest elements within you. Regardless of how wonderful things are and regardless of how painful things are, your self-respect is strong enough to maintain your sense of integrity. That integrity does not mean having your way, or winning or succeeding or anything like that. It means being sincere about who you are and acting in ways that reflect your essential human values.

Having self-respect, self-consideration, and self-love means doing and learning whatever is needed to maintain that integrity and self-respect. It means that if something needs to be learned, you go ahead and learn it; if something needs to be done, you go ahead and do it; and if something needs to be said, you go ahead and say it. To have self-respect and integrity means not complaining about how things are. It means acting towards others with respect and consideration regardless of what you feel.

Having self-respect means that even if you are dying, you are still considerate and respectful towards yourself and other people, because who you are is much more important than whether you are going to die. It is much more important than whether you' are losing your business or losing your boyfriend or girlfriend. Human dignity is much more precious than any of these things.

This is why we sometimes practice the nonexpression of automatic emotions. When you do this, you not only pay attention to yourself by sensing yourself continually, but you also pay attention so that you do not express any automatic emotion that you feel. Keep it to yourself, feel it, understand it, and use it as a fuel for your presence and your understanding. You might not be able to do this all the time and it is important not to attack yourself when you cannot do it perfectly; the point is to put forth as much conscious effort and dedication as possible.

This means that if you are angry for some unconscious reason, you do not just yell at someone; you keep it to yourself for your understanding. If you are hurt because someone is rejecting you, you keep it to yourself. You do not tell the other person, "You are rejecting me and I think you are terrible." You let yourself feel rejected, you work to understand it by yourself or with your teacher if you are working with a teacher. You use the energy, the fuel, the heat that comes out of that Work with the intention of keeping it to yourself for your presence, for your understanding, for the transformation of your personality.

All kinds of emotions can be automatic—for example, hopelessness or despair. Not acting on these feelings means that even though you might wake up in the morning feeling that your life is pointless and hopeless, you get out of bed and go to your job anyway. Not acting on automatic emotions means that if a friend comes by and you are feeling lonely and needy and you want a hug, you do not act on that desire—you just feel it, because you know that that desire is to fill an automatic and elementary need.

It might take time for you to understand what the non-expression of automatic emotions entails, and that is fine. What is entailed in not indulging in your automatic emotions is being conscious all the time. We are not talking about suppressing the emotions, we're talking about not expressing them. To express them discharges them, and that stops you from really understanding and going deeper. Expressing emotions stops the process of transformation, because a truly mature human being does not act on these emotions. This practice is most important; doing it will teach us a lot. It might be hard to understand what it involves, but you need to persist anyway. If you want to grow up to be who you truly are, you have to learn to do these things. Indulgence will not help you. Indulgence just feeds the elementary needs and values, and perpetuates them.

To do this practice, we need to use all the awareness and all the will that we have developed. We have to consciously take our transformation into our own hands. A human being who has true self-respect does not declare his or her enlightenment, nor want to be seen. The more real you are, the more invisible you are, because you keep your realization to yourself. Desires to show it or expose it or impress others are desires to satisfy elementary and childish needs, and the true human being does not act according to those needs, and in time does not have them. A mature adult human being just goes about his or her business without trying to please anybody.

This practice is not about stopping the emotions. It is about stopping acting on them (or from them) because we recognize that they come from that part of us which is elementary, primitive, and childish. This is just like raising a child: You don't let the child do whatever he wants, because if you do, he will make a mess of your house and probably hurt himself, right? It is the same with yourself: You don't let the childish part do whatever it wants to do because it will make a mess of your life and it will hurt you. It is as simple as that, you have to discipline it. This childish part of you will have to learn that its behaviors are not grown-up ones, that there is no use for them, and that they are just destructive. If a baby is angry, he might drop his bottle and break it or throw things, and that feels good to him. He does not understand why you want to stop him, and he gets more angry when you try to stop him. It is the same thing with yourself: You might say that it feels good to express your anger, and that might be true, but it is also destructive to yourself and to humanity in general. Expressing anger is an automatic reaction, and just like a baby, in order to grow up you need to learn not to do it. It doesn't matter whether expressing it feels good or bad—that's not the point. The point is integrity, self-respect, maturity, humanity, and truth.

FOUR

Maturity and Truth

S ometimes I think that many of you are here for the wrong reasons. Many of you persist in wanting and trying to get things from the Work that it is not the job of the Work to provide. Students bring in problems and want me to solve them. Certainly each of us needs to solve his problems, but that is not the interest of the Work, nor is it my interest in working with people. When I am working with someone it is generally not my concern to solve problems. Not only is it not my concern, but I find the situation of being expected to solve problems for people, or even with them, very boring and unrewarding. It misses the point. Resolving specific problems is not the most important thing, because problems will continue to arise. Life is full of problems. If you dedicate your life to solving problems, you will have your hands full for the rest of your life. Certainly, there is a place for problem-solving in life. However, students often believe that solving one problem after another will eventually eradicate all problems and lead to happiness. That is not what happens.

The attitude of wanting to eradicate one's problems strengthens the attachment to problems. You keep generating problems one after another, since that is what you know how to do, and what you expect. It is easy to generate problems and issues. When that mechanism is dominating your work, problems will remain the focus of your attention while other things become less important.

I understand that once in a while someone has something very pressing, some problem that needs to be resolved. That is fine and I am sometimes willing to help in that way. But that is not the function of the teacher or of our work here. I am more interested in the process that happens when I am working with someone, and understanding the workings of the process, rather than the result. I don't look at the resolution; instead, I look at how the student is handling the problem or situation. How is he struggling with it? What kind of attitude does he have about it? That is how I can tell how much the person has learned. I find it much more rewarding to work with a student when the student is not as interested in solving the problem as they are curious about the truth of the situation.

Our Work is motivated by certain values, and it has its own principles and aesthetics. These principles, values, and aesthetics are different from those involved in eliminating difficulties. If my purpose were to help people solve problems, I wouldn't last more than a year or two in this work. I would be like a mother with a hundred children, who has to take care of them and make them feel better every time they cry. I am not a mother; and even in dealing with children, I expect some level of responsibility from them. Even with a child, I don't automatically try to help every time he cries and demands help. Sometimes the most loving thing to do is to allow a child to go as far as he can by himself, to allow him to mature. The same is true for adults. It is demeaning to be constantly concerned with problems; human beings have more dignity than that, and a higher purpose. If problems are all you are concerned with, you will see everything according to this preoccupation. This is a waste of our human potential. In our Work we emphasize working to understand ourselves and the nature of reality. It is true that as we become more objective and more free, some problems might be resolved. However, this is a side-effect of becoming aligned with the truth of who we are, since so many of our problems result from our ignorance about who we are.

However, if our motive is to be rid of problems and suffering, they will only get worse, and you will become more frustrated. The suffering and frustration are there because of the motivation to get rid of them. That is how the suffering began and it is how it perpetuates itself.

A mature human being with self-respect and dignity will learn to tolerate and accept some problems, live with some frustrations, and still manage to appreciate the finer things that are there. Something immature and petty is happening when someone experiences a subtle perception, an essential state, or some understanding, but only sees the possibility of either pleasure or gratification, missing the substance of the experience or process. This is a common occurrence. One such reaction is excitement because it feels good, or another might be to discard the experience because it is not what was expected. "I don't care because my boyfriend still doesn't love me." There is no openness to the moment then, only an infant's wish for gratification. The Work is not a magic wand.

What I look for is a certain appreciation for the process of what we have done together, not a result. There is a certain exquisiteness in the interaction; it has a beauty of its own, apart from gratification. Feeling good is only one of the elements that I perceive in the situation; in fact, the result becomes simply interesting. I see how I feel in that state, and how I feel about my boyfriend or girlfriend not loving me. I find it very fascinating when I experience a state like that, and I don't care whether someone loves me or not. That is very significant. This does not mean that there will not be emotions of loss and grief when a relationship ends; feelings will be there as usual. But the significance of the Work is beyond loss or gain. The significance lies in the freedom that results from the sincere desire for truth.

When there is sincerity about understanding the truth, there is beauty and appreciation in the process for both the teacher and the student. My own essence does not respond when someone is only interested in getting rid of discomfort. The session becomes boring and not aesthetically appealing to me. When the student is interested in a mature way in the process, and is sincere and curious, then there is some kind of dance, an exchange that is real and intimate. The real world becomes more the center than the world of personality. Even when concerns of the personality arise, they are viewed from the perspective of the truth. Even personality stops being a source of irritation. There arises an appreciation of the intricacy and complexity that is the process of understanding, loving the dance and process, rather than wanting to be rid of something. This appreciation results in true dignity and integrity by being aware of the personality without going along with it. There is a beauty to the human being who experiences his or her suffering without indulging, and getting lost in it. Truth sometimes leads to the elimination of suffering, but it can also lead to pain. Whichever results, if the student allows the perspective of love and appreciation for reality, for truth—whether it brings joy or pain—a feeling of deep intimacy within will result. You could be intimate with yourself, which is satisfying and fulfilling, regardless of whether the outcome of the problem results in pain or pleasure. Either pain or pleasure, grumbling that you didn't get what you wanted or being elated that you got your way, could distract you from the deeper significance of working on yourself. This is the deeper satisfaction of inner intimacy. This attitude of truth frees us from our usual childish desires, needs, dreams, and wants. When you appreciate the truth and yourself in that process, you exercise this intimacy with yourself, a capacity and a fulfillment you may not have known was possible. This fulfillment is clearly so much more to the point than being seen, feeling important, feeling better than others, having power, riches—all the things that we usually seek. The more you feel this intimacy, the more you see that these desires are vacuous. Even if you reached all these goals and desires, they would never compare to the riches of the heart, this intimacy with yourself.

This perspective of love and truth also brings humility, not because a person wants to be humble, but because humility is a part of this intimacy, and it is very human and satisfying. Getting your way, being right, or getting something you want, are part of life, but these things are not central to our deeper interests because they don't take you closer to the truth, nor to yourself.

It is up to each of us to decide what values govern our lives. We can allow our lives to be governed by the pursuit of pleasure, avoiding and trying to get rid of difficulties, or we can allow our lives to be focused on loving understanding and truth. If we are going to wait for the pain to disappear before we come to appreciate truth or to love reality, that will rarely happen.

You will have problems, issues, conflicts, and misunderstandings in your life, and in your work here. These are to be seen as only part of the picture, not the focus and center of our Work. These things need to be looked at when they present a barrier. Even when you are looking at an issue, it is more to the point to focus on the mechanisms of the mind with an attitude of appreciation for the process of understanding. This focuses on the truth in the issue, rather than on getting rid of the problem. This may seem to be an insignificant or subtle distinction, but it makes a big difference in the outcome of the work. One perspective is alive and dynamic; the other remains boring and static.

If you want to live a more fulfilling life, you have to develop a taste for certain values, a taste for truth and understanding, depth and profundity, precision and exquisiteness, dignity and integrity. These refined values are subtle rather than gross. They will lead to a refined human life, infused with natural beauty, colorful and rich. All of these things are present all the time—you don't have to achieve them, you just need to appreciate them. You need to begin to love them and orient yourself towards them so that you allow yourself the time and opportunity for them to emerge.

It is also important to see that the result of the orientation towards solving problems, conflicts, and tensions, is an infantile sort of dependency on the teacher. If the student learns to appreciate the process of understanding and supports the truth, then the student is an adult and an equal with his or her teacher. There will be collaboration and an enjoyable interaction, an artistic, creative flow. The world is full of all kinds of miraculous things and beautiful subtleties. When it is not focused on and limited by the perspective of getting rid of the problem, this entire process—including the problem—can become a source of fulfillment.

Often, there is an attitude that "Nothing good is going to happen until I get rid of this problem." This attitude eliminates any openness to what might arise in the moment. If people are going to be heavy, waiting to solve their problems, there will be no happy people left. We're talking about a certain focus, a persistent stubbornness, a narrow-minded view of wanting only what you have in your mind, what you think is good. You are saying then, "I know what is best and I'll close my eyes to anything else that is there." This only leads to suffering, frustration, and tension.

You will be much more compassionate and kind, both towards yourself and others, if you just learn to relax. Say, "What is this? Why am I driving myself crazy? Why not relax and have a cup of tea?" Take a walk, forget about all the problems for a while. Why do you think you can only enjoy yourself if there are no problems? Why do you have to wait until you get enlightened? Don't wait for the mantle of loving kindness to drop on your shoulders before you can be nice to yourself and everyone else. Why wait for it to drop spontaneously, so that you begin to do everything right all of a sudden? That's not how human life is. You have to work at certain things, exert effort, deal with problems here and there. There will be pleasures, enjoyments, and fulfillment which will help you in dealing with the problems.

Who are you when you are dealing with your problems? When you see your deficiencies and frustrations, do you relate to them with dignity, or with demands and a temper tantrum? Are you interested in complaining, or in giving yourself the time to learn what you need to know to work with problems intelligently. Certain things need to be done; other things you can only allow as part of your life. When the roof is leaking, it is not intelligent to respond with a fit—you do not find someone to blame. It is a hassle, but there are certain things that need to be done, so you do them with the right attitude at the right time. If you make yourself miserable, hating your house and your responsibilities and wondering why God made rain, you will only end up with frustration. You must accept that these things happen and you must attend to them.

A mature human being is not a person who does not have problems; a mature human being is one who handles problems maturely, taking into consideration everything he or she knows and then acting accordingly. This replaces the behavior of persisting in infantile tendencies which can only lead to frustration and even more problems. The mature human being can accept difficulties as part of life, and is willing to deal with them appropriately. There are things to be taken care of, but you can enjoy the things that you need to do. Life does not start after the chores are done. When someone matures and feels happier and more fulfilled, it is not because they have solved their problems. It is because they have accepted the way things are. Problems exist and work needs to be done to deal with each one of these problems or issues. Maturity entails finding whatever knowledge is needed to develop the expertise to do what is needed. The mature person goes about doing this quietly, as part of his life.

In time, a mature person attains joy in wholeheartedly dealing with whatever arises in life. Life is a much larger thing; these are only incidental parts of it. If you learn that, you will see that a certain integrity is implicit in that acceptance, and that you can enjoy your own capacity to deal with it. From this attitude of acceptance and appreciation of life, there arises a kind of autonomy and independence. We no longer need to be nursed all the time like children.

FIVE

The Integrated Human Being

Human life can be lived with beauty, grace, and dignity. But this refined mode of life is not easy to come by. The point of being human is not to achieve success, riches, comfort, or security. These things may be important or necessary, but only to the grosser side of human life. When there is disharmony or imbalance in one's consciousness, one's values tend towards the grosser side of human nature. The refinement of human consciousness requires harmonization and balancing of all the human elements. The more harmony and balance in one's consciousness and in one's life, the more it will become a life of beauty, grace, dignity, and efficiency.

We are not saying that there is something bad about ordinary human life, nor that one should seek something better.

It is a matter of harmonization and balance. The absence of that balance or harmony predisposes us towards certain assumptions, certain expectations of what our lives should be like. Then our consciousness becomes stabilized with the idealizations of certain elements to the exclusion of others, which only leads to more imbalance and disharmony. That is why a consciousness that is not balanced usually does not know how to balance itself, for this consciousness can see things only from an imbalanced perspective. In turn, what this consciousness believes or feels that it needs and wants is determined by that perspective. The consciousness first needs to be balanced and harmonized before it can see what is truly needed.

One element of imbalanced consciousness is the dream of a magical event, an idealized intervention, a romantic experience or a person that will suddenly make things wonderful. Of course, the fantasized situation is wonderful only from the perspective of that imbalanced consciousness. Since reality is mostly not like that, things do not generally turn out according to our expectations, and then we feel disappointment. The hopeful expectation of a miraculous event or person typically manifests in ordinary life as an idealization of success or fame, or sometimes an idealization of a person, perhaps a prince charming who will come along and enable us to live happily ever after.

When someone enters the Work, this tendency becomes displaced on the Work, the school, the teacher, or the method. This happens with any form of work, essential, spiritual, or psychological. With psychological work, you are looking for the magical cure. With spiritual work, you are looking for the magical experience which is usually called enlightenment. From the balanced perspective, one sees that these experiences do exist but are not magical in the way that the imbalanced consciousness believes. There do exist experiences of realization and enlightenment and the like, but these are only some of the initial elements needed for a balanced consciousness. They are not the only elements, nor the end, of spiritual work. In other words, for a balanced consciousness that lives in a balanced, harmonious, and mature way as a human being, enlightenment is not enough. It is a beginning. Realization is also only one experience among many others that are needed for a person to develop a capacity to live correctly. Many people who have been engaged in spiritual work can see that their experiences have not necessarily transformed the way they live their lives. One way of seeing the guidance in our Work here is that there is a continual movement of balancing and rebalancing the individual, the groups, and the school as a whole. Whenever there is an imbalance in a certain direction, something needs to happen from the other direction to balance what is happening. What could result if things remain imbalanced is tantamount to a malignant growth.

From the perspective of our Work, generally speaking, three elements need to be balanced or need to stay in balance as a person is engaged in the process of development. Basically, the three things are understanding, being, and doing. Most individuals tend to emphasize one of these over the other two. Some people are more balanced towards the understanding aspect of human experience. Some people are balanced more towards the being element, the actual felt experience part. And some people are balanced more towards the action, the doing part of human experience. This imbalance creates a disharmony that affects all three elements. Our work involves developing these three elements into a harmonious unity, and this involves balancing them. A constant balancing needs to happen again and again, whenever an imbalance appears in either the individual or in the group. Otherwise, development could happen in an imbalanced way. It is possible for a person to develop one part but not the others. Although this can be fine in itself, it does not lead to an integrated human life. It does not lead to the state of maturity.

Some of the activities in our work are oriented towards understanding our personal situation, and through that process towards a knowledge of reality and truth. For a long time, understanding will in large part reveal that the personality, the false personality, and the life of that personality, are empty. Realizing that the normal personality, which dominates the experience of conventional life is actually empty, will lead to the awareness of the fullness of Being, which is the second element. We come to know the actual experience of Being, the feeling of beingness, the state of being, the realization of presence. This state is called various things—enlightenment, or self-realization, or the state of unity, or oneness of being. We then discover that the state of being, although wonderful, is still not the totality of a human consciousness. This state of being and the understanding accompanying it need to be embodied, to be integrated into one's life.

This is when the role of action becomes important. It is not enough to have understanding of yourself. It is not enough to realize the presence of Being. For full integration, these need to manifest in your life in action. They must appear in your actions so that you live your life according to that understanding, and from that state of beingness. Of course, some individuals are satisfied with the mere understanding of things, and continue only to seek insights and realizations. It is absolutely necessary to have this understanding, these insights, realizations, perceptions, and all the knowledge of the different states and conditions of human life. However, there is a need for the actual experience of Being itself, and that has to do with the essential states, ultimately, and with a state of being. Being is really the central part of all those three elements; it is the heart of the matter. In fact, it has to do with the heart. Although Being is primary, it is not enough for living on earth, because life also involves action and doing. To live a mature life means not only to live, but to live according to this state of being. If a person doesn't live according to the understanding that comes from the realization of beingness, then the realization or development is restricted to certain experiences and does not touch the person's soul deeply enough to allow the integration necessary for maturity.

Of course, all three elements exist on a conventional level, too. The ordinary, undeveloped, unrefined human life has in it understanding, being and doing but they are fake. The usual understanding and conventional wisdom are the usual beliefs, assumptions and preconceptions, and the usual information of the personality. The experience of being human is equated with the usual emotional, mental and physical experiences. The action on the personality level is simply the way people live their lives. When I refer to essential doing or action, I do not mean just any action; many people, in fact the majority of humankind, are action-oriented. People do all kind of actions, but this is not what we are talking about. We are talking about action that embodies Being, about doing which is real action. This real action is what differentiates a developed human being from an undeveloped one.

In other words, human development has three elements or three stages. One is that of understanding and knowledge, as in insights and intuitions. Then there is realization, which is abiding in beingness. After that is the state of doing, which is the embodiment of the beingness and the knowledge in your life, in how you live your life. If you come to the group or to your session and you have wonderful insights and realizations, and experiences of boundless love and infinite presence or whatever, but then you go through the rest of your life and live according to the usual personality, it's as if it has not happened. Essential experiences or realizations need to affect all your life, to permeate everything, until they are embodied. A maturing person needs to live according to those experiences and those insights. A person who has not had these experiences and insights will be unable to live in a mature way. So all of the three elements are necessary. If a person is oriented only towards action, to live her life and be successful, it doesn't matter what she does. If there is no true beingness and no real understanding, then her action is not to the point, her life is not in harmony, and she will be oriented towards satisfying the desires of the dream, the magical expectations of the personality.

We do our work here so that in time, there will arise in your consciousness many insights and understandings of the personality, of your life, of your past, and of the mind. This understanding will reveal the false elements, and unveil the dimension of Essence. Together with this process of insight and understanding, the path will reveal Being in many kinds of experiences. There will be a series of experiences of different dimensions, and different levels of realization. All these insights and all these experiences are needed for full development, and, at some point, need to be integrated with action. If it does not happen spontaneously, a person will need to intentionally live life according to what has been learned and what has been experienced. This might not necessarily happen by itself.

Some insights, realizations, and even actions, will come to you as gifts that just happen, but some of them you will have to work for. You will have to put in the effort to regulate and balance yourself. That is the reality of human life. If you are open, if you are interested in the truth, things will happen to you, but not everything. For some things, you will have to take action, you will have to make greater effort. Both elements are needed: the spontaneous arising and the effort, the expenditure of energy. The first part of understanding is the easiest part. It is sometimes difficult to see the significance of states of being and to allow oneself to abide in these various states of being. Then, the most difficult task is to embody being in action.

Carrying the understanding and being into action is the primary and most powerful integrative process of both understanding and being. If you do not take the action, if you do not try to live your life according to what you have learned, according to what you have experienced, then there is a tendency not to integrate the various elements. There is a tendency to create a split between different parts. There is the wonderful part of you, and then there is the rest of your life which is a mess—full of frustrations, problems, complaints, or indulgences.

But when a person begins taking action according to what they know, what they have experienced, rather than rote, automatic action based on their conditioning and patterns, then those insights and experiences will be integrated into the soul itself. The soul will transform by metabolizing the old personality patterns, and will thus mature. The personality is not something that needs to die or to be thrown away; the personality needs to develop in time, to be refined, and integrated with the sense of beingness. This integration is necessary for wholeness and totality, for an integrated soul in which Being and personality are not at war. The usual personality is nothing but a conditioned part of the soul. This conditioned part can be transformed only as the result of impact from insights and states of being, leading to the integration and maturity of the soul. Otherwise, it is possible for a person to put aside the personality and just develop the state of beingness. Some spiritual systems are oriented in this way so a person has the understanding, the realization and various wonderful experiences, and can remain in those states. But these are people who are not in the world. Such a person might have achieved a mature state of being, but they have to be sitting on their ass to experience it. They cannot go into the marketplace with it.

The further step to be taken cannot happen by just sitting on your ass, or by just meditating, staying away from everyone, or just by understanding some part of yourself in sessions with your teacher. You actually have to take action. And your actions have to be real actions that take into consideration everything you have learned: all the insights, all the knowledge, all the experiences. Only then will all the elements be integrated so that you can become a more and more integrated and balanced human being.

So, in a sense, this Work is like a kind of a building, a development of one's self and one's life. You are not going to be doing a certain kind of work and then be automatically rewarded with wonderful things; this is the expectation of many people. Things do not happen that way. A person can have insights and experiences and perceive them as rewards, as goodies, as candy. But if you just eat the candy and that is all, you will be a dependent infant who goes back to sessions only to get more candy. A person who is interested in really developing understanding, becoming complete as a mature, balanced human being, will use those experiences in life to transform.

Something I have noticed which is unfortunate and frustrating, but inevitable, is that for a long time when people experience states of being, they see those states as a kind of food, some kind of reward or acknowledgment of success. The experience of Essence or Being *is* a kind of food, but these experiences arise from something much more fundamental and important. Those experiences are supposed to transform you. They do not arise for you just to consume them, but for you to digest and metabolize them. It is not enough to have the experience, "Oh how nice, how wonderful, I feel so sweet now. I feel so full now." For a long time I wondered about this. Not everyone has this pattern, like that, but I would say the majority do. When a student experiences a certain state, for instance, a state of Will, there is a feeling of strength, solidity, and support. The deficiency of Will and support is gone. It may be wonderful, but it is not enough. Usually, when I experience a state of support, a state of Will, that is not my only concern: there are a lot of other things that one could see and understand, and other benefits from that experience. It is not just that a little bit of my suffering is gone. I wonder, "What does this mean, when suddenly a certain state arises and my lack of support or my weakness is all gone? How did that happen? What does that mean about my life? What does that mean about how I'm going to live my life? What is this that makes me feel strong?" You need to get so curious about it that you spend some time looking at it under the microscope, trying to investigate every atom of it: "What is this? It's some new thing I've never seen before." But what I noticed is that when many people have a new experience, say the experience of essential Strength, the only thing they like about it is that they feel strong, the pleasure of it, and that's it. The person was only interested in eliminating his state of weakness. He is not interested in the truth of the situation, nor in the truth of the experience. When a certain state arises there is a truth there, a nutrition for your soul; it is not just to eliminate a certain hunger in you, although it can do that. Truth can nourish you in a very deep way that will transform you fundamentally, permanently, if you really get interested in it.

Or someone might experience a state of Personal Love, feel sweet, fluffy, and delicate and say, "Oh good, now I feel love. I don't care about someone loving me, just so I don't feel rejected or hurt," and that's it; you leave the session. This is what many people do, in fact, but it seems to me that you could say, "What is that? What is love? I'm experiencing a state of love, but what is that?" You look at it. It feels so delicate. "How can something in my chest taste sweet? Sweet is usually a taste in my mouth." For the first time in your life, you feel sweetness in your heart. But you don't question why you feel sweetness in your heart or why you have never felt it before. You believe it is totally unimportant; what is important is that you feel love now. Why not ask yourself: "How is it that I can experience something that seems fundamentally true and contradicts all of my ideas and assumptions about things, but I don't even look at it?" Why is it that usually you believe there is no such thing as experiencing sweetness in your chest even when this assumption has been contradicted by your experience? What does that mean? What does that entail for your beliefs and ideas, for the way you live your life?

Besides the actual investigation, the actual interest, the actual involvement with the experience, you need to get into it and feel it and understand it, to see how it feels, how it tastes, how it affects your mind, how it affects your action, how you can take it into your life. There are a lot of things to digest from even one simple experience. Five minutes of one experience could take a person months and months before they actually get nutrition from it. Otherwise, a person may believe, "No, I had the experience. Next week I am going to come and get another one," when this experience has not been digested yet. After a while the result is a state of constipation, being bloated and constipated with a great frustration because there are no new experiences of realization, while each one of those experiences could transform consciousness in a fundamental way.

Although unfortunate, these limitations are inevitable because of the tendencies in the unbalanced consciousness. The unbalanced consciousness might be interested only in the sense of pleasure or security in the experience, and that's all. So we could say that the soul has tunnel vision. The soul looks at one element of an experience and eliminates everything else. Then, of course, the person misses the true benefits, the complete impact of these experiences. It is only by immersing oneself in these fundamental states of consciousness that the soul will be transformed. Your soul is the consciousness in which all states of consciousness arise. When deep states arise, they can transform your soul. The mere arising of an experience, and liking it or not liking it, is not enough to transform the consciousness. The consciousness has to get into it and be touched, be burned by it. Otherwise, it cannot transform.

In my experience, the effects of certain experiences change from one person to another. Some people experience the state of Personal Essence and see their lives and consciousness becoming transformed in a big way. Some people experience it as if nothing at all has happened. This might seem surprising. You might think, "How can that be?" I was surprised too, but I learned that some people experience fundamental states of existence as just one more thing in their everyday life. Like another hamburger, or an entertaining movie. This is not detachment, but a lack of recognition of the true nature of such revelation.

Experiencing an essential state affects some people in such a way that the experience deeply transforms their life, shifting their whole orientation and perspective. Whether this happens seems to have to do with expectations the person has, or what the person is already valuing and idealizing. It has to do with the person's focus. Some people are looking for a certain thing; other people are looking for other things. Also, it depends on the depth of a person's interest and love for the truth itself. Many people are not interested in the truth. Many people are interested in experiences of security, or simply the pleasure or the comfort of these realizations. In traditional schools, in some of the old schools, people are not allowed to have these experiences because it is seen as a waste. The least that could happen is that it could be a waste. The worst that can happen is an imbalanced development.

If we look at understanding from a perspective that will tend naturally and spontaneously to go towards balance and harmony, we find that understanding needs to be motivated by love of the truth for its own sake. The experience, or the beingness, is the experience of the truth. That's what a person needs to learn over and over again. When you are in a state of being, what you are experiencing is the truth: the truth of who you are. Your experience is not a candy, or a goody, it's not a reward for being good or for having done your work. No; you are experiencing the fundamental truth, and that needs to be seen, understood, imbibed and absorbed; then action will come from the place of this truth.

No one has said this is an easy thing to do. As you see, It is quite an endeavor. The creation of the beautiful, graceful, true, and mature human life requires work at many levels. It requires dedication, sincerity, and a commitment to that endeavor. This kind of life is possible, but only for the person who really wants it. It will not happen if the person wants something else. It's as simple as that. It is not that you are going to be punished if you don't pursue this life. If you don't work for it, you don't get it.

Think of living as a mature human being in terms of the truth—the truth is the basic thread, the basic element, the unifier, because it is the heart of the whole matter. If you do not want the truth, you cannot get the truth. It is of the very nature of truth that you cannot lie to yourself about the truth. You cannot try to get truth by pretending that you want it when you don't want it, because then what you get is falsehood. So a person who gets the truth is a person who is worthy of the truth. A person is worthy of the truth if he or she prefers, wants, and loves the truth for its own sake, more than anything else. Otherwise, what you get is something else. Truth is not accessible except to the one who wants to do all that is required. Otherwise, the veils and illusions of the idealized preconceptions remain in the way. Who is interested in spending the time, the energy, the effort, without complaining, with a great deal of graciousness and generosity? Only that person will be able to realize the truth. Without this level of effort, it just will not happen; it does not have to happen.

No one says that every human being should live for the truth. For many people, it is not of interest, it is not what they want. They want something else, which is fine. If an individual is interested more in stabilizing around some kind of security, or in achieving a certain accomplishment or some kind of recognition or whatever, that is fine. It is fine; but this is not the interest of the Work. A person would need to go to a different kind of teacher or school to help them get those things. They are certainly valid things to want and to have. However, a work school like ours is oriented towards accomplishing something specific. It is not oriented towards giving a person pleasure or security or recognition or love, or anything like that. That is not our concern. We do not judge these things as good or bad. That is just not our orientation. If a person needs some kind of recognition, that is fine, but he should understand that he must look for it elsewhere. If a person wants pleasure, he needs to understand that there are places other than here to find merely pleasure.

What you get here is truth. That's what we are doing here. Our work has to do with the pursuit of truth. When I say there are three elements that need to be balanced, these elements are not necessarily separate and delineated from one another. Understanding involves states of being, and being involves action; they are all connected. But at different times or for different people, there is more of a focus in each one of these elements. Each of us needs to examine our work and our attitude from that perspective; how are we imbalanced? Which of these elements we value and go towards and automatically develop at the expense of the others? You will notice that the group itself, or the various groups, sometimes focus on one of those elements more, depending on the individual or the composition of the group. This comes up when there is an imbalance in terms of the three elements. Some groups are balanced more towards one than the other. It is most useful for a group to be balanced in terms of these elements. If not, then of course, that group will have to be exposed to various corrective factors.

The teaching formats in the school are important and necessary for the balanced development of the group. Some students prefer certain formats or structures over others. Some people only like the small group meetings. You can talk about things, you understand things; it's wonderful. Some people love the Sunday morning meditation. Some people like Sunday work afternoons. They feel happier, more at home there. Now, because of the perspective of balance, you should know that the places where you have the hardest times are the places where you need the most work. If you find that you have the most difficulty with Sunday morning, that's where you need to do most of the work. If you have the most difficulty in small group, or on Sunday afternoons, that's where you need to do most of the work. A group is like an individual in this respect, so the same holds true for groups. That is why, in our work here, you will notice that in the groups I do different things every once in a while, I change something. I bring in a different perspective. I start talking about new things or do new things. The main reason for this has to do with balancing. Many times a group will be going in a certain direction. Everyone may be happy and think it is wonderful, but then I shift things. People may feel disappointed, angry, hurt, abandoned, and all that, thinking that I am not going to give them something or that I am punishing them, or I am mad at them, or something like that. But what is happening is that I see that the group is going a certain way, and I am trying to bring it back into balance, and that will necessitate certain processes or certain emphases or certain activities.

If you consider the various activities that we do in the groups, you will see that they also involve the three elements. There are the small group meetings, which are oriented more towards the understanding. There are the meditations that you do yourself and in the group, which are oriented more towards the being, the experience. There are other times, like Sunday afternoons, that have to do more with doing. Some people tend not to like Sunday afternoon because it feels like it goes against the grain, in a sense. But that is exactly what needs to happen. That is exactly the imbalance that needs to be corrected. You might not like it for a long time, but it is exactly the most beneficial thing for you. You will see that this perspective explains many things about yourself and many people. Usually, it is rationalized the other way: "I like to have more big group meetings because I like these insights, because that's what is really important. The insights and the realizations and the connection are the most important things." Of course you think that way because your consciousness is imbalanced in that direction. Some people say, "No, we have to do things. Otherwise it won't work." This may be true, but it might be the student's position only because that is what he has always valued. Therefore, that student probably doesn't need so much work on action. They need more in other areas so that their action becomes more truly attuned, more oriented towards the truth.

One result of the balancing, one way you know that the balancing is happening more and more, is your attitude towards it, your personal attitude towards truth. It's not only that truth leads to the balancing, which it does, but the balancing also leads to the truth. Balancing does not lead only to the truth; it leads to the correct relationship to the truth. The more your consciousness is balanced, the more you cannot help but like the truth. You don't like it because it is good to like the truth. You don't like it simply because it is useful to like the truth, or because it is more spiritual to like the truth, or because it is more practical to like the truth. You just like it. It is the nature of the balanced human consciousness, the nature of the soul—when it is acting normally in its natural functioning—to love truth, because truth is the very nature of the soul and of all reality. The more the consciousness is balanced, the more it is integrated, the more it is completed, the more you will notice that you naturally love the truth and love people who love the truth.

You will see how your value and respect, your consideration and love towards people, depends on the truth. You will see that when you see someone loving the truth, you will naturally tend to love them more. It's as simple as that—not because it is good to love them, but because you can't help it; it's a natural thing. You notice that the more you love the truth, the more you respect yourself, and you cannot help but respect other people who love the truth. It is natural to love the truth when the state of balance is reached. It is not something that *should* happen, not a moral or a judgmental perspective. What makes things beautiful, what brings grace and dignity, is truth; balance is the spontaneous, natural result. Truth has these three elements, as well as others. What makes something beautiful is the truth in it. What makes something graceful is the truth in it. What makes something dignified is the truth in it. Falseness brings in ugliness, awkwardness, and indulgence and lack of self-respect.

The more a person loves the truth, the more she will naturally and spontaneously want to live her life according to the truth. The truth is not just something you understand or something you experience. Truth begins to influence and determine and govern your life. It is in the living and the doing of life according to the love of truth that makes one's life a life of beauty, grace, and dignity. You can understand your measure of balance, and your measure of development and refinement, just by seeing what you do in your life. Do you live your life according to the truth? How much do you live your life according to the truth? Do you live according to preconceived ideas that you already know are preconceived ideas? Do you live according to patterns that you already know are patterns? Do you live according to indulgences that takes only a little bit of awareness to know are indulgences? When you see that you are indulging in your life instead of living it according to the truth that you already know, then the work starts: You know you are responsible. You cannot blame anyone or anything else.

Some people think that enlightenment is when all of your problems end. But enlightenment is really when your problems start. Enlightenment is partly the realization that you are responsible in your life, that your life is *completely* your responsibility, and you are the one who really has to live it. You have to live life the way you know you ought to do it. It's not going to just happen. God is not going to do it *to* you because ultimately, you are God. You cannot say, "Okay, maybe God will do it." Who is God? When you know the truth, God is not separate from you. You cannot say, "I'm going to wait for God to do it for me." There is no God separate from you, and there is no grace separate from your heart. When you see that you are ultimately responsible, that is where the true Work starts.

Of course, the way you want to live your life is up to you. There is no general rule for everyone. It depends on the person and the situation you find yourself in. It depends on what you want to do in your life. So there is no spiritual rule about ownership or non-ownership, relationship or no relationship, marriage or no marriage, business or no business. It depends on what you want. It depends on what your work is, what happens to be your contribution. Living your life, then, and taking all these things into consideration, is where grace happens, where beauty happens. You need to understand how to take action, how to arrange the situation, how to arrange your life in a way to reflect the truth that you already know and experience. If your work requires a lot of action, a lot of strength, you need to live your life so that will happen. If your work requires a lot of subtlety and refinement, how do you live your life to make that more and more possible? It won't just happen. When a person truly begins to work on the embodiment and actualization of their knowledge and understanding, a great deal of resistance comes up. This resistance manifests in many ways, but especially as an indulgence in conditioned experience, even after it is recognized as such.

Once a person has a certain amount of understanding, a certain amount of experience, at some point they need to start to take action. That knowledge and experience has to come out in life; it has to manifest. If not, the imbalance will increase. The imbalance will be exaggerated and as a result you will experience more dissatisfaction and more frustration, even though you might have had wonderful experiences and insights. But if you continue to live your life from an imbalanced perspective, all those experiences and insights will only enhance the state of imbalance. If you do not learn from these experiences, and you merely take from them exactly what you have already decided you want to take, rather than allowing the complete impact of the experience, you will tend to increase the imbalance. Anything you do can increase your imbalance, even experiences of self-realization, enlightenment, being, and insight. I think many people already know this.

It is a natural law that the more you experience, the more understanding you have, and the more you need to live your life accordingly. At some point, you will have insights, understanding, and experiences on many dimensions, on many levels. Your way of living needs to take into consideration all these levels and dimensions, in terms of what you do in your life and how you do it. The way you live your life needs to embody all these dimensions. If you know there is a subtle dimension, an essential dimension, and a supreme dimension and so on, you can no longer live just according to the mental dimension; that would be crazy. You are not taking reality into consideration. The moment you know these things, they will have to affect your action. If that does not happen spontaneously, you have to ask yourself: "Why not?", and try to find out how to do it. You know there is truth. You know what love is. You know what independence is. But you continue to relate to your love partner as if these things were not true. What are you doing when you do that? You are not living according to the truth that you already know, and thus you are increasing your imbalance.

Insight and realization can be used to magnify imbalance, or to balance and harmonize the consciousness. A primary component of this balance is doing, action. Understanding is also very important because you can experience a state of being without understanding. Many people experience all kind of states of realization, but they do not understand what those states are about; they are not interested in understanding. That is just as detrimental as not embodying these states in one's life. It is possible to block the flow of understanding. When there is a state of being that is not yet understood, whatever understanding can come from it needs to flow, and then the whole thing needs to come out in action. It has to seep completely into your life to transform your life.

There is no reason why a human being cannot live a life of truth, love, strength, impeccability, dignity, and self-respect. You do not need any special situation. You do not need any unusual occasion. Any interaction, any transaction, is a place for you to be that way, and that is when you see the grace and the beauty of life.

S: Could you say something about how to use the Work as a way of bringing Being and understanding into action?

AHA: Well, we already know that our physical work session is set up for that to happen. In those sessions, people are engaged in various tasks, the actual practice of doing something. But they are ideally supposed to do this practice in a state of awareness and presence. The attempt to be as fully aware and as fully present as possible in your task, is the necessary effort needed. Of course, as you are doing that, there might arise many kinds of things that you can look at, understand, let go of, and so on. In time, all of your experience, all of your understanding, should be integrated, should manifest in action. Manifestation does not come about merely by thinking about it, because one person has millions of insights. You cannot just use your mind to figure out how all these insights and realizations relate to living life. You cannot integrate them into living by thinking about them, or by merely having more insights. They will be the insights of a couch potato. You cannot do it that way.

However, when you put forth the effort to be present, to be aware, to be essentially in action, the awareness becomes the understanding part, and the presence, the Being part of action. You will encounter difficulties and barriers to being present and aware in action. Learning how to deal with these barriers is the actual Work. From this come observations and issues that you might have to work on for some time afterwards. Overcoming these barriers, through continual practice of presence and understanding, will integrate your realization into action. You might not be able to actually do it in one Sunday afternoon, but you might start becoming aware of the difficulties, the barriers, your preferences, and your prejudices, and of how your imbalance shows and presents itself.

As I have said many times, when we are engaged in physical tasks on Sunday afternoon, we are not just doing these tasks. You can do them anywhere else in your life as you do anyway. We are trying to perform everyday tasks from a real perspective. It's a practice in actualization, in embodiment. This is a very important element of our Work, regardless of how you feel about it. So on Sunday afternoon, the Work is that there should be awareness, there should be presence, there should be action; but the action should also be efficient and economical, and it should be done the best way you can do it while maintaining presence and awareness. It won't work to think: "If I'm aware and present, it doesn't matter if I do the job." That is not true. This is because you can sit down and just be aware and do nothing, which is not the point. We try to hold this presence and awareness in action. And action can manifest with beauty, grace, and dignity. You have to do whatever job you are doing the best way you can. Not the best you can do according to some kind of standard, or for being good, successful, wonderful; no, but because that is the expression of the excellence of who you are. The "good job" is the reflection of the excellence of your being and your consciousness. So if you're doing something and you're doing it precisely, and effectively, that usually is accompanied by a certain consciousness, a certain state of being. The two things are the expression of the same realization. That is how the integration happens. That is how the personality and the being begin to interpenetrate and become one functioning unity: a developed soul.

S: I think that most of my life, I've done things well and precisely but out of the personality.

AHA: Yes. That's why I said that the understanding and experiences of Being are necessary. Many people do a "good job," are "successful" in their lives, and are very efficient and all that, but they are also disconnected from their actions.

S: There might be a period of feeling awkward. . .

AHA: Of course, that's what will happen, sure: awkwardness and states of deficiency and helplessness. Sometimes that is what arises, a state of being awkward: "I don't know how to do it," "I'm not up to it. It's a grown-up job. I'm only a little kid. My fingers are not long enough." All those kind of things will happen. It's amazing what happens in people's minds.

S: Is the point of this segment of the Work to carry it into our daily life all the time?

AHA: Hopefully, yes, all the time. Otherwise, what's the point? The doing is the exercise for the muscles of the soul. Usually, doing from the ordinary perspective is separated and split-off from Being. There is the doing of the personality while Being is somewhere else, not involved. There is a gap. What we are learning to do is the being and doing together: being in action. Being flows into the action, and that way the action is efficient and beautiful and graceful.

S: I realize that when I focus on doing, my tendency is to want my understanding and my experience of being to tell me what to do or what direction to be going in. But it sounds like that's not it.

AHA: Well, it is not exactly like that. Being knows how to do things with grace, with beauty, with power, with effectiveness, with precision. However, Being does not know about how to fix a window. Your true self has nothing to do with windows; it does not know about windows. It does not know how to water plants. That is where your consciousness, your personality, comes in. But when you are watering plants, Being certainly knows how to do it the best way, in terms of the sense, of how to hold yourself, how much effort to exert, how to do things in such a way that you feel integrated within yourself. Being shows you how to manifest the beauty outside. There has to be a coordination and a working together, and ultimately a harmonization, a balance, because we are not just talking about a state of being; we are talking about living. That is the Work we have in our life. We are already beings. Before we are born, we are beings. The story then is how to bring this Being into living. That is the task we have in this life: to learn how to live on earth in physical bodies, do things and enjoy things that the inner being is usually not concerned with. In other words, how can essential Being manifest as a human being? What we are doing—the task of life—is developing Being into a human being. That is the stage of evolution we are engaged in. Being is already here; you come as Being. It is true that you forget, and you forget because you still learning how to bring this Being into life. However, in the case of conventional life, the necessary knowledge and guidance are absent, so a split develops. After the splitting occurs, a part of the consciousness goes on doing and living life, separate from Being. As a result, we need to regain access to our being, and then harmonize that being with living. Regaining of Being, which is enlightenment, is not the end; it is the beginning, which is how we started anyway. But we need to grow up, and learn how to be as mature human beings.

S: If your work—what you're doing for a living—supports a particular imbalance, what's an efficient way to work with that?

AHA: Well, if your work supports a certain imbalance in your personality, then, of course, one thing you can do is find another kind of work that doesn't do that. Or you can pay more attention while you're doing it, to see how that imbalance happens or doesn't happen. Or you could get engaged in other activities to counteract these forces. There might be other ways, but these are what I can think of now. Many people cannot help that they have a job that is not oriented towards balancing them but is continuing their imbalance. Frequently, these people cannot get disengaged from this particular kind of work, so they have to engage in other activities that will bring in that balance. Someone whose work is sedentary, for instance, where they sit in an office and type all the time, may need to do more exercise at other times.

The perception of balance and harmony is simple, common sense, very practical, down to earth. It is the truth behind the falsehood. In other words, it is the truth that the falsehood is trying to imitate. The personality is trying to imitate the real life but doing it wrongly because it is disconnected from Being. But the personality is trying to do the real thing. It is trying to live a certain life, have a certain kind of work, certain accomplishments, certain relationships—that is part of the real life. But the personality cannot go about it correctly because it is missing an element. The balanced life is a life that involves human interactions, human relationships, work, creativity, all kinds of activity and enjoyment. All that the personality has developed like sports, arts, literature, recreation, philosophy and science: all these are true human activities but they need to be filled with the human Essence for them to be real. A true human life is not a life devoid of these things. If we are living, what we do can be done in a real way. You can be married in a real way or in a false way. You can do a certain job in a real way or in a false way, and the false is usually an attempt to do it the real way. But because there isn't the necessary knowledge and experience, the person cannot do it the real way. I do not go along with the usual spiritual perspective that you have to renounce your life, live simply, and forget about living well or doing things in your life. It is not true, you can be successful. You can live in a comfortable way, you can live in a refined way, enjoy the good things on earth, and still be one hundred percent spiritual. The real integration is a complete integration between materialism and spirituality. Wholeness is when the completely material endeavors become completely spiritual endeavors, at the same time— when there isn't the slightest distinction, completely, not the slightest distinction. Otherwise, you are still not a complete human being. You are half. You are one way or the other.

A true human being is not somebody who does not like sex, for instance, or does not have any sex. A true human being is somebody who is engaged in sex in a certain way, in a real way. A true human being is not somebody who does not care about food. A true human being is somebody who likes food, but likes and enjoys it in a certain way, the way it should be enjoyed.

So, when I talk about balance and integration, I am not saying throw away part of your life, renounce this and embrace that. No, there is no such thing. What you renounce is the falsehood. What you embrace is the truth. It is much easier usually to renounce certain things in your life in order to have certain kinds of experiences. To say, "I'm just going to live in a monastery. Just meditate or whatever and I'll be enlightened." You can do that, but that's a cop out. It's not a complete life yet. You see, you can do it, and some people do it, that's fine, that's what they want to do. But that is half of the human life. That is the side of being. But how about the action part? To actually go into the store, buy the stuff, cook it and go to work tomorrow. That is the other half. While you are sitting in your monastery, some people are cooking for you and bringing your food to your door and you are eating it and you do one specific thing every day. That is not human life. That is not really it. Neither is the human life just going to your work, becoming successful, making money and getting married, and so on. That is also not the human life, that is half of it. It is like one is the inner of it, one is the outer of it, and they should both be there, the inside and the outside. Otherwise, there is no integration; there is a split. And that integration is not simple. It is not easy at all; in fact, I would say it is rare. Very rare.

To meet a human being who is really a mature human being is a very rare thing. It is not the same thing as meeting an enlightened human being. It is a different story. From the perspective of a mature human being, enlightenment is one of the necessary ingredients needed but it is not enough, not sufficient. It allows possibilities that the person didn't see before. The more a human being is mature and complete, the more he is neither selfish nor selfless. A spiritual person is selfless, always giving for the other. A worldly human being is always selfish, always taking. For a true human being, within the same action there is giving and taking. Something for oneself and something for the other without any contradiction whatsoever.

So, there is no place for morality here. You do not say that it's good to give. Yes, it *is* good to give, but it is also good to receive. You need to serve and serve humanity, but if everybody is just serving humanity, who is living it? If you sacrifice your life for your children and your children for their children, whoever gets to live a life? There has to be a balance between the two. And the balance will be the natural thing. When a true human being is giving, he does not feel he is giving. When he is taking, he does not feel he is taking. A true human being simply experiences himself as doing something that needs to be done. When the situation requires that such and such a thing be done, the integrated human being does it. Who it is for isn't important because that action takes into consideration all levels, all dimensions, physical, emotional, personality, Essence, Being, the present, the future, all these things.

However, that kind of action does not happen by calculation. It needs a balanced consciousness to do it. In action, the being flows and the flow of being is the doing. The intelligence of Being is functioning at all dimensions, all in the same act. Its intelligence is beyond the mind, beyond the awareness. But as I said, although it is the ideal thing and it is possible, a lot of work is needed to realize it. It might take all your life to do it. It is not a matter of getting from here to there. It is a matter of continual development. It does not have an end. You can grow and grow and grow and grow. There is no end to human maturing.

Your work on yourself does not end by the end of this group, for instance, or by the end of your work here. Your work continues for the rest of your life. It is just like being a painter. Is there a point when you become the perfect painter and that's it? A good painter is always becoming a better painter. You don't say, "OK, now I've got it. I'm a good painter." There is always a place for more excellence, more refinement. There is no end to it. You can always break new ground. So, to think of an end of a development in that way does not make sense because the development is a growth, an evolution. There is an end maybe for the state of disharmony but there is no end to the state of development itself, in the sense that a completely integrated human being at the age of thirty is not the same as a completely integrated human being at the age of forty. They are not the same thing. And a completely integrated human being at the age of thirty in the twentieth century is not the same thing as a completely integrated human being at the age of thirty in the first century because the human race as a totality has developed.

So, hopefully this talk will dispel many kinds of preconceptions about getting something, or arriving some place, and bring us to a more correct, more mature perspective. A more balanced one.

SIX

Oneness and Human Life

The goal of our Work is not to help you get a job, or a mate, or to help with other worldly situations. There are many resources in this society which support people's external lives—schools, trainings, therapies, professional institutes—to help people survive and live successfully. Our Work is definitely not to help you survive. If, in the course of doing this Work, you become more effective in your functioning, and resolve some of your problems in life, this is a secondary effect. It is not the primary thrust of the Work. The function of the Work has to do with the quality of life we live, with bringing into our lives the higher human values of kindness, gentleness, appreciation, respect, consideration, and the capacity to love and enjoy.

Of course, if a student is having difficulty in her work or relationships, the teacher will do whatever he can to help the student understand her difficulties. But resolving difficulties is not our primary purpose, and the Work should not be approached for that purpose. We inquire into the situations in our lives to bring about a transformation of the quality of life itself. We look at our relationships, our work, our interests, to learn about what kind of people we are, what kind of situations we live in, what is the quality of our life. There is no need for work as fine, intricate, and as deep as ours to solve the problems in our lives.

We are interested in discovering how to live life in a way that is more human, more humane. We are seeking more value, more depth, more refinement in our lives, and this means becoming more human. It is in the very nature of human beings to be loving and gentle, and to have the capacity to enjoy and appreciate. So this Work is really a matter of uncovering or revealing these parts of us: our human capacities. These are not capacities you are going to be given or that you are just going to get. They are part of you. The Work is a process of revealing your human nature to yourself, so you can live increasingly in accordance with your essential nature. As you understand and realize the essential human values, your life will come to have a different meaning, as will your work, your relationships, and your family. You will be living your life, then, from a perspective completely different from the conventional one, although the external appearance of your life might be the same.

The task is to live an ordinary life and be truly human at the same time. To be human obviously means more than just surviving, because if we just needed to survive, there would be no need for all this evolution. We could have stayed at the level of crocodiles, and survived pretty well. If you think your life is just about survival, you are missing the point of your whole life on earth. Survival is not a big issue for most people in our culture, although it still is in some parts of the world. To be human means to be able to participate in existence in a way that is not available to other creatures. Our evolution has a lot to do with refinement—refinement of our senses, refinement of our minds, refinement of our capacities. So if you come to this Work in order to find a job or acquire a boyfriend or a girlfriend or have children, you are missing the point. The majority of humankind already does these things; they do not need a work school like this to do them. I am not saying that these things are not important; they are the content of a human life, and as such, they are important and necessary.

What we are exploring today is the quality of that life. What is the quality of interaction, the quality of existence, the quality of relationship, the quality of contact and experience, the quality of communication in your family, at your job, with your friends? That is what matters here for us. That is where this Work is useful. In this Work, our development is not a matter of going away from this life, nor of transcending it to depart for some spiritual domain. It is a teaching of how to live this life in a genuine way. The more we realize the true, essential elements of our inherent human nature, the more we can see and understand what there can be in life, how we can live, and how we can be, as human beings. Until then, we only know what we have heard or what we have seen, we do not know for ourselves. Neither is the Work here a matter of working on yourself simply to see through psychological issues so that you can realize certain states. That is not the point. The point is living. The point is manifesting your understanding and capacities in your life. If you are learning about love, and every session you go to you are experiencing all this wonderful love, yet you leave the room and your relationships with people are full of anger and resentment, your work has no fruition. It is a lie. If you come here and learn about peace, and then go home and live chaotically, your life will be full of agitation regardless of what you learn about peace. You are missing the point; what are you learning it for, then? It is not entertainment. This is not like going to a movie and going back home to resume the usual. A person's development, or level of refinement, will manifest in the way he lives his life, and the way he relates to others.

We are also not here to learn to appear a certain way. That is what most of society learns: to appear human, to appear generous, to appear strong. The idea is to really live that way, not so that someone will see you that way, or so that people will recognize you, or so that you will be more successful. The point is to live; that's it. To be human is to be human.

Human values can generally be understood by looking clearly at the personality, or the ego, from a simple perspective. The usual way of living life, the undeveloped way, operates from the perspective of the personality, of the ego-self. If you envision it as a circle, it can be divided into two primary elements: the circumference or periphery of the circle, and the center of that circle. This is a good metaphor for the nature of the ego-self: The center is what we call the sense of self, the "I" that you take yourself to be. When you say, "I will do that," or "I want this," that is the center of the personality, not the whole of the personality, only its identity. The other element of the personality, the circumference, is the individuality, the sense of being an individual. So the center is the identity, and the circumference is the individuality. If you look at your experience of yourself and the way you live your life, you notice that usually it can be seen from these two perspectives. Either you are concerned about who you are, your sense of identity, the feeling of self, the center of operation, your center; or you are thinking of yourself in terms of boundaries, in terms of being an individual, separate from other individuals. You notice that you are an individual, and as an individual you have a certain quality which is your identity. The fact that you are an individual does not affect what quality the self is. So the personality is like an individuality with a certain color, a certain quality that defines it, and a name. At the most superficial level of these two elements, the shape of a human being gives you a sense of individuality, and your name gives a sense of identity. You are usually willing to fight for your name, and for your sense of individuality. These two elements are the major ego structures which pattern the flow of your experience, pattern your soul, and they are, of course, intertwined.

Living your life from the perspective of being an individual who has a sense of identity is the primary source of all personality problems and issues and misunderstandings, because these two things just do not exist. They are figments of your imagination, and of the collective imagination of the human race. If you are always having to protect and operate from that center of self, that personality, that identity, that is what is called self-centered or selfish. You are concerned only for yourself. If the individuality is defined by your boundaries, then the concern is about how big your territory is, what it includes, what it excludes?

It is not easy to understand the structure of one's personality. It takes a lot of work to expose the various constituents, delusions, and structures. The process requires a lot of inquiry, taking you through successive experiences, different kinds of experiences on different levels, exposing the reality of the situation. The experiences in your process tend to reveal over and over that the components of your ego structure do not actually exist, and at the same time tend to reveal to you what is real, what is actually there, rather than only personality structures created by mind. These experiences can transform your life.

This transformation will come to pass, however, only to the extent that you actually live according to the understanding you have achieved. The experience of the identity or the sense of the self—the belief in the self, the belief that you are the center that is operating, commenting, judging, choosing, that is active, doing, rejecting and accepting—is easier to deal with than the circumference. Ego activity is the inner experience of the center: the cycle of rejection, hope, and desire constitutes this identity. The significant experience which exposes the falseness of the belief in this center is the experience of Essence. The moment you experience Essence as your nature, and you feel, "This is me, this Essence is what I am made of," the ground of that center is shaken. Before this, you always believed firmly in that identity, that that is who you are. So when Essence manifests, when you are experiencing Essence in any of its aspects, you realize, "No, I'm made out of something else, I'm not this feverish activity, I'm not this center that's always accepting and rejecting, wanting and not wanting, afraid and angry and all of that. My nature is something else, like the nature of love or the nature of peace, the nature of existence." This is the primary experience that jolts our identity. It begins a process we call self-realization. The experience of yourself as Essence does not always eliminate the ego identity right away. It depends on the person, and on how deeply entrenched the identity is.

After this beginning experience of one's true nature, then the essential journey begins—the essential journey which will bring about a more complete understanding of that central identity and eliminate it, bringing in its place the true identity, the essential self. This is the journey of self-realization. You realize at some point that you are a simple presence that does not think or feel or judge or choose, but that simply is, a timeless existence. The main work of the Diamond Approach is to deal with that journey. Our approach is quite complete, and very effective, for this part of the journey. But dealing with the center does not remove our belief in the reality of the circumference, our notion of ourselves as separate individuals. As long as the circumference still exists, the circumference will tend to define the center, to bring that identity back. So the sense of territoriality is not yet gone. Maybe now you do not need your territory to be a certain color, but you still a need a territory of your own. So the content of your experience might change, but you are still taking it to be separate from the rest of the universe.

As I said, this process that makes up the first half of the journey takes a lot of understanding, time, and energy. To actualize this realization is the easier part of our Work. The other part, dealing with the circumference, understanding the sense of separateness, the sense of being an individual in your own right, is harder. These issues of the sense of individuality become the focus of the Work once the first part of the journey has been actualized. And in this particular culture, the work on the individuality is different. It is well known that America is the place that most values individuality; this is where individuality is most supported and idealized. Here everyone is trying to achieve an independent, autonomous life, and build on it as much as they can. This is true in the rest of the world, but here it is a societal ideal.

Actually, dealing with the individuality is difficult anywhere, because the whole species of human beings believes that to be human means to be an individual, demarcated from others and from the rest of existence. That is really the deeper part of the personality, the basis of the personality, that in time builds an identity and a name. It is this sense of a separate individuality that is very hard for most people to let go of, because we do not understand how else it could be. It is very difficult for us to understand: How can I be a human being if I have no circumference? So after self-realization a whole dimension of Work commences to confront and eliminate the delusion of the circumference.

Can we truly understand what it means to live the life of a human being, even when we have reached self-realization? It is not enough to be essential; you have to stop taking yourself to be a separate entity. Of course, everyone will react to this notion; it sounds like a big loss. What is left then? It seems like I've never really existed at all! What's so wonderful about that? How could I live my life? How could I move my arms? How could I eat? Why would I eat, if I don't exist as a separate individual? This is a mystery until it is understood. And working with this question will bring in the second primary experience that will shake that sense of individuality, that will have as much of a jarring effect on your mind as the first experience, because your mind is based on that sense of individuality, of a separate existence. You cannot conceive of the possibility of it being otherwise. It seems preposterous, unimaginable, and completely undesirable.

So, just as the first journey starts with the experience of Essence and ends with becoming the Essence, the second part of the journey goes to another dimension, which is called the Supreme level, the dimension of pure Being. Essence is Being; however, it is qualified Being, in the sense that it has various aspects, which can be experienced in and as the human being, even though a person still believes she is separate from the rest of existence. The dimension that deals with and eliminates the sense of boundaries is Being as such, Being without qualifications, which we call the Supreme. The experience of the Supreme corrects our perspective on reality and reveals to us the unreality of boundaries; it is the experience of oneness.

The experience of oneness eliminates our sense that we have a territory. It is not that you exist as someone who does not have a territory; it is more that you exist as a totality of territory. You lose a boundary and gain a totality. We typically live our lives on the assumption that we are separate individuals—this is my thing, this is your thing, and I'm different than you, and if you are a nice person, it is all right for you to have your life the way you want it, and I will have my life the way I want it. However, this perception of separateness is not the most objective perception.

In the experience of unity, the objective perception of reality is that the boundaries that you see are actually creations of your mind. They are figments of your imagination. You have created this image and idea in your mind, and then said, "That's me. I end here, and the other person starts there. I end here, and the chair starts there. You start over there, and you end over there." That is how we experience ourselves. But what if it is not really like that? You just think it is that way, and because you think it is that way, you see reality that way. Of course, if you see reality through the idea that you start here and end here—of course, you will live your life in a certain way. The interests of other people might not be your interests, and your interests might conflict with the interests of others, and then comes the issue of what's mine and what's yours. Can I have my share, can you have your share? With the assumption of separateness come the issues of giving and receiving, loving and being loved, having and acquiring, and all of that. All these things which are the causes of people's problems are based on the assumption that we have a circumference.

If you have no circumference, all these concerns go. Then you do not say, "I want you to love me." "I want you to love me" means there is a person here, and that person over there is going to love this person here. But there isn't that boundary; there is only one, there is only a oneness. In that unity, what could it mean that you want someone to love you? What could it mean that you are going to love someone?

What does it mean that you are going to give anything to anyone? What does it mean that you are going to get anything from the universe? You are the universe. The experience of oneness is not like all of humanity are all one and we know it in some deep place. No, the experience of oneness includes everything: all that you see, all that your senses are capable of perceiving. This is the world of appearance, the creation.

In the experience of oneness, all that you see is perceived as your own body. Then you truly know that the notion, "This small body is my body and that one is your body," is a figment of your imagination. It does not actually exist. My body is all that there is, and it is your body, too, and who we are is not this limited individual: Who we are is everything. We do not exist separate from each other, we do not exist separate from the environment that we live in. We are all one. The separateness that you perceive just does not objectively exist: it is not there. Just as when you are dreaming—you go to sleep and dream that you are this person here, and in the dream there are people, cities, universes, airplanes; you could marry, you could get divorced, you work, you have a wonderful time or a miserable time. . . . Right? And it feels completely real; in the dream it feels absolutely real. You wake up and it is gone. It was never really there. All of it was just ideas; you created all of this in your mind. But in the dream, you do not question it, you do not say it is a dream. You are dead sure it is reality. So that is the way I see the situation right now—all of you are dreaming, and are dead sure it is reality. And you believe that you are there and that person is there, and you are talking to that person. But when you wake up, you realize, no, it is actually all in one place, in your mind. These people do not exist, not in the sense that we usually think. That is why it is said that most people live a dream life, live the life of illusion.

When I say that when you wake up from this dream and you realize that all that you believe is not true, it does not mean that you no longer see people. You continue to perceive people, but you realize that there is only one. It is not that I have Essence inside me and you have Essence inside you and we know we are connected because it is the same kind of Essence. That is the experience of the first dimension, the realization that we are essential. What I am talking about now is that not only what is in you is what is in me, but that what is between us is also the same thing, and our skin is made out of the same thing. It is one block. There is utterly no separateness. We are actually all one thing that cannot be divided; we are indivisible. This realization becomes possible when we finally recognize our true nature.

The moment you have the experience of self-realization, if it happens completely, you are automatically catapulted into this experience of unity. Then you realize, not just that, "I am free and I am a simple sense of being;" no, everything is this being. This chair is the same thing as I am; in fact, it is me just as I am it. I mean this in the simplest, most fundamental sense, that we are actually the same thing, actually made out of the same consciousness, the same kind of existence. What you see as differences are just a kind of surface, a paint, as if there is just one thing painted over with different things. There is cream color there, blue color there; it looks like all kinds of things, but it is really one thing. So the experience of unity is a matter of recognizing the presence that is the nature of everything.

Also, the experience of oneness is not a good experience which you have once in a while. No, you realize that it is a fact. It is reality, not just a passing experience. What is actually transitory is our usual experience. It is not that you are a person who experiences oneness. No, you *are* a oneness, and at some point you will wake up to this reality. When you do, you realize, "All this time I had this strange idea in my mind that I exist as a person, that I am an individual separate from other individuals, and I have my own things and they have their own things." You realize what a gross lie it is, what a gross falsification. You realize that the truth is not such that it can be divided. And when you realize this, you realize that it makes sense, that that's how it should be and it is the best way it could be, and that you wouldn't want it any other way. When you realize oneness, you realize there are no issues, there are no problems, because all your problems relate to yourself. If there is no you, what problem have you got? You realize you cannot die, that nothing can actually happen to you. The worst thing that can happen to you is that your colors and forms will change; one day you look like a human being, the next you look like a tree. Your very nature, who you are, is the same; it is the totality of all of that. It is not actually precise to say that one day you look like a human being and the next day you look like a tree; it is actually more like a little part of you, one cell of you, at some point looks like a human being, and the next day looks like a tree. The rest of you is the totality of the universe.

From this perspective, it is clear that to think you are going to die is ridiculous. What's going to die? It is like the paint is being changed. You erase a certain picture. There is no sense of death, so there is no sense of fear, no sense of loss, no sense of pain. You do not need to be loved, you do not need to love anyone, you do not need to get anything, you do not need to give anything to anyone. Saying you want someone to love you is just like your nose saying, "I want my knee to love me." The nose is protesting, hates the knee for not loving it. That's how ridiculous it looks. Or your ear says, "I'm going to have my own life. I do not care about the legs. I'm going to be independent from my legs from now on. I'm an ear; I can hear very well, so let these legs go their own way. I'll let them be in peace, but

I'm going to have my own life and make myself bigger."
That's actually how it looks when you see people fighting
with each other. It is that absurd.

Finally, when you see your fundamental nature, which
is the nature of all that exists, you can no longer live your
life the way you have been living. That doesn't mean you
do not have relationships or you do not have work. All this
will continue; the movie goes on. The ideas that I'm going
to be independent from this person, I do not like this person, I want this person to love me, I'm afraid of becoming
poor, I'm afraid of dying; none of this makes sense. Saying,
"I hate this person because this person doesn't love me,"
is a strange idea. It is like you are sleeping and you are
dreaming that someone hates someone else, and there is
a big trouble there. You wake up and realize, "Hell, I don't
care. I'm going to have my breakfast. It is nothing. It is just
a movie that doesn't actually exist." But, you see, we are
always living the life that supports the lie. We are always
believing that our hatred is real, that our wanting something from someone is real, that we had better be a certain
kind of person, we should be able to do this or that. We
believe these things are real, and we live according to that
belief. This is how we completely eliminate the possibility
of seeing life as it is, as a oneness, an indivisible oneness,
that reality is one infinite solid block.

If you think about your life, with its problems and issues,
from the perspective of unity, you tend not to take things
so seriously. It is from this perspective that true human values emerge. Love, compassion, truth, and appreciation
come naturally. You are not loving someone else; you are
loving yourself all the time. You never love someone else.
No one ever loves you. There is only oneness, one reality,
and part of this reality is love. Part of this reality is truth.
Part of this reality is compassion, gentleness, and beauty.
It is not yours, it is not mine. It doesn't belong to anyone.

Essence doesn't belong to you. You do not *have* your essence. It is a mistake if you think you are going to *get* "your" essence. "I'm going to do my session and get another part of my essence." Nobody *has* an essence. There is only one Essence. You might become aware of it: It is as if one part of your body experiences Essence, and another part of your body doesn't experience Essence. What would you say? Would you say, "I should keep it in my left leg? I shouldn't let my heart have it? I should have more and more Essence in my leg." The moment you see that Essence is part of your body, don't you naturally want to experience it everywhere? The leg doesn't say, "It is mine. I shouldn't share it with the arms and the head." The natural thing is for it to be everywhere. In reality, it is the same thing. You do not experience your essence just for you. Self-realization is not for yourself alone. Self-realization is for everyone and everything, because it is not just yours. It is inaccurate to say that it is your essence, you are going to have your essence, it is your life, and you are going to have only your life, so you will use this essence to make your life nice. Your life is connected with everyone else's life. There is only one Being, and our lives are the life of that Being. When you look at things from this perspective, it is natural to be loving. It is natural to be helpful and generous, because the other person is actually you, is very much a part of you, is as much you as you are you, not one iota less.

I do not see you as separate from me, so your getting something is the same thing as me getting something. We are like different cells of the same body. This essential work cannot be done in isolation. You cannot have it just for yourself. You can do it to some extent in that way, but you'll run into trouble because you are fighting reality. In actuality, things do not exist separately; no one has more or less Essence than another. All of Essence is there is for everyone, all the time. It is never not like that. It is only when we are dreaming that we think , "I'm getting more, or the other person is getting more." Of course, we get into a lot of trouble when we look at it from this incorrect perspective.

The perception of reality—which is more objective than the perception of separateness—is the perception of oneness: the direct knowledge that there is only one, one beingness, one existence, indivisible, eternal. If we do not see that, if we do not experience that, if we do not live according to that, then we are still believing certain lies. There are things we do not see about reality. There are illusions in our individual minds that we haven't penetrated yet. So the goal of someone who is sincerely doing inner work is oneness, or unity, which means that it is not just for you. It is everyone and everything, and it is *for* everyone and everything.

The nature of this oneness is absolute goodness. It is the source of all love, compassion, color, beauty, peace—all inner richness and fulfillment. The oneness is the source of all the Essence that you know, all the goodness, all the beauty you've experienced in your life. In fact, it is the source of everything. It also *is* everything. So to believe that you are an individual little thing, and you are going to get your share of life, of reality, is to isolate yourself from this rich, immense reality, and to make yourself poor, small, and insignificant.

Oneness is not something you are going to accomplish one of these days; the oneness is already you; it always has been, and it always will be. What is needed is to wake up, to see things the way they are, instead of viewing them through distorting lenses. Oneness is absolute freedom, absolute release, absolute delight. It is a newness that is ever new. So wherever you go, there you are. Whatever you see, you see yourself. Whatever you touch, you are touching yourself. Whoever you talk to, you are talking to yourself.

I am talking about the objective perception of reality. I'm not saying that it is easy to perceive. It is difficult to come to a place where you perceive it, because of the accumulated ignorance that is based on the belief in separateness. Although we say that it is difficult to come to a place where we perceive the Supreme reality, we also know that there is no method to achieve this, because employing a method assumes that there is someone there, someone who is trying to get somewhere. By its very nature, method indicates a belief in separateness. So there is no technique, no method, no understanding that will precipitate the perception of oneness. If you do anything to get there, then you must be seeing yourself as a separate person, acting according to that separateness, and trying to get oneness—which is impossible. Still the perception of oneness does happen, because it is a fact, it is the reality. It happens when we relax, when we abandon our beliefs and our ideas and our defensiveness and our fears, when we do not need to constantly be protecting ourselves and pushing away the outside, when we are not busy enhancing ourselves and thinking of ourselves.

When you relax, it is possible to realize that you are everywhere, and then you might realize that it is not that you are everywhere: Everything is just one thing, an undivided whole. Seeing the oneness jolts your mind out of a deep groove, because your mind has been in this groove for all your life, believing you are a separate person, and that one of these days you are going to get something or arrive somewhere. Then you realize that all of that is not true; it is completely false. You do not need to get anywhere, you just need to forget about what you think you are. You just need to relax the tension that you call your boundaries. Of course, there is a need to continue, to do your work , to actualize the human life. It is living the true human life which allows the possibility of the arising of the perception of oneness. You have to live a life that is conducive to the experience of oneness, a life that doesn't resist that perception.

You need to live a life that doesn't depend on separateness, but on oneness, although you might not yet experience the oneness. The Chinese Taoist teacher, Lao Tsu, described the Four Virtues of what he called the virtuous life. If you live according to them, you will be living the true human life, which will predispose you to the experience and the realization of oneness. That means it is not just understanding yourself, not just having certain experiences; it means living, acting, interacting in a certain way.

So what are these four virtues? The first has to do with love and respect for your Essence and Being: to live a life that implicitly loves and respects what is genuine in you and everyone. If you do not live your life from the perspective of loving and respecting the beingness that you want and are, then all your understanding and essential experiences are useless; they can have no fruition. So this virtue has to do with living in a way that does not take you away from the perception of your essence, your true nature. You do not live a life that insults or devalues your being, or other people's being. And although I am saying that is a virtue that you need to develop and need to work on, it is actually a capacity that is inherent in the depths of the soul. We cannot help but feel this love and respect when we finally get closer to the true nature of oneness. Oneness becomes your primary love when you realize that it is what you really love. Everything else is nothing compared to this. But even if you do not actually perceive this, you need to work on having that attitude of love and respect for Essence everywhere in your life, because if you do not love and respect what is real, there is no way you are going to realize oneness. Without that attitude, in fact, you are saying "No" to the reality of oneness, and saying "Yes" to the false. You are living the life of separateness, the life of lies.

Another of the four virtues is sincerity: being sincere in your life, not lying to yourself. To be sincere is to be earnest about exposing your self-deceptions about who you really are, what you want and do not want, what you feel and do not feel, what scares you and what doesn't, about what is actually happening in you and in your situation. You need the utmost genuineness and dedication to the truth, and you need to live a life based on this sincerity and earnestness. Then you are living a life of truth, and loving truth. When I say you need to be earnest about being truthful, I do not mean simply that you need to tell the truth; I mean you need to see the truth, and live according to it, not to lie to yourself or to deceive yourself about what is actually happening. This development requires sincerity in all of your life. If you want something, let yourself know that, "Yes, I want something." If you are mad about something, let yourself know, "Yes, I'm mad about something." Let yourself recognize the truth, because oneness is a manifestation of ultimate truth. When you are completely sincere, you realize that oneness is the real state of the world. It is what exists; you are a universal person. That is a deep truth. When you are really sincere with yourself, and not trying to be anything else, then you realize your truth. When you are insincere, you are not letting yourself be who you really are. It is very important to work on developing sincerity.

The third virtue or quality is what is called delicacy. It is the nature of the ego-self or personality that it is thick-skinned, thick-headed, hard, and tough. This hardness, toughness, thickness, and dullness is the circumference, or the boundary between you and everyone else and the rest of the universe. So that's why you need to become more refined, more delicate. You need to have more gentleness, more vulnerability, more receptivity and permeability. You need gentleness and consideration, a kind understanding of yourself and other people and other beings. If you treat yourself or other people roughly, gruffly, or unkindly, you are making your boundaries thicker. You are not only hurting other people; you are hurting yourself. So the gentler you are, the simpler you are, the more delicate you are, the more sensitive you are, the closer you are to the reality of oneness.

Delicacy also means treating other people as though they are as valuable, as good, and as worthy of everything as you are. You are not putting up thick barriers between you and other human beings. Other human beings are not seen as enemies or adversaries. They are seen as a reflection of who you are, part of you, just like you, of the same nature, like fingers of the same hand. You do not want to be rough to your fingers; you want to be gentle, considerate, perceptive, and aware. So we are seeing that gentleness here, or delicacy, is of paramount importance because it is working on boundaries directly. It is actually letting go of the thickness that is the belief in your separateness. All the thickness, all the dullness, all the grossness, the aggressiveness, is ultimately an attempt to create or protect boundaries. The thickness is a protective thing, because you believe there is something there that you need to protect, so you keep building walls, one after the other, until you are thick, dense, insensitive, callous, loud, and gross. Life has to be lived to support inner unfoldment: the way you live, the way you move, the way you eat, the kind of environment you have; all these need to have this sense of delicacy, the sense of refinement, gentleness and sensitivity. You can actually work on developing and appreciating all these in your life. You need to be earnest enough to pay attention to that aspect of reality, learning to be sensitive to perceive and respond to, and be affected by, the finer elements, the subtler elements, because oneness is one of the most subtle things there is. It is one of the subtlest perceptions. So you need to be very gentle, very refined, very soft and malleable, to develop that sensitive perception, that sensitivity.

The fourth quality or virtue is what is called helpfulness. Obviously, helpfulness is based on oneness itself. To be helpful means that you are aware that you do not work only for yourself; your work is for everyone. If you only work on yourself without helping other people, you are not doing the Work. It is as simple as that. You cannot genuinely work on yourself without helping other people in one way or another. Helping other people does not necessarily mean working with them. It means to be aware of, sensitive to, concerned about other people's problems, issues, difficulties. In fact, it means always being generous, because other people are not separate from you. There are no other people. If you do your work from the perspective that you are freeing yourself, but you believe that it is not the same as freeing other people, then you are approaching it from the wrong premise. What you will reap is a lot of trouble. Nor can you approach it by trying to help other people so that you'll be doing the right thing in order to realize oneness. The helpfulness we are talking about is genuinely seeing that another human being is just as valuable as you are, and they need help as much as you need it. Your heart opens spontaneously to give, to consider, and to help. Helping other people only as a technique to get to oneness actually reinforces your belief in your separateness. You are not seeing that other people, other beings, are of the same nature.

Although helpfulness is good for you, it is also good for other people. You do it because it is good for you and because it is good for other people, too; it is intrinsically good for them. But not because ultimately it is going to be good for you; no, you want to be really generous regardless of whether it is going to be good for you or not. You want to help; You are not thinking of yourself. You are giving of yourself all the time, as much as possible, and giving of yourself in the sense that you are trying to be as helpful as possible. The development of this virtue means developing yourself, learning what you can, learning all the capacities you can, to be as objective as possible, as sensitive as possible, as generous as possible, so you can help in the best way. Your life then could be oriented towards helping, towards being a generous person, not because of the pleasure of helping; no, you genuinely want to help. Don't you feel that way sometimes? That sometimes you are genuinely interested in one person, one being, and you want to help so that person will have a better life?

The helpfulness needs to be genuine, and you actually have to work on it and orient your life that way. Your life should not be oriented towards making yourself richer and better; your life should be oriented towards becoming more generous. This does not mean that you need to forget about yourself, or sacrifice yourself, because you are a part of the oneness. You are as worthy as any other human being, just as any human being is as worthy as you are, and as valuable as you are. All people are absolutely equal, because there is absolute oneness.

These four virtues indicate what qualities we need in order to live a genuine human life, a life that can lead us to the deepest truth. If we have love and respect for Being, sincerity and earnestness about reality and truth, if we have delicacy and refinement, and if we are helpful and generous, then the major obstacles that block the perception of oneness are removed. When I say that the truth is our oneness, or that there is no separateness, I am not saying that when you realize this truth, you will disappear as an individual. You might take oneness to be a loss of who you are; you might fear that you are going to disappear. The condition of oneness can either be the sense that you are the oneness, the undivided Supreme Being, or that you are a unique individual who is inseparable from the Supreme oneness. Your individuality remains, but you as an individual are part of the totality. You realize you are a cell in a bigger body, that your body is a cell in a bigger body. It is not that your body will be erased, nor that you as a unique human being will disappear. No, you remain a unique human being, but that unique human being is an expression of the oneness, is supported by the oneness, and is part of the oneness, one cell in the larger cosmic body. So you are not less and you are not more than anyone or anything because everything is of the same nature. You cannot be more and you cannot be less.

When there are no boundaries, what naturally arises is love, abundance, and generosity, because what blocks love are the boundaries. There is no sense then that you are going to love someone, or that you want someone to love you. You are just you; you are natural, you are just living a human life, and there is love in it, naturally. You do not say, "I want to do this because I want to be loving." You just do it naturally. You are loving, without having to think about it. You do not have to feel compassionate to be helpful. You are helpful regardless of whether you feel helpful or not. Compassion might be present; you might not even care about it. You are just helpful. So, in a sense, in the Work, nothing is for you; at the same time, everything is for you because you are everything. Each one of us can come to see that these are not ideas, that this is not a point of view. This is actually the fact, this is the state of affairs; it is how things are when your mind is not interpreting things.

The way we usually see reality is determined by the ideas and beliefs and patterns of our minds. When the mind stops, when the ego stops, and you let perception be there, clear and cleansed and pure, then reality is what is seen. Everything else is an interpretation, and there are many levels of interpretation. There are many levels of consciousness, many levels of reality. But ultimately, when you completely let go of that interpretation, of the desire to interpret, it is possible to see things as they are.

Oneness is not a mental idea. It is not an idea that everything is one. The *idea* of oneness is not the same thing as the *experience* of oneness. The oneness is that you do not feel you end here or there; you do not end anywhere. You continue on and on and on, through everything. In the normal ego state, you can observe that your sense of self always includes a sense of boundaries. But when the perception of oneness is there, you do not feel anything like that. It is as if there is just air there, where your boundaries used to be. You feel yourself extended, continued through the air, through other people, through the walls, through the mountains, through everything. It is all one nature, one thing, and that is your nature. When you recognize yourself ultimately, what are you, ultimately? When you go to the deepest self-realization, then suddenly everything is one nature. Every atom that exists anywhere is that, and it is not an idea, it is not a point of view, it is not a perspective, so it cannot change. You might not see it, but that does not mean it is not there.

As you consider this perception of oneness, you will see that in a very deep place in you, in the deepest part of your heart, there is a very deep grief, the deepest wound, the wound of the separation from oneness. And there is longing in our hearts, the deepest longing, the deepest yearning. The most powerful desire we have, in the deepest part of our hearts, is the longing to cease as a separate individual; to be united, to see that there is really only one because it is our ultimate nature. If it is cut off from our perception, there has to be a sense of loss, a deep, gaping wound that does not heal, and there inevitably arises an immense longing, a very deep ache, so that no matter what you experience or feel, there is dissatisfaction and discontent. Your heart does not allow itself to be completely happy because this oneness is what your heart ultimately wants, and everything else it wants is just a little reflection of this. You might think your heart wants this and that, and it is all true, but these all are superficial wants. What will make your heart dance in happiness is this perception of one-ness, your direct knowledge of the unity of yourself and everything in one nature.

S: It seems that once you wake up, or at least feel that you have this experience, you go back into deep sleep again. For instance, how you can have this direct experience while you are watching television? Can you continue to have that all the time, can you access that all the time?

AHA: If you still believe that you are an individual person, you lose this realization. If you see that is the fact, that is how things are, and you are completely convinced, then the experience stays. But there is no way that you could try to get to it. You just live a decent life, a virtuous life, as Lao Tsu defined it.

S: So if that experience doesn't stay there, then that might mean that one was not fully convinced.

AHA: Yes. It means you are still identified with a separate kind of self, and you still take that to be the true identity. If you are still experiencing yourself as separate, you must still believe that is how things are, at some very deep place in you. You might not even be aware of it, but it must be there. You see, just saying that you are there and you get away from that, indicates that you see yourself separate from oneness. In oneness, there is nobody there experienc-ing oneness. There is nobody there that leaves oneness. Everything is one. The experience of oneness is not, "Oh, here I am experiencing oneness." If I say that, there is a duality there. Oneness is just the perception of how things are. The boundaries, the sense of limitations, are not created by the center, by the self; the boundaries exist in you before your sense of identity. That's why it is possible to experience oneself without self, but still existing as an individual.

S: When did we separate? You say that in fact we are, have always been, one, so there must have been a oneness and a separation.

AHA: Separation happens in very early childhood, in the first year of life or so. When babies are first born, they do not experience themselves as separate. Being separate has to do with a creation of the mind. As your mind develops, and has concepts, you conceptualize an entity that is you, that is based on the perception of your body. Before that happens, there is oneness. Oneness is nothing but the experience of reality without the intervention of the mind, without concepts. Oneness is nonconceptual reality. What are concepts? Concepts are nothing but boundaries. You take something and conceptualize it, and you create boundaries around it. This is a human being, this is a tree, this is a house, this is a feeling, this is a sensation: All these are concepts. When you are not doing that, all separateness disappears. Then it is possible to see reality as it is. That's why it is hopeless to *do* anything to experience oneness, because the moment you try to do anything, you are doing it according to your mind. How else can you do it? The moment you try to do anything to get to oneness, you are doing it according to your mind; then oneness is still an idea, a concept. If you are living according to your mind, you are going to perpetuate your mind, and in perpetuating your mind, you are not going to see reality completely naked. Oneness happens by complete relaxation, not by going after anything. We have always been going after something since the moment we developed a mind. In oneness, there is no going after anything, no seeking whatsoever. That is why the center needs to be dealt with first, because that center is the seeker. When the center is quiet, it is possible to become aware of the boundaries, and to see that the boundaries are the barrier. Then you live a life according to boundlessness.

As you may notice, the notion of oneness has quite an impact on your mind; it is a possibility that your mind doesn't usually conceive of. The idea of it has an impact.

Now, imagine what the experience is like. The more the person has an experience of oneness, the more the person will be walking around with a question mark: How can that be? What does that mean? You are eating your food, and you ask, "What am I eating? I am eating myself." For your mind, it is completely incomprehensible. It takes time for the mind to get used to it, to adjust itself, to realize, "Yeah, I do not really have to think the way I usually think, I do not really have to go about my life the way I usually go about it. Things are not really like that." The goodness and abundance is in every point and all of existence. It is not here or there.

S: It seems like separateness and oneness exist simultaneously, but that they're different dimensions, because if you look at the state of humanity, and ourselves, myself, what I really experience is the separateness. And in dealing with people, that's what comes up: the separateness. So what kept coming up for me when you were talking was that if I experience unity with the rest of humanity, what comes up is strife and suffering, things like that.

AHA: Well, let's put it this way—is your heart separate from your liver? I mean, if your heart has a mind, it says, "Yeah, I'm here, and there is the liver over there—we're two separate things." That's one way of looking at it, but is that the correct way? Or you could look at it even more closely. Suppose you can be aware of the cells in your body. Of course, each cell has its own boundaries, separate from other cells. So each cell says, "Well I'm separate." Looking at it from the perspective of the cell, you could say that the cell is separate, but when you are aware of your whole body, you do not experience the cells as separate. Some of the cells might be having a hard time instead of having a good time, and someplace in your body there could be a party, while in another place, there is death and stagnation, but it is all one body. You do not say, "No, those parts are separate, those cells are dying and this part here that's happy is me." It is all one thing. The oneness is something that is even more one, more connected than how the cells are connected, much more. There is absolutely nothing in between because everything that is between two things is the same thing as those two things.

S: You said earlier that if we blew the world up, the oneness would stay there, and I can't get far enough to understand that.

AHA: There are many teachings that say that the world has been destroyed many times before. This world might be blown up, and some other world might take its place. But when you see yourself, and you see your true nature, then the whole world is a certain form of the totality. It is like humanity: some people are born, some people die. The human race continues as a human race, the nature of humanity continues. Now, there is the nature of everything that is beyond the nature of humanity, where, just like one person is a part of humanity, humanity is one thing. The human race as a whole is one thing, part of a bigger thing. So even if it goes, the bigger body continues.

S: So Essence is a part of that oneness?

AHA: Essence is a part of that oneness. Oneness means there is nothing apart from it. There is nothing apart. Everything is part of it. Nothing is excluded absolutely; the good and the bad are all part of it. Oneness itself does not discriminate between good and bad. The Supreme is pure being: It is just the existence of things, how things exist. Everything exists. This existence, the existence of everything: that is the oneness.

Oneness is not concerned about individuals, about the separateness. It does not say, "Oh, this person is suffering, that person is having a good time, let me do something about this." Oneness doesn't do anything. It is not of its nature to be concerned, yet it is also the source of all love and all goodness. But the love and goodness of oneness are a natural arising, just like the sun has light. It is not that the sun is concerned about us and says, "Well, the human race needs a little more heat, so let me pump a little more heat." The nature of the oneness is that it is a source of love, gentleness and humanness, and all of that. It doesn't have to be concerned. It is bigger than being concerned.

In fact, the whole universe is the expression of the love of that oneness. The world that you see is like the robe that this oneness is wearing. And this robe is beauty and grace, made out of love and Essence, but it is also part of the oneness. Oneness as a concept is very difficult to think about, because to do that, you need to contrast it with other things. The oneness means there is nothing else to contrast it with. It does not exclude anything. The moment it excludes something, it is not oneness. There are two things then.

S: When you were talking about being helping and being generous, what if you do not know what that is? If you do not know what it is to truly help someone?

AHA: Then you try to learn to know.

S: Before you try to help them?

AHA: Help comes in many dimensions, on many levels. When you see somebody lying in the street sick, it is obvious what to do to help them. So you help according to your level of understanding. Part of helpfulness and generosity is to increase your level of understanding so that you could be more helpful, in a more real way. But there is always some kind of understanding, some kind of humanity, from which you could help. Helpfulness means you are loving the other. It also means you are not separate from the other. Helpfulness means that everything around you is part of your family. You all make one family. Helpfulness does not mean just blindly giving away everything you've got. If you do that, you might not be able to help anyone. It means using all your intelligence, all your capacity to help the best way possible. Developing helpfulness also means developing spontaneous helpfulness. It is not saying, "I want to help because it is good." You need to learn to develop yourself so that you feel helpful spontaneously. If spontaneous helpfulness is there, what needs to develop next is your capacity to help, ways of helping and assisting. And one of those capacities, obviously, is gentleness, delicacy.

You might notice, for instance, that when people understand themselves and like themselves more, it becomes natural for them to want to help; it just arises by itself. The more you are in touch with your love, the more you naturally want to go outside, to others. Essence operates according to the objective law that it is not you, but everything, that is valuable. You are not special. Nobody is special, absolutely. But the whole totality is the most special and the most exquisite.

SEVEN

Realization of Absence

S: I've recently been transcribing the tape on Will and Support, and one of the last things you said on that tape was that real Will has an absence of effort. When you are making an effort, that's not real Will? I feel that if I don't effort, I won't do anything.

AHA: We say that real Will is effortlessness, but that does not mean that effort is not useful sometimes. You are usually efforting unconsciously, so if you don't put in some conscious effort, that unconscious effort will be the dominant force that runs your life.

S: Is that related to effort in the Gurdjieff sense?

AHA: Effort in the Gurdjieff sense is conscious, but it is still effort. In the Work, there is need for effort, for some time. Effort is needed because there is already unconscious effort; if there were no unconscious effort, then one could not effort at all, at any time.

S: The unconscious effort often feels like lethargy so that I can't do anything.

AHA: Unconscious effort is really a resistance, saying no. You have some internal resistance that you might not be aware of. The presence of any mechanism of inner action indicates effort. You can't have resistance, or unconscious defending, without there being some effort involved; resistance is not the natural state.

If there is really no unconscious effort, there will be no resistance against anything in you. So the conscious effort is needed to expose the unconscious effort. Once the unconscious effort is exposed, then continuing to make effort is just resistance, which blocks the true Will. Sometimes we need to make an effort and sometimes we need to stop the efforting, depending on the situation. To really work on oneself efficiently and intelligently means to know when to use effort and when not to use effort.

S: Are there any guideposts?

AHA: There are no formulas for it. You have to use your intelligence. When you are aware that there is something unconscious in you but you are not putting in any effort, that's a time to put in effort. And when you are aware that you are not influenced by such unconsciousness, and you seem to be present and clear, then it is a time not to effort: to just let go, to flow. Ultimately, effort is against true Will because effort indicates that there is a person there who is efforting. Efforting indicates that you are identifying with some image. You take yourself to be a person separate from the rest of the universe. You take yourself to be a separate person, an individual with her own mind and her own will. In this situation it is inevitable that you will make efforts. But what if the deeper truth is that you are not a separate individual with your own mind and will?

S: That's something I've never experienced.

AHA: Yes, I know. That is why you believe you have your own will and why it's hard not to effort, because at this moment you believe you are a separate individual with your own mind and your own volition. To continue to be separate takes effort because you are maintaining your differences from the rest of the universe. Since you have your own preferences, your own choices, that might not go along with the rest of the universe, then there is a place for effort. You make efforts in order to push your own preferences which you see as different from the rest of the universe. But when you realize that you are not truly separate, then you can relax the effort and return to a more relaxed, natural state.

S: For me, all it seems to come down to is survival: Just feeding myself takes effort.

AHA: This is generally true for human beings, but the delusion of separateness is universal. Concern for survival also indicates that you believe you are a separate individual with your own separate life.

S: Yes, I definitely have that belief.

AHA: Right. So survival of the individual becomes very important. But the fact is that you are not that individual. You have never been that individual. It is a figment of your imagination. Without this delusion, survival will mean something different, and will involve less effort.

S: Who's in this chair?

AHA: The imagination of the universal mind. It is not your own imagination. You are being imagined all the time, so is the chair and everything else, just like being a figure in a dream, and the figure in the dream believes he or she is real. Imagine you have a dream where you see people and one of those people believes that they are really real while they are being dreamed by you. Your situation is exactly like that. Exactly. This is what is referred to as the universal mind, or the Divine Mind.

S: I have a question about this, about the combination of love and movement and effort. I don't know exactly what my question is. It's not exactly, "How do you know when you are moving from your heart?" but something like that.

AHA: Sometimes you believe you are moving from your heart, but you never do. It depends on what level of experience you find your identity. If you are still operating from the perspective of being an individual entity, then you will feel sometimes you are coming from your heart, or head, or belly. When your identity moves deeper, you realize yourself on a more boundless dimension; you experience the universe as your body. Then it makes no sense to come from the little place of the heart. You realize that nobody ever moved from their heart. Do you know why? Because there is nobody there to have a heart. The heart is all of existence. That is the real heart. All that you see around you is the heart of the universe. When you believe you are a separate person, you take a little part of that and say, "That is my heart."

S: Then how do you know you are living as the heart of the universe?

AHA: When you are not making any effort and there is no unconscious effort, when there is no effort at all—just spontaneous movement, the movement flows and there is true love. There is only a flow and no conflict. You are probably not even thinking about it then; it just happens. This is similar to what you do most of the time. For instance, when you get up to go someplace, is there effort? Some of the time, maybe, but most of the time there isn't. If you want to get a drink, you just get up and get a drink of water. Where is the effort? It is a very spontaneous, smooth movement. That is similar to the movement of love.

S: Is that different from being present?

AHA: Why do you say that?

S: While I get a drink of water I may be thinking so that I'm somewhere totally out of my body while I'm doing it. Then it doesn't feel like I am present with that action.

AHA: That's true, but sometimes you are being sponta- neous and present at the same time; even while thinking, you are thinking spontaneously. However, there is always the activity of self-reflection, which is mostly preconscious. It's not exactly unconscious or repressed, but it is not explicit in your awareness. This self-reflection always identifies you as the self which is a separate entity. This makes it impos- sible to be completely spontaneous. The only problem hap- pens when you reflect back on what you are doing. If you don't reflect on it, then everything is happening sponta- neously; you just do it. If you never think about it, no prob- lem, you just do what you do and that's it. It's only when you start thinking about yourself: Should I do this? Should I control myself? Should I do that? Is this going to be right? Is this going to be wrong? Then conflict or dichotomy arises. If you don't think about it, you just do it, then spontaneous activity is a natural thing.

S: Then what is the difference between love and just existence?

AHA: From the perspective of objective reality, there is no difference. We tend to think of Love only in a specific way, connecting it with specific feelings we call love. But Love is really all of existence. When you recognize this, it becomes easy to let yourself be spontaneous, just let yourself be, with- out reflecting about who you are or what you are going to do. You just do it, spontaneously, completely without thinking. Everything is Love then, and that is the movement of Love. Love doesn't reflect on itself. Love just moves. What reflects on itself is the mind. But the mind is also the expression of Love in the end. The mind is also a manifestation of love.

Mind acts as a mirror of Love so that Love knows itself. This brings us a mixed blessing: a blessing and a curse at the same time. There is the possibility of knowing who you are, but there is also the possibility of creating a mess out of your life. If you look at it, you see that the situation is actually about the mind. The mind can look at itself, while Love doesn't look at itself. Love is just there and flows. Mind is there for Love to see itself.

S: Sounds like the garden of Eden . . . and the loss of it.

AHA: Yes, that's one way the mind is very clever; it creates ideas like loss of God and Eden and all of these things. What we are saying here is that self-reflection brings self-awareness, but it also brings conflict. The central manifestation of this conflict is identifying with being a separate entity that has its own will and doership. We are completely free when we don't reflect on ourselves, just like little children. Little children don't reflect on themselves. They don't even look at themselves. They don't know who they are, or whether they exist or not. When their minds start developing and they begin to reflect on themselves: "I am this, I am that, I am good, I am bad . . ." then the trouble starts. When they begin to attempt to control themselves and reality, that is false will. That's the effort. But if there isn't that division between who you are and who looks at you, there is just one who doesn't look at herself. There is no effort.

S: Spontaneous activity seems effortless. Often, automatic behavior is too, but I'm getting a sense that as I become aware of my automatic patterns, then I am beginning to sense the effort in them, for there is self-consciousness.

AHA: Automatic patterns are a kind of false spontaneity. They are not really spontaneous. The person is still reflecting on herself, is behaving still in a way to be good, or to do this or that. This is still a judgment and a discrimination of oneself, and the person might not be aware of it. But they are doing it anyway, maybe preconsciously and not consciously. When I say spontaneously, I mean you are really not aware of it at all. You just do it with absolutely no self-reflection, absolutely, just like when you are falling asleep.

Usually when you are falling asleep, you are not aware of it. You are just falling asleep. You know you are lying there thinking about something, and then suddenly you wake up in the morning. What happened? That's how it happens usually, that is, very spontaneous. If falling asleep is not spontaneous, you can't fall asleep. Try to fall sleep, you'll never make it. Anyone who tries to go to sleep, can't go to sleep. Only when you forget about yourself do you fall asleep. That is similar to the true flow of love. So when you live your life like that it's just like falling asleep. That is when you are free.

S: You always talk about us waking up, though.

AHA: Yes, we have talked many times in the past about waking up. In our Work we use ideas appropriate to the specific teaching, appropriate to the particular time, place, and people. A mother tells a three-year-old never to cross the street, but tells an older child to look both ways before crossing the street. At a certain stage, experience is different and so our concepts are different.

Here, we are changing the terminology from what we have been using. To be free means to be completely unconscious of yourself because at the deepest level there is no self to be conscious of. You don't know who you are. You don't know what you're doing. You are just doing it. You are not even doing it: it just happens. You'll be eating and suddenly you realize that you are eating, and then you can reflect on yourself. But most of the time that you are eating you don't know that you are eating or that somebody is eating. There is eating; that's all. There is an awareness of the food but there is no awareness of your mouth or anything like that. You are not seeing your image if you are completely spontaneous. No, there is just the process of eating. This is a fact: It is only when you reflect on yourself and think about things that you feel there is a person there. There is a body there, and there is food. If you just let everything be there on its own, get it out of your mind completely, you will simply know the process of eating.

This is the spontaneous life that is both Existence and Love. Imagine a child who is about six months old, who is eating. Does she know she is sitting there and that she is eating? Does she know she is eating? No, not mentally. Infants do not have the self-reflection that you have; they do not have the notion that there is a person who is there, there is food there, they are eating, and eating is for such and such. All these things are in your mind, but if your mind is silent, none of that is there. I'm not saying that there is no food going in the stomach. The whole thing is a process; that's all.

S: Isn't there something that we have as adults but we don't have as children? Some kinds of presence or awareness?

AHA: We develop many things as adults, many capacities that infants do not have. Among these are capacities for thinking, for conceiving of things. But presence and awareness are not thinking. They are there if they are allowed without trying to figure them out. Awareness is not interested in looking at itself. Awareness has nothing to do with conceptualizing and knowing: Awareness is completely spontaneous. That is called living without mind. When you look at me right now and don't think, is there anyone there looking at me?

S: How does that connect with feeling? When you feel something, you do not necessarily think of it.

AHA: Yes, you do think about it. Feelings go along with thoughts. They are actually determined by thoughts.

S: What about sensation?

AHA: Sensations go along with thoughts. When there are absolutely no thoughts, there are no sensations. In your nature there are ultimately no thoughts, no feelings, no sensations. You're mind is 100 percent still. You see no thoughts, no feelings, no sensations, and no you.

There is a state of complete absence, and there is also absence of the awareness of absence. There is no one and nothing there. And there is nobody there to be aware that there's nobody and there's nothing—complete absence of consciousness. That is the most awakened state.

S: I'm confused.

AHA: There's no way not to be confused if you start with the word I. That's the initial confusion. If you start with confusion, how is it possible not to be confused?

We got into this by talking about effort: how effortlessness is spontaneity and spontaneity means no reflection on yourself. The moment you reflect on yourself, there is no spontaneity. There is recognition, and then there is deliberation—thinking about what you are doing. The interesting thing is that most of the time we are actually like that, but not when we are thinking about ourselves. When you are reflecting on yourself, you are not being spontaneous.

Much of the time you are spontaneous, but at that time you don't know it. There is harmony, but you don't know it because you aren't thinking about yourself. You're not reflecting on yourself so you don't know if you are happy or not. When you are thinking about yourself, then, of course, you think, "No, I'm not happy." Most of the time when you are thinking about yourself, you are not happy, but you are not aware of the times when you are not thinking about yourself. Try to remember a time when you weren't reflecting on yourself. It happens a lot during the day. Were you happy? Were you unhappy? You don't know. There is harmony in it. You don't know if you were happy. You don't know if you were unhappy. You don't know what you were. You don't even know if you were existing or not.

S: I always thought of that as a definition of being a human being. When I came to, and wondered where was "I", I thought there was something wrong with my brain.

AHA: Asking that question doesn't mean there is something wrong with your brain. It is part of the development of a human being. Ego development is a natural stage of the development of the soul. This development depends on self-reflection, which is the basis of most human knowledge. The problem is that we forget how to be ourselves without this self-reflection. We lose the immediacy of true nature, and we forget the deepest secret essence of this nature, which is absolute absence.

S: Is this absence the absence of awareness?

AHA: Absence of awareness of oneself.

S: But there is awareness?

AHA: There is awareness of everything else.

S: I thought essence was the one thing that really existed.

AHA: Yes, this is true, but there is what we call the secret or mystery of essence, which is ultimately who you truly are. Knowing the deepest mystery of true nature is a matter of shedding subtler layers of mind. When Essence is reflecting on itself it is not just Essence by itself; there is a mind there. Essence manifests in many dimensions of increasing subtlety. When mind is completely shed, self-reflection ceases.

S: I've had experiences when I don't feel like there are any thoughts, but my awareness is sensations and feelings in my body and outside the room and there is an evenness everywhere.

AHA: If there aren't thoughts, how do you know that there is an inside and an outside?

S: I don't have a feeling of having an inside or an outside.

AHA: So what's there, then?

S: A lot that I sense.

AHA: Like what?

S: I sense the floor, I sense the connection between.

AHA: So you are aware that there is a floor. How do you know there is a floor if there is no thought of a floor?

S: I don't know. I just experience it.

AHA: Yes. That means there is a very subtle thought still. When you are aware of the floor, then obviously, there must be a thought of the floor someplace because who says that it is a floor? How do you know that it is a floor and not something else? The floor is a concept, an idea. Otherwise, it could not arise in perception as something distinct from other objects.

S: Well, I know that I have experienced it.

AHA: How do you know that you are not sensing the wall? They feel the same.

S: I didn't experience them as names. I experienced them as sensation.

AHA: But how do you know it was the floor?

S: I don't have names for them in that state. I was sitting here, and after I came to, I saw that I was sitting on the floor.

AHA: Why do you assume that you were sitting on the floor? Maybe you were sitting on something else. You are assuming that it was the floor that you were sensing. You were aware of some kind of sensation, no? Later on, when your mind came back, you thought this was the floor that you were sensing. It is possible that you were wrong.

S: Well, there is also some way in which I feel that when I'm in that state, there are two different things: I have the experience of everything as I have always experienced it, and at the same time I experience that it is not real at all, that there is some other level or some other dimension that I'm experiencing there. But I feel them both at the same time. It is not that the normal one disappears and suddenly I'm in a different state.

AHA: Yes, I understand; there is that perception, that experience. When that happens, the concepts and thoughts are still there in a subtle way. Even so, what you are describing is more real than the usual experience.

S: I have a question about something. You once made a distinction between fear and terror. It seems that in fear there is some unconscious material wanting to come through. Why would fear turn to terror?

AHA: Terror usually has to do with survival, so it is not just a matter of unconscious material. When people have terror, they are afraid that they are going to die, or that they are going to disappear. The loss of the sense of self comes after that. The self in the beginning is an ego self, what is called the personality, with its identity. If you follow it, you realize that it can go, disappear, and there is a terror about letting go of that. That is when you shake in your boots.

When that goes, there is peace. Then there is the discovery of the essential or true self. The real self is made out of pure essence and consciousness. It is luminous and pure and a source of love, compassion and goodness, with a sense of timelessness and spacelessness. That identity can go too. When that goes, there is another experience of peace which has to do with nonexistence. When that happens, there is the possibility of the arising of another identity, which we call the Supreme identity, for this identity is the self of the whole universe. The true identity is a reflection of a more universal, boundless identity, which is the nature of all that there is. You see yourself as everything, as the source of everything, not merely the source of your own body and thoughts. Then there is the possibility of losing even this cosmic self. This results in a new experience of peace, which is the experience of selflessness. Then there is no self to see you or anything: All that exists is ultimately empty and self-less. Then even that can go. The selflessness can go, which means going through fear and terror again. The selflessness goes because even selflessness is a concept. What is left then is absence, which is not anything left.

You could say that is who you are, but there is nobody there to say that is who you are. It will be exactly the same as deep sleep, except that you are awake. You don't know yourself: You don't say whether there is a self or whether there isn't a self.

As you see, self-realization goes through many stages. The sense of self, the sense of identity is the last thing to go. We don't say it is real or it is not real. There is a real self, the true self, the essential self. Everybody has that self. You can't be a human being without having a true self which is not your own production. It has nothing to do with your childhood conditioning. You were born with it. But it is possible to see that you can go beyond that. The true self is needed, and must be realized for a person to move to the Supreme or universal self, because these are sparks of the same light.

What you usually take yourself to be is the most external of these, which is the psychological sense of self. And that exists in its own level. If you look at it from the level of the personality, there is a psychological self. You experience it and you can even feel it physically. So whether there is a self or not is not the relevant question. It is not that there is or there is not a self. It depends on which level of discourse you are operating on. At each transition, there is terror and the fear of losing what you have; you feel that you are going to die. People feel that they are going to disappear or vanish. There is nothing abnormal about being terrified when you are going to die. There is fear until you get to the selfless stage, when you see that there is no need to have a self. You realize that there is life, there is functioning, everything is as usual without having to fear the loss of self. A self can arise which you could call a self, but there is no need for it. And selflessness is really essential. There is still an awareness of experience, of consciousness, and there is no self. There is consciousness and a kind of emptiness, a void that has no sense of self and no need for a sense of self.

The step after that is the loss of consciousness of no-self, and when that consciousness is gone, then there is no consciousness of self, or no self and no knowing that there is no consciousness of self or no self. This is the absence of mind, consciousness, and sensation. When that happens, it is then possible to be truly spontaneous because there is no self there to reflect on. If you reflect on yourself in this state, the only thing that happens is that you realize your head is turned around and that you are looking outside. There is nothing else to look into; you can only look outward.

The main barrier to all these transitions is the belief that you are the person that is connected to the body. You are taking what we call the shell (because it functions as a defensive shell) to be you. Identifying with this shell brings the terror that you are going to lose the sense of being a person. But what you actually are is not a person; you are a window to the universe.

S: In my experience, when my body is in balance, I lose a sense of my boundaries, the body boundaries that make me feel I am a separate entity.

AHA: Exactly. When the body is relaxed and balanced and has no tension, there are no boundaries. Boundaries are tensions in the body. The experience of boundaries goes along with tensions in the body. The body armor is the boundary. When the body is balanced, relaxed, there is no need for boundaries. So you could say that some self-realization can be done physically. In the end, self-realization is the completely relaxed body, nothing else. When the body is completely relaxed, it is a window to the universe. That window allows the possibility of perception, awareness and experience. When the body goes, the window is gone, which is a further development, a greater opening.

It does not mean that the window is closed; it means that the whole universe becomes the window. Then there is nothing to see. And each transition brings a deeper peace. Each time there is a loss of self or self-identity there is a deeper peace. Peace and stillness. Until you get to the complete absence; then peace is absolute because there is absolutely nothing to disturb it. Absolutely nothing, not even the knowing that there is peace. The moment that you know there is peace, there is a little disturbance someplace because there is self-reflection. But absolute peace means that there is absolute peace without the awareness that there is peace. Complete unification, no reflection. And when the peace is absolute, the clarity is absolute. When there is absence, there is absolute clarity. Clarity is everywhere and everything.

S: You are saying that what a human really is, is absolute clarity?

AHA: Not only a human being. Everything is.

S: Even the personality and its most dark and most congested places?

AHA: Its true nature is.

S: Its true nature?

AHA: The true nature of everything including the personality is the same. For instance, if you are looking at only a physical object like this rug you say it is white and soft and all of that. That is looking at it externally. Looking at its deepest nature, you will see that it is clarity. But if you look at it from the external perspective, it looks like it is a white, soft, fluffy thing.

S: What makes for the difference? Why don't I experience it as clarity?

AHA: Because you are looking at the appearance and taking that to be true nature. The more you believe the appearance to be real, the more it looks real. This is my experience: When I look at the appearance, the body, the physical thing, the more I think they are real and the more they solidify. The more I look beyond the appearance at something deeper, and see its substantiality, the less real the surface looks and the more insubstantial it becomes.

S: What is the difference between clarity and unity?

AHA: In absolute clarity, there is no unity and no absence of unity.

S: There is no unity and no absence of unity?

AHA: Unity is a very deep experience. It is the absence of boundaries. When boundaries are completely gone, you don't experience yourself as a separate individual, and there is no boundary between one thing and another. There is unity: This is the universal identity. When you feel that you are everything, that everything is one, still there is a concept, the concept of unity. Beyond that concept, however, the way reality ultimately is, is neither unity, nor non-unity. The way things are is just the way things are. Saying it is unity is your own comment.

S: Saying things are clarity. . .

AHA: . . . is also your comment. This is why I call it absence. The absolute clarity is just the reflection of the true reality.

If awareness is still there, there is not complete absence. There is consciousness. There is something there cognizant of absence, so that is not absolute absence yet. When it is absolute absence, what do you call it? Absence? You might, if you approximate it. It seems the more I get into it, the more it is absence. But when you are gone, maybe it changes then, maybe it does not. Who knows? Hence, it is unknowable.

S: It sounds like the absence is from before you were born.

AHA: Not only before you were born, before anything was born. You, as an individual, were born out of unity, but before unity was born, what was that?

S: I don't understand what you mean that I was born out of unity.

AHA: You are thinking of yourself as an individual separate from everything else. That sense of being a person, being an individual, is born out of unity. Before you developed a sense of individuality, there was oneness, there were no boundaries, and before that perception of oneness there was the sense of the absence of oneness, neither oneness nor division. But then before that, what do you say?

S: I think we're always looking backwards.

AHA: In one sense, you keep looking backwards, until finally you get to the most backward; then you realize that you are looking forward. When you reach the complete back of reality, then you can only look forward. There isn't anything to look back to. So the only thing left is to look forward, and that is spontaneity.

Self-realization, which is the realization of true identity, goes through regressive movements. There is a greater and greater loss of what you think you are. One after another, always a loss, and the more there is a loss of what you think you are, the more freedom there is.

S: So there is a maturing and a regressing? Is there any difference?

AHA: Maturing is living according to the wisdom gained from regression, which is more of a shedding of accumulated concepts about reality. Shall I repeat it? If you have learned from the regression, and that is incorporated in the way you live, that is maturity. Maturity is connected with wisdom, and wisdom is connected with the integration of what you have learned and what you have experienced. If you have not integrated what you learned from experience, then there is no wisdom. When experience is integrated, it becomes wisdom; wisdom is living according to what you have learned. When you live according to what you have learned, you are mature.

S: What does integrated mean?

AHA: Integrated means your life flows according to your understanding. If you have some experience of reality but you don't live according to that perception, that means that perception has not been integrated. Integrated means it is naturally, implicitly there, in what you do, how you think, how you operate.

You notice the first experiences in learning. During the first steps you have certain experiences and you realize, "This is real, I know what love is now," for instance. Then the next day you act as if love was not that. That means that the experience of love is not integrated yet. There has to be a process of integration: When it is integrated you not only know love, but you are wise about love. Then you act with maturity and love with maturity. Maturity is not an absolute term. It depends on what understanding has been integrated, so there is no end to it.

S: Is maturing assumed to come after from a point when we have a sense of our personality developing?

AHA: Maturing has to do with the true development of who you are. It is not the development of the inner child; the inner child cannot develop because the child does not exist now. It is only an image in your mind. How can an image in your mind develop? Your body was the body of a child thirty years ago. It isn't now. So if you take yourself now to be a child, how can that grow? It cannot grow because it's an image. It's not real. What develops is what is real in you, your Personal Essence. That is what goes through the personal development to maturity.

S: Because the world that we live in is always reinforcing the idea of separateness and individuality, progress and all of that, the question that comes up for me is what are conducive ways of living to integrate that understanding?

AHA: Clearly, the most obvious thing is what all the traditions and teachings have said, which is to live selflessly: to give of oneself instead of accumulating for oneself. The more you give, the more generous you are, the more compassionate, the more loving, the more selfless you are, the less there is an identification with the person because the person is an experience of being an island. An island needs to be protected and enhanced, but if you don't try to protect it or enhance it, then the generosity will tend to eliminate the boundaries. Generosity is a good word because generosity is an openness. There is no holding back in true generosity. I don't mean simply open and giving physically, but in all ways. It means not protecting yourself. I don't mean not protecting yourself in the sense of not closing your doors at night. Not protecting yourself means not trying to build psychological boundaries, not trying to thicken your boundaries, but working on dissolving those boundaries. Generosity really is the heart of the oneness or the unity. When there is the experience of oneness, the heart is experienced as absolute generosity. There is absolutely no holding back. Whatever is there—love, compassion, understanding, knowledge, help—just flows out. But there is a tendency to protect yourself because of a lack understanding . It is not because you are bad. In a relative way, you exist, but if you think of who you are ultimately, you are not a person; yet a person is one of your manifestations.

We can manifest as a person, or as love, joy, or compassion. The person is just one of the essential aspects. Being a person is the most difficult of the essential aspects to understand because we have lived an imitation of it which is the false person, the personality. In being a person, there is a true person, and the true person is what I call the Personal Essence, an expression or manifestation of your true nature. Just like love is an expression of who you are. But if we believe that ultimately we are the person, then we form a false personality. We form boundaries. So the person is not something to be rejected or put down or hated.

The person is as precious as love is. The person is the way that who we truly are manifests on earth. Who we truly are cannot live on earth because we are nonphysical and have no form, so for true nature to have a window on creation, it manifests as a person.

When you realize the true person, the essential person, then you realize one of the essential aspects. This means that sometimes you are person and sometimes you are not. Just like when you experience your true nature as love, you don't have to have love all the time. Sometimes there is love, sometimes there is compassion, sometimes there is will. You can't say, "I have to have love all the time. I have to have will all the time." The same thing is true of the person: sometimes there is a person, sometimes there isn't a person. This is also true of the true self. Sometimes there is a true self; sometimes there isn't a true self, depending on the need because you are the source of all these things. If the true person which is made of consciousness and essence is not being protected, then the true person does not feel itself separated and isolated from other persons. There is a sense of true contact and true concern.

As I have always said, there is a true individuality, which I call the Personal Essence, and because it is an essential aspect, all the laws that govern essential aspects will govern the aspect of the person. Just like the the aspects of Strength, Will, and Compassion, those natural laws also apply to the aspect of the person. Usually, however, we want to hold on to the aspect of the person all the time. This is the same thing as trying to hold on to Compassion all the time, and then it becomes fake compassion. Our human conditioning is that we should be a person all the time. This conditioning exists in the genes, in a sense; it is a whole species-wide conditioning. Everywhere in the world, all human beings have this conditioning. It is there because we have bodies, individual bodies. Because we have individual bodies, we believe that the person is outlined by the body and that the person goes with the body. The person is bigger than that; it goes beyond the body and can be much bigger than the body. Personal Essence can be experienced as filling the whole room and beyond.

S: Is there a time that we have to release that feeling somehow to get into another place?

AHA: Yes. It is the feeling that you are a person all the time. This feeling needs to be experienced, thoroughly experienced, accepted, allowed, and understood to death. Nothing will happen through rejection or anger. No, but through love and understanding of the person, the hold is released.

If you look at it that way, you see that there are many dimensions. As long as you are operating from a certain dimension, that dimension seems to be real. If you go to a deeper dimension, the first dimension seems unreal. If you take all that into consideration and integrate it, then the knowledge of all dimensions of reality gets deeper, and deeper dimensions become accessible. Do not take one dimension to be the only thing there is.

If that knowledge is integrated, then the maturity that happens is what I call the objective person. You are a person in an objective way. Then maturity is the expression of the wisdom of the different dimensions. The problem is that when you take only one dimension to be reality, for instance, if you take the physical dimension and say this is the most real thing, that is only true from the perspective of the physical dimension. If you go to another dimension, then the physical dimension will not seem so real. You don't say that the physical dimension is not real, but you say that the physical dimension is real from its own perspective. If you go to the essential perspective, then the physical dimension is not that real. So which one is more real? You don't make a judgment. Who are you to say which is more real? You are just aware that this is how things appear depending on where you are operating from. You are free from opinions and from positions. Absence does not comment.

EIGHT

Bare Bottoms on Ice

I t is our lot as human beings to fall into a momentous error. This error is so momentous that we not only end up not knowing and not recognizing who or what we are, but we end up not seeing the world around us as it is. We are born with physical bodies, and we grow up little by little to become independent, functioning human beings, and through this long process mind develops. At some point we see ourselves not as the reality that we truly are, that we were born as, but we start seeing and believing the reality which is our conditioned mind.

Our awareness of our true reality and potential is so fragile, so delicate, so pure, that even in the moment we notice it, it disappears. The moment you begin knowing you are here, the moment consciousness dawns and self-reflection starts and knowing happens, you're gone, you're lost. What you are, what reality is—gone. Completely gone. You cannot say that it is forgotten, because it is not really a content of your mind. It just becomes unperceived and unperceivable.

A certain natural development of the mind, of our cognitive and functional capacities, is necessary to enable us to live and to function. However, this development tends to establish us in a perspective which is not an accurate reflection of reality. This perspective tends to exclude some aspects of reality and emphasize others, and the perspective that allows us to function in the world tends to become the only reality that we perceive. We take a very small part to be the whole. This loss is much more momentous than can be imagined from the perspective of conventional reality.

So your mind and personality develop, and you end up being the personality, the ego-self, living in the world of the mind. The personality is the creation of the mind. The representational mind is itself a mental creation. So you end up being a ghost, living in a ghost world. That ghost world is dark compared to reality—not only dark, but dank and old. It is merely a repeat of previous thoughts.

We forget reality so thoroughly that we live our lives completely seeking the values of our conditioned mind, one conditioned goal after another, whether we call it goodness, love, success, or happiness. All these are creations of our minds. They do not exist; they never existed. They exist only in our minds. They are mirages. We seek them all our lives, and when we find them, we find that there is nothing there. They do not quench our thirst, because they are not really there. When you believe you have found one of these elusive conditioned goals, all you can do is attempt to perpetuate it in your mind, to solidify and support it, which means to perpetuate the dank, old world that we believe exists.

We can never think of reality as it is. We can never imagine it; we will never know it. The moment you know it, you kill it. The moment you know it, what you end up with is an idea in your mind, an old, dank idea that you will perpetuate. You are preoccupied with the various creations of your mind. Of course, your mind is interacting with lots of other minds, and the creations of other minds in our society; mind begets mind. And you are trying to live according to the contents of this mind, your mind in conjunction with the collective one. But it is a dream life, a ghost life. It isn't really there.

You believe this mind so completely that you invest all your energy in it until after awhile it appears to be solid and real. We believe the content of our minds to be reality. We completely believe our thoughts, our ideas, our beliefs, and our dreams, and we make them solid by continuing to see them and believing them to be reality. If you consider the world you live in, the kind of things you pursue, the kinds of things you like, the kinds of things you want, they are nothing but repetitions of the past. There is nothing new in them. Even what you think is new is a combination of things from the past, and since it is a repetition of the past, it is not real, it is not alive, it is not what is there. It is a content of your mind. That content of mind is a prison. But the person in that prison is so mesmerized, the bars appear so powerful and strong, that you take the bars of the prison to be what you want, what you seek, and what you want to strengthen.

So you end up living a life in which you are continuously supporting and strengthening the bars of your prison. You will never know these bars as bars, and you will never know what is truly there, until you are capable of throwing off the whole thing—everything that you know, that you've ever known; everything that you want, that you like or dislike—until you're willing to throw away your mind completely.

To throw away your mind means to throw away what you think you are, what you think the world is, what you think is there, what is not there, what is good, what is not good—to throw it away, all of it. Otherwise, what you will perceive, what you will be experiencing, is nothing but parts of your mind, a continuation of the past coming from your own memory. When I say the world is old, or that what we see is old, I do not mean old in the sense that it has grown in time. I mean old in the sense that it has stopped growing. It is dead in its old form, the way you constructed it years and years ago. The mind perpetuates ghosts, dead things; there is no life in them. They're not light—they're heavy, dark, dank, old, and musty. They are stale.

In that dark, old, dank world, you suffer. The suffering is felt mostly because we still believe that old, dark, dead world to be reality, and we live as if it is reality, wanting one part of it, not wanting another part of it, putting part of it against another part of it. You are putting this dead body against another dead body, not liking this dead thing, liking the other dead thing. When you want something because you have experienced it in the past, what you are wanting is a corpse. It is already dead. If you think what will give you happiness and release is something you know, then what you are looking for is a corpse, a dead thing. You can never know in your mind what you truly want, what it is that will give you release. You can only work to let go, to slough off the universe that you know, the totality of your mind.

You cannot go about looking for reality by looking for something you know, because what you know is a memory of what you perceived in the past. A memory is already something dead. And since you are remembering it, even if you are remembering some experience of reality, the memory is not the reality. The reality cannot be remembered because it cannot be put into words, images, or concepts. The reality itself is the very explosion, the very incineration of those ideas and concepts, so how could you remember it?

You can only learn to forget. You can forget what you know, forget what you want, and continue forgetting until you have no mind whatsoever—until you become like a newborn baby. Only when your mind becomes as innocent as that of a newborn baby is it possible to see what is here, what you actually are, and what reality is. When you see it, you do not really know it; it is more like you smell it, you taste it, but you can never say what it is. The moment you are about to know it, it is old. So what we really know of the world we live in is a continuation of the past, which means it is in the mind. It is completely in the mind.

When we look at something, we do not see with fresh eyes, we see through the veil of the totality of our past. When you look at a table or at a person you know, at yourself, at your life, at your future, you do not see them with fresh eyes. You do not see anything with openness. You look at things with all the ideas and feelings and knowledge and memories of the past. So you are looking at reality through layers of dead matter. So you see darkly, as if through many heavy veils. You do not see reality at all; you see that deadness, and after a while you take that deadness to be reality. You believe it so completely that that deadness becomes even more solid and real. So what you wake up to every morning is deadness again.

Once you can see reality, when you wake up in the morning you won't see anything you've ever seen before. When you can truly see, perceive, and taste something, you will see that you have never actually seen it before. Then you know you are looking without your mind. But as long as you recognize something, in the sense of remembering it, in the sense of giving it names and labels, then it is not reality yet and you are not yet truly seeing. To penetrate to reality involves a process of unlearning, a shedding or a dropping-away of mind, getting rid of all that we know.

I am not saying that you need to get rid of all you know so that you cannot go do your shopping. We're talking about perceiving, penetrating to what is, to reality. We are inquiring into the nature of reality, we are not making assertions about what is needed for practical living. It is true that you need your mind, you need what you know to be able to tell which store to go to buy what you want. But that does not mean that you need that knowledge to look at reality. When you are looking at a pool of water and you see a reflection, you know the reflected object is not really there, it is just a reflection. You know that what is there is water. It is the same thing with the mind: When you look, you see the content of mind, but you know it is a reflection. You know the reality is there, not the reflection. We take the reflection in the water to be what is there most of the time, and we forget the water. After a while we take our minds to be what is there and we forget the true reality.

This is why I say we need to become like babies, in several ways. One way is that they have no idea what the hell it is all about. When you are a baby, you are completely unknowing. It is not that you stop thinking, or that you have forgotten; you haven't begun to know yet. You are completely untouched. You have to become virginal again before you see things as they are. Not only do you not think, you do not know: you do not know anything. If you know anything, what you know is old. So you have to be like a baby in the sense that you do not know. You do not know what you are, you do not know what is there, you do not know who's there, or if there is such a thing as who or what. The rules of grammar do not make sense. There is no such thing as subject or object or verb—none of these make sense yet. There is no "you" and "me" and "he" and "she" or "yesterday" or "tomorrow." There is nothing good and nothing bad and nothing in between. There is nothing that you want—without feeling that there is nothing that you want. The moment you feel you want something you already know, it is the past, the corpse again.

So when you experience desire, your desire is for nothing but the past. The moment you want something, what you want is something in your mind. The moment you have a dissatisfaction, it is a product of your mind. The moment you have a hope, you're hoping for something that you already know in your mind. You're hoping to get some kind of a corpse and live with it.

To be like a real baby means to not know, and to not know that you do not know. You do not want and you do not know that you do not want. You do not know what to do, and you do not know whether there is something to do or there isn't anything to do. The moment you know what to do, you are already using the past. You are already taking direction. You've already separated things: you are choosing one part of your mind over another when you say ,"I know what to do." Knowing reality, knowing what to do about it, wanting something from reality, desiring it, feeling dissatisfied by it—all these are indications of living in the old, dead world. All these things merely perpetuate the dead and make it more dead. If you really let it be, let yourself penetrate to reality, let your perception penetrate to reality, reality is absolute virginity. Reality is total innocence, so innocent that you do not know anything and you do not know whether it is important to know anything or not. You do not know what to do and you cannot say anything about that, good or bad.

This innocence, this virginity, this newness, is delicate, very, very delicate. The slightest idea arises about it and it is gone, erased. To be completely innocent means to perceive newly, freshly. Reality, right now, has nothing to do with what I remember from yesterday. To perceive reality, you need to be innocent in the sense that you do not know anything, you do not know what reality is, and you do not know whether there is such a thing. You do not know whether there is something there to look for or not look for—you are completely innocent. You haven't known anything yet. You are there, you are being there, but you aren't feeling that you are being there. You do not even know that. It is mysterious. It is not mysterious because it is obscure or hidden; it is mysterious because it is so totally new. It is totally new and you do not even know it when you see it; it is a direct tasting. If you know it, you make it old.

So if you continue to perceive reality without knowing it, what is that? It is mysterious. Because we believe our dead world, our dead mind, we are afraid of this innocence. This innocence scares the hell out of us, scares the hell out of the person in the mind, because when it appears, this innocence has an effect like the sun coming out from behind a cloud: immediate incineration of the dark world. More specifically, to be innocent like that, to understand or to be in that condition of absolute innocence, also means that we must be defenseless; we cannot be innocent and have defenses. We have to be absolutely without protection—even the protection of our ideas. We have to be completely vulnerable.

To penetrate, to look at reality directly, to have immediate contact, means nothing in between, no veils, no clouds. It means no protection whatsoever, no defenses whatsoever, no cushioning. It is like sitting with your bare ass on ice—it stings, and that's how you know it. You cannot try to be comfortable and cozy, and hope to penetrate, to look directly at the fresh reality. You need to throw away all your comfort, all your props, all your coziness, all ideas and feelings and objects that give you warmth and coziness and familiarity. Coziness and warmth are familiar; we like to be cozy because it perpetuates the familiar. Coziness perpetuates the familiar and the familiar is the old, dead world. To look directly at the innocent reality, you have to take off everything and be completely naked, and allow your skin to come in contact with ice. The ice will touch you so immediately that for a second you do not even know what hit you. It is just a coolness and a freshness. There is no way that you can manipulate it to be able to look at it directly, no way that you can do anything, to try to apply any method, any technique, to align with any path, any direction. If you take any direction, it is a direction in your mind, which is dead. If you take any action, it is according to the ideas of the past which, again, will perpetuate that past. To be in direct contact with reality is to be absolutely naked, with no props, because the moment you are using a prop you are using the past. If you use the past, that's what you will see—the past.

Innocence means no knowing, complete naiveté. It is to be completely naive, as if you've never known anything. It is not that your mind is quiet; your mind hasn't begun. There is consciousness, but prior to knowing. Your brain cells do not have information in them at all. Not only are you not thinking, thoughts are not in the brain cells. A cold wind has passed through your brain cells and cleansed them; they have become translucent. You need to be naive, completely helpless; but in a sense you are not helpless because you do not feel as if there is anything to do. You do not even know whether there is something to do or not do. You don't even know what that means, to do or not do. Not only do you not know what that means, you haven't even contemplated the question. You haven't arrived at the place where you can think there is such a thing as doing. Your mind still hasn't gotten to the future where there is something in the future that needs to be done. It is absolutely now, so completely now that not only are you in the present, so much now that there isn't even the feeling that it is the present. You are without even the slightest, the vaguest beginning of an idea of future, or of time.

We can see more clearly now the momentous error I talked about at the beginning; you fall into this error by taking the reflection to be the reality. The world you see is a reflection like a reflection in water. You want to solidify the reflection to make it reality, but then you are not seeing what reality is, without which there would be no reflection. Reality has nothing to do with what will happen and what will not happen, what has happened and what is going to happen; here, even the word "happen" has no meaning. It is possible to be aware of reality before having words of any sort, before the dawn of cognition, before the beginning of thinking and conceptualization. Everything else is a repetition of the past, of ideas, images, and feelings from the past.

You might remember that when you were a very young child things seemed to be new. Things were fresh, they had some kind of openness and excitement about them. As a child, every time you go somewhere that you have never seen before—oh, new!—it is exciting. So maybe there is a wisp of a memory of what freshness is, of what innocence is. You have to be naive, unknowing, completely helpless, utterly defenseless. You have to be absolutely vulnerable. There is a sense of innocence and virginity, with the sense that everything is new and nothing has yet happened. So who you are is a very original reality—it hasn't been broken.

You become a window through which the day breaks. It is like the first moment of knowing there is anything. It is the dawn of consciousness, the daybreak of consciousness. There is just the slightest glimmer of perception, before you know that there is perception, before the mind creeps in with a layer of deadness. This is original reality, our original face. Clearly, there is no way that we can penetrate or open our eyes to that totally fresh, totally virginal, absolutely innocent reality unless we let ourselves be completely defenseless and vulnerable, with no ideas or preconceptions, without even a movement of mind or consciousness.

Whatever we are, whatever we see, is spontaneous, the completely uncontrollable wild explosiveness of reality. Every second is a big bang, before anything got formulated yet. That's what it means not to look through the mind. That's what it means to be fresh; that's what it means to regain our original innocence.

Your original innocence is a continually exploding freshness, an ever-new innocence that never knows anything, that never lives in time, because there is no time that passes yet. Time is part of your mind. You have to think to be able to have time, and your innocent, original nature precedes that. That's why I call it explosions: It is just a continual exploding; you do not even have time to realize what happened. What is it even before you ask what it is? The explosion happens and your mind hasn't even collected itself to ask the question yet. This is our nature, all the time: that much freshness, that much newness.

Reality is not only our nature, it is what is there all of the time. It is what is there that makes us see the reflection. What we see is there, but it is a reflection. And if you see that it is a reflection, it will be penetrated by the freshness of the innocent reality, and the whole thing will look much lighter, much more brilliant, cool, and refreshing. Everything you see, you will see with the eyes of the newly born awareness. You've never known it. You look at the table and do not know it is a table; you have not yet known that there are such things as tables. You look at people, you do not even start to ask questions, you are just dumbfounded, struck with awe.

I'm saying all this to give a little hint of the kind of depth our inquiry can reach, to give a taste of what it is we are really doing. This gives us a sense of where we are going so that we do not delude ourselves with believing that we know where we are going, and we do not delude ourselves in pursuing things that we already know, that we already have planned and mapped. This is the true function of knowledge. True knowledge is not an accumulation. When true knowledge arises, it might answer your questions, but at the same time it will open up a thousand others. Understanding is a continual process of opening up more and more questions. When you have absolute knowledge, it is one huge, infinite question. You do not know something; you are just staring at reality.

Knowledge is not to close something, to end something, or to come to conclusions. The true function of the mind is not to come to conclusions, and true knowledge is not comprised of conclusions. True knowledge is the opening of questions. In the dead world, we want knowledge that will silence our questions. We want our questions to be answered for good; we want to have no more questions. The fact is that true knowledge just opens up more questions. It just shows you more and more that you do not know. When you have the next insight, you have just found out something, but at that same instant you realize how much more you do not know. And it should continue that way—seeing how much more you do not know, until finally, you realize you do not know anything. When you finally see that you know absolutely nothing, then maybe it is possible to be innocent.

True knowledge does not give us comfort. In fact, it frees us from the need for comfort. It does not make us more secure and cozy; it makes us more and more insecure. True knowledge causes us to lose our ground more and more because the ground we are standing on is fake. This Work is not an easy thing from the perspective of the dead world. It is very difficult and frightening. It is terrifying. It looks impossible because we look at it from the perspective of the mind; from that perspective it is not possible. But it is possible because the true reality is there. That's what makes it possible. It is not because our mind thinks it is possible or not. Its possibility is its reality. It is what is; that's why it is possible to perceive it.

From the perspective of the mind, how can we allow ourselves not to know? It seems impossible, terrifying. How can we be willing to not know, to leave ourselves alone, to not even assume that we exist or do not exist? How can we not assume that we are human beings or not human beings? How can we not assume that this is my body or not my body? How is it possible to not assume that there are people? To not assume there is good or bad? It is terrifying. All these assumptions that we make indicate that we believe that we know. These assumptions are the darkness; they are the veils. This is the staleness, the darkness that obscures the freshness. Reality is so fresh it cannot be approached through the mind. The mind will have to dissolve, thin away, because reality is like a sun of ice, a radiant sun of ice. It radiates coolness, freshness, crystalline clarity. There is no place for coziness, familiarity, comfort of the usual kind. No hiding, covering this corner or that corner, with dust here, a little old thing saved over there—none of that. Our Work reveals the perception and understanding that we are freshness, we are innocence. We are an unknowableness.

True inquiry results in an unveiling, a penetration, a dropping-away, and seeing through things. Everything that you can see, that you can know, fine; know it, see it, understand it, and let it go. It is not the end of the journey yet. The true journey, the journey that will arrive at the direct perception of what is, is a journey that will penetrate without going anywhere. It is like running in place. It is not that you are going anywhere; the running will just consume the darkness. There is nowhere to go. It is just the process of understanding that is important. When you are understanding, you are not going anywhere, you are just penetrating. There is no direction that you are going. That's what I mean when I say running in place.

S: You've mentioned how terrifying it is when a person begins to let go of their defenses and experiences a lot of fear and terror. It reminds me of Maslow's hierarchy of needs in *Toward a Psychology of Being,* in which he talks about how self-actualization happens after a person develops a strong personality, and that somewhere along the line you've had the experience of feeling love from someone. I'm wondering, using that example of someone that hasn't ever felt loved by a parent or someone close, it seems like it would be very difficult for that type of person to let go of wanting that. And so does not a certain amount of development have to have taken place, does not a person have to develop certain strengths before they can begin to let go of those things? Then it seems like there are two things going on at the same time: one is the development of the self and the other is a complete letting go of it at the same time, which can appear paradoxical.

AHA: It does appear paradoxical. It is true, there is a development, a person has to go through the different layers and levels of development, but that's the process of running in place. We believe we're going somewhere. We think we're getting love, or we're getting this or that. That's fine, that's as far as we could see. It is possible to work on yourself in developing the different parts, satisfying the various needs. These things need to be done, but if they are done within the context of a larger view, then we do not waste our time—it is more efficient. It is true that for someone who never felt love, it would be hard for them to let go of the need for love. It is much easier for a person to let go of the need for love when they have experienced it.

When a person knows love completely and embodies it, the next step is to let go of it. That is the natural process. It is the same thing when you realize that the various levels of realization are nothing but a process of actualizing the concepts of the mind. You actualize love; you actualize success; you actualize happiness; you actualize this and that. Every time you actualize something completely, when you really have it, that's when you realize that it is really an idea in your mind. You cannot tell before that; only when you have it completely can you see that it is an idea. The moment you know that it is an idea—pop—it is gone. Then the next one comes and you seek it and you actualize it, and when it is completely there—pop—it is gone. The need for love goes, but you continue to be a source of love, without even thinking about it.

The process of development is the same thing as the process of unveiling or shedding at the same time. The development and the actualization of a state is what is needed to go beyond it. They are not two separate things. You cannot go beyond self until you actualize self. For instance, when finally you know your true self, you are it, you realize in the same instant that you've gone beyond it. You do not need it any more because you've got it. That is the hierarchy of needs—when you do not have it, you need it. You must look for it, but the moment you get it, get it completely, you do not need it any longer. It is not exactly that you do not need it any longer; you realize that it is not important. You realize that it is an idea in your mind anyway. But you do not know that it is just an idea in your mind until you get it.

The process of the satisfaction of the needs, the totality of the hierarchy, is the same process as the process of unveiling or shedding. So it looks paradoxical but it is really not a paradox; it is the same thing. When I say you need to let go of your desires, how do you do that? You do not let go by saying you are going to let go; you let go by actualizing them, by understanding them completely. In my opinion, there is no other way than by completely experiencing them. Complete understanding and actualization opens the door for transcendence, for Being to take consciousness further. You cannot let go of self until you completely have self. You cannot let go of your own will until you completely have your will. You cannot let go of love until you have love. That is the natural process of penetrating, of unveiling. If we remember that this is a process, that the actualization is at the same time a loss, a going beyond, that will help us to not get so frustrated and suffer so much. If people believe that they're going to actualize love and have love, and actualize self in order to have self, and actualize pleasure to have pleasure, then they will be disappointed in the process. When you actualize it you lose it at the same time. That is the trick that reality plays on us. We want it, we have to have it, but when we completely get it, it is gone. It is gone to allow space for the next revelation of reality. If we do not know that that is what happens, we could get very disappointed and angry at God and reality. "What's this—it is unfair! I've worked all these years, finally I'm happy, and now it is gone?" But when we know that this is what happens, that it is the natural process of growth just as the fruit comes out of the flower, then you do not feel disappointed, angry, and hurt that you lost the flower.

You have to let go of the flower to have the fruit; you have to leave the flower of actualization before you can have the fruit. It is possible to understand this process of penetration of veils if you look at it from the perspective of reality. If you are looking at it from the other side, from the perspective of the world, it is not possible to see because things are only seen as gains and losses. It will look as if you are always either gaining something or losing something. From the perspective of no mind, you will see it is not a gain or loss, but a matter of unveiling, a matter of discovery, and that is the process that happens. The unveiling, the discovery and penetration, is a process of becoming more and more naked until your bare bottom hits ice. Then you get stung directly—not through the mind, through your bottom. That's when you really know. As long as you know it with your mind, it is an old idea. When you really sit on it with your bare bottom, it stings and burns you; then you know something. You know it without having to look back at it, without self-reflection—it just stings.

Losing your mind means losing direction, inner direction. It means being completely lost. You do not know what is happening and you do not know what is supposed to happen. You do not know what you need to do or how to go about it, and you accept it completely. If you have any direction, any preference of one thing over another in your experience, it is still the realm of the mind and there is no innocence. Innocence means innocence—you really do not know what it is. You are completely open. Nothing has happened yet.

S: So what if you notice that your preference is for comfortable dead things, and you find that you keep going along with that?

AHA: That is fine; however, if you just do that, that's it, no freshness for you. Things will get more and more dull, darker and darker. Cozier but more crowded. Less light and less freshness. I'm not saying no to comfort or that it is bad to choose comfort. I'm saying that to penetrate to reality, comfort has to be dropped. We do need comfort for the physical body. The comforts I'm talking about are mostly mental comforts—the ideas we tell ourselves, almost all that we know. That is the greatest comfort, the biggest blanket that we have.

S: I was thinking more in terms of not taking chances, or not taking risks. Choosing to be more comfortable . . .

AHA: That's part of it, to let go of comfort starts with things like taking risks, allowing yourself to be in the cold wind, getting lost. So in the beginning it feels like that. You might have to do it physically, to work on not having so much comfort, to minimize your need for comfort and pleasure. To minimize your need for love and company and entertainment. Everything will have to be minimized. It does not have to be completely eliminated, but all of these need to be balanced in some way—there needs to be no excess in these realms. To not have excess means there is a detachment about these things. You have them and you like them but you are not attached. You might have comfort, but you are not really attached, you do not feel that you are going to die if you do not have it. Compulsion and attachment indicate preferences in the mind; they mean you are living in the realm of the past. That's why some paths utilize the fact that a practical way to work on yourself or to seek reality is to find balance, to learn not to have excess in anything—neither for nor against anything.

It is fine to have pleasure, but you do not have to make it so important. It is okay to have food, but you do not have to eat too much. It is all right to exercise, but not to be obsessed with it. It is fine to have company, but not all the time. It is okay to be alone, but not always. With this balance, there is a freedom in the mind. You are not attached to one channel; you are not hooked. You can flow back and forth between many things; that indicates non-attachment. Non-attachment means you are starting to be free from the conceptualizations and divisions of the mind.

S: It seems that I had an experience of something like what you are talking about, and it seems that on one side is absolutely nothing, non-existence, and what comes up on the other side is just the total extreme manifestation of all the uncomfortable parts of the personality. There was a terror—this came as a result of getting something that I thought I wanted, and realizing that I didn't want it, and that it was there was just totally terrifying. It felt like I had a lot of conflict about that. My reaction was that I just wanted to fight my desires, and fight getting them, and totally push everything away. But at the same time, I felt like

I was subverting myself because it seemed that on the other side was what would be death or nothingness. I do not really have a question except what do you do about that?

AHA: If you have desires, the desire is going to come out. There is nothing you can do about it. You cannot just eliminate your desires. If you have needs, the needs are going to come out. Especially when you penetrate deeper into reality, all the veils and layers that were there are going to come back with force if they have not been worked through. They will come back as all kinds of issues and fears and difficulties. That is the normal thing. Every time a person has an experience of unveiling, after that they have some kind of difficulties and issues and difficult feelings and so on. That means there are some layers on top of that dimension of reality that haven't been cleared, haven't been understood and seen through. The natural process is that as you understand them, they thin away. At the same time your personality is going to do what it wants to do. You are not going to stop it. The best thing you can do is to let it do it—let the personality run its course. Let the mind think the way it thinks. Let them do their jobs—but know they are not you. It is just like seeing a child doing its thing; you'll stop the child at certain limits, but since it has to do its thing, let it. Let it think the way it thinks, feel what it wants to feel, try to get what it wants and desires, and so on. Just watch it happen; it is not you.

S: It seems like the terror is so real that I cannot disidentify.

AHA: Do not disidentify. Let it run its course. You cannot disidentify because you are not separate from it, in a sense. There is no you without the terror. If you do not take yourself to be that way, there will be no terror anyway because the terror is a result of that self-image. Feeling terror means you are losing your fake support. You are beginning to see that the reality you've been taking to be real is not real. The moment you see that it is not real, the ground starts shaking.

In one minute it might disappear, and you might feel that you are falling. Or you might realize that there is nothing there to fall. If you take yourself to be the personality, you will experience it as falling. If you realize it is not you, you become the emptiness itself. But all these events are in the realm of the mind.

S: My mind has a searching quality, it wants to know what that other would be like. And I know there is no way that it can conceive it.

AHA: So let it seek. Just watch your mind seeking, day and night. You are not going to be able to stop it, so let it happen. Ultimately, it is not a matter of seeking, it is ceasing the seeking. Seeking indicates going in a certain direction, towards something you want, something you can get. There isn't anything like that. Whatever you want is part of your mind anyway. If you seek nothingness, nothingness is part of your mind. Reality is not nothingness, but it is also not a thingness. It is prior to nothingness and thingness. But you will experience nothingness sometimes. That's part of the deeper layer of the mind, and it is fine to go through each layer.

Do not ever let yourself feel you've arrived. The moment you feel you've arrived, penetrate deeper, until there comes a time when you do not care whether you've arrived or not. Then you have arrived, but you do not think you have arrived. You just do not care. You haven't the slightest interest in whether you have arrived somewhere or not. That means the mind is finally quiet. As long as you care whether you have arrived or not, you haven't. You might have had some experience, but the experience is not complete unless there is complete innocence, the way a baby is innocent—without the vaguest idea about reality or enlightenment. What's that? I do not know—nothing, as far as I know. Innocence is before the whole thing developed: pre-mind.

S: It sounds like we might have a chance to get post-mortem.

AHA: An interesting idea: post-mortem. It is already "mortem," so after that it is post-mortem. Really, a person hasn't the vaguest idea how dead the world is. It looks real and alive with a lot of things in it. When you have that little glimpse of freshness you realize, "God, this old world stinks." The world is like an area of your room that hasn't seen sunlight in a million years. With innocence, there is sunlight, and suddenly everything is fresh and alive.

NINE

The Creative Now

Creativity is everything. Everything you see, whatever you think, wherever you go—there is creativity; something new is being created. There are three *dimensions*, three *levels* to the journey of this Work, and we can look at the question of creativity from these three levels. The first dimension is that you are in the world and are of it. In the second dimension, you are in the world but not of it. And in the third dimension you are part of the world but not of it.

The first level—you are in the world and of it—is the conventional perspective. Most people experience themselves in the world and of it. How is creativity seen from this perspective? Creativity is seen as someone doing something new: whenever there is a creation, an idea, or production such as a painting, sculpture, design, poem, music, that hasn't been done before. From this perspective, the more you are different from other people the more creative you are. Sometimes the weirder you are, the more creative.

Many artists fall into this category. But often in art, creativity is nothing but the expression of the unconscious. Something is inside you that you're not aware of, so you express it by a creative act. The creativity brings out the unconscious and expresses it through some artistic production. In that sense it is good, in that it allows your unconscious to come out and be seen and expressed.

The second dimension has to do with being in the world but not of it. Creativity here means expressing the part of you that is not of the world. This means the part of you that is really you, that is not part of the conventional world of human conditioning—the expression of this is the *process* of creativity.

If you are self-realized, you are in a constant process of creativity. The true self is always being lived out. You are being your true self and just living. And living yourself out is a creative act, it is creativity, because who you are is always new (always new, but not necessarily different). You might simply be sipping a cup of tea, but you are being creative, because it is like the first time you have done it, very new, fresh, very clean. So there is creativity in it. For instance, you make yourself an egg in the morning, and because you are what is really you, you are artistic and creative in the way you do it. You do it delicately, precisely, with great beauty. You are there, you're aware, and everything is perceived in a very delicate way. Being yourself means being present. Creativity is the living out of your presence. The more you are yourself, the more you're being naturally creative. Creativity then is the process of living, the process of understanding.

In the third dimension, when you are part of the world but not in it, creativity is all that you see, everything that you see. It is like a dream, in that when you dream, you are creating the dream. You are creating the whole world. Everything you see around you is in the process of creativity, is in the process of being, or coming into being: creation. That is actually the objective situation—everything that you see around you is being created every second. This world that you see—all these people, this house, the floor, the light, the plants—are not products of the past; they are being created right at this moment, constantly, always being generated. The world is not a product of the past, and you are not the product of your past. You think you are there because you were born and grew up. In a sense this is true; however, right at this moment where do you come from? You don't come from your mother's womb at this moment. So at this second where do you come from? To see the answer is to know and participate in what creativity is, what creation is. This is the greatest creativity, the greatest art.

Right at this second, you are appearing from out of nowhere, manifesting out of nothing, and you exist, you are here. Forget about the past, don't think of time. Think about right now. How do you come to be here? What makes you appear to yourself, what makes other people appear to you? There is a constant process of magical creation every second. And this process includes everything; everything you can see, everything you can experience is always the creativity.

If you see from this perspective, there is a sense of newness. Everything is newly created, not only what we call the essential dimension; even the physical dimension is appearing out of nowhere, right now. You will see this the moment you forget about the dimension of time. If you don't think in terms of time, but consider the situation simply in terms of now, it's an amazing thing. Where does all this come from? People and things and sky and wind and trees—what makes them be present?

It's a miracle. It's happening all the time, but usually we block this perception by thinking that this came from yesterday, this came from the day before, and so on. We are convinced that we came from the past. We convince ourselves, our minds, that's how we came. We were born, and before we were born we were a fetus, and we grew up and lived all this life story, and now we're here. We think that's where everything came from, and that's not true, because the past doesn't exist now. It actually isn't here; what is here is now. So what you see must be coming from something that is here right now. If you consider your source, where are you coming from right at *this very second*? Right now you are coming from somewhere, you're being created from somewhere; there's a source. Do you see that? What is that something that is the source of everything here? That is ultimate nature. It makes sense when you realize that the past is not here; how could it be producing this? The past is completely gone, is absolutely truly gone—logically, rationally, it's all gone. So it can't be producing what you see right now. Something right now must be producing what you see right now.

This present arising is creativity, and in this sense, everything is creativity. The whole thing is in a constant process of creation. Everything is being created every second, every split second. You are being created; so is everything. We have been lulled into the conventional belief that we come from the past—from our father and mother, from childhood experiences, and from our history. Our mind uses this story so that we don't look at the issue of our origin more directly. The mind is habituated to think that the past is where everything comes from. But that is illogical because the past actually doesn't exist. It's completely illogical and irrational to think that you came from the past, from your mother and father. Right at this moment, you are not coming from them; you're coming from something right here, right now, in the present. What is giving you existence can't be something that does not exist, like the past.

If you recognize what it is that you are coming from right at this second, you will recognize your true nature and the nature of everything. When you realize that, then you realize that you are not in the world. It's actually like the world is not you. If you recognize your true nature that is constantly creating what you see, then you realize that all that you see is in that true nature; that everything you see—the whole world, is in you, not the other way around. This process of creativity is seen then as obvious and normal—there is nothing special about it. It is happening all the time; it is happening to everyone and to everything at every second. You don't see it because you are accustomed to thinking that you are a body that continues in time.

The second level of creativity, when you are being your true self (being who you are in the world), is just the same as the third level but experienced in a limited way. You see yourself as an individual in the world, but the individual is real and this reality is what is being created. This reality comes from the ultimate reality, from the nature of everything.

S: Why then do we look for past psychological causes for present effects?

AHA: We don't necessarily have to. However, if you take yourself to be a separate individual with your own mind and will, it will be very difficult for you to be able to perceive the nowness and to operate from that perspective. It's much easier for a separate individual to look at things from the perspective of time, to use time to get out of time. When you see yourself as an individual just like everyone else (which means you have a history), it is easier for you to deal with that, because you can relate to it, although it's not completely true. You can relate to it, you can work through it, and you can go from one dimension to another. Ultimately, if you go through your own history, you realize that your personality—the way you think of yourself as an individual—is also oriented in terms of time and is a result of what happened to you in your childhood. There is psychological cause and there is phenomenological cause. To address the psychodynamic cause requires time.

The phenomenological cause is what's happening right now. Most spiritual teachings do not address the psychodynamic cause; they just try to operate from the perspective of nowness rather than the past. From what we see, that's not as effective. A lot of people, especially in the West, can't relate to that: it doesn't make any sense to them. Students need to explore a lot of things, and expose who and what they believe they are. Little by little, by working on your past, you are exposing what you take yourself to be. Ultimately, you realize that what you took yourself to be is what you see. That is the ultimate conditioning. It's not absolutely necessary to look at the past, and many people could actually work on themselves without having to look at the past. But using the past is a very useful, effective method, although ultimately it is part of the illusion. Any method is part of the illusion anyway—but some of them seem more useful than others. As long as you do anything, the moment you do anything, you are believing yourself to be an individual with a separate life and will. You're operating from a delusion, and we bring in the psychodynamics so that you will question why you have to regard yourself that way? By exploring your past, by uncovering your unconscious, you discover the beliefs, fears, and conflicts that make you feel you have to operate as a separate individual. As your need to assert your will and your separateness is eliminated, the need to operate as a separate, isolated center of action gets less and less. Then, it becomes more possible to let go of the boundaries of the separate self.

TEN

The Two Realities

We will talk today about a perspective that will help you to be nicer to yourselves in doing your work, and not to push yourselves too hard. The Work we are engaged in is not easy; in fact, it is very difficult, more difficult even than you know yet.

Two main motivations bring people into work like this. One motivation is the awareness of suffering in one's life and in the lives of other people, along with a desire to be free from suffering. This is the motivation of compassion. The other motivation is wanting to know the truth. You want to know, "What is really happening here? What is the truth about who I am? What is reality?" This is the motivation of love.

One motivation is to be free from something; the other is wanting to move towards the truth. Practically speaking, these motives cannot be completely differentiated, because to some extent they accomplish the same thing. It is best if a person has both motives. Wanting to be free from suffering is actually not only an attitude of compassion; it is also motivated by love. You want to be free from suffering because you love yourself, and this love takes the form of compassion towards yourself.

To be a student in this Work, you need these two motivations—love and compassion—from beginning to end. This is very tough work. To do the Work with love and compassion means to appreciate that this process is tough; it is an almost impossible task we are undertaking. So it is best not to give yourself a hard time about it. You need to learn to be patient, to not judge or criticize yourself when things do not happen the way you think they should. You need to not be too pessimistic, and also not too optimistic. If you are too pessimistic, you will create a lot of heaviness in your process. If you are too optimistic , you will create too many disappointments. Balance is the best way.

It is not useful to look at yourself from one day or one week to the next and make a judgment: "I haven't changed. I've been meditating for two months, and nothing has happened." This is not being kind to yourself. You are not taking the nature of the task into consideration. If you want to consider changes, or improvement, you need to not look from one week to the next, but consider a span of several years. Fundamental changes do not happen in a short time. Transitory or superficial changes can happen in a short time, but real changes, fundamental changes that will last forever, take years of work.

If you consider yourself as you were three years ago, for example, and see a difference compared to now, that might encourage you. In the shorter term there are always ups and downs; you might be in a difficulty or a hole for weeks or even months at a time. To consider the way changes happen over a long period of time is to be compassionate and loving towards yourself. You need to encourage yourself, instead of discouraging yourself. You need all the encouragement you can get. So patience is of the utmost importance. Enjoy your life as you go. You are not just working towards a goal and forgetting about what you are doing in your life now. This work is going to take a long time.

This Work is not something you can do as a seminar or a workshop; it is not something you can do for a year or so and that's it. To look at it that way is to not understand the nature of the task. The nature of the task is not to achieve a particular goal or a certain state. It is about growing up, becoming more of a human being, and actualizing your potential. It is not useful to think that you should be able to attend one weekend class and then be able to actualize your potential, and beat yourself up if that's not happening.

Today we will explore why this Work is so difficult. This understanding should help convince you about the need to be more compassionate and patient with yourselves. The difficulty comes from the fact that there appear to be two realities or two truths. It seems that reality is not just one thing, but two things. The first is appearance, or what we call conventional truth. The second is fundamental truth. The appearance of reality is what you perceive all the time, what you see and experience. Everything that appears to your senses is the conventional truth. That's why we call it appearance—it appears to your consciousness. The more basic reason it is called appearance is that in relation to the ultimate or fundamental truth—which is the reality itself—it is clear that conventional truth is only the way things appear. It is not really how things are. We need to understand as deeply as possible that the appearance of things—of everyone and everything, of the whole universe—is not reality.

Clearly, if you take the appearance of things to be reality, there will be suffering, ignorance, and delusion. Suppose, for instance, that an elephant is taking itself to be a mosquito. Imagine what kind of trouble the elephant would get into! This is just a hint of the kind of difficulty we face. It is actually much worse than that. Just imagine what the elephant will go through, in its delusion that it is a mosquito. It will eat the wrong food; it will feel hungry all the time. It will always be doing the wrong thing, and always feel dissatisfied. The elephant will want to find help. It will go to therapy, get body work, do psychoanalysis, thinking that it is an unhappy mosquito. And the elephant is actually being a mosquito in his own experience. So this mosquito wants to go to a therapist so that he can become a happy mosquito. This is clearly not going to work. Maybe he will go through all the therapies, then realize that maybe he should do spiritual work, and find out who he really is. He expects to contact the real mosquito essence, the inner mosquito. Then he will be realized!

This is what everyone believes: I will work on myself and find the real me, the good me, which will be a very nice, colorful, pretty, and happy mosquito. But the mosquito is in for a shock! If it goes to a real teacher, it will start to see some of the truth. Suddenly, the mosquito has this big trunk, these giant ears. No wonder it has been having trouble. It will see that there is a big problem here. It is not a matter of doing therapy, of changing a little something. It is not a matter of getting what you want. Maybe the mosquito has been looking for a mosquito soulmate, for example, and has been thinking he's unhappy because he hasn't found the right mate. He goes from one mosquito to another, always disappointed. Sometimes he blames himself, and sometimes he blames the other mosquito.

Now the situation is even more confusing because the other mosquito also happens to really be an elephant who believes it is a mosquito. Neither mosquito has any way of knowing what is really happening. They wonder what is happening, they read all the self-help books, and find out a great deal about mosquitoes. But they just cannot become successful, happy mosquitoes.

This gives us a hint about the problem. It tells us something about why we have so much suffering and dissatisfaction, and about why this Work is not easy. We think that when we do this Work, we will find something in us that is a good person, an efficient human being, a successful person—whatever it is we think we want—and we think that will release us. If that were the case, therapy would be more effective than it usually is, and this Work would be much easier.

As we have seen, the ultimate objective of the Work is not to solve the usual emotional problems that everyone has. If we made such problems the focus of the Work, that would be like trying to heal the mosquito by solving its mosquito problems, while the fundamental problem is not a mosquito problem, but an identity problem. The mosquito will continue having trouble until it realizes that it is an elephant.

A human being will continue to have emotional problems until the basis of these problems is eliminated. The basis of all emotional problems, of all mental suffering, is taking appearance to be the only, fundamental reality. Emotional problems and psychological issues need to be worked on, explored and understood, so that you have an opportunity to do the more fundamental work, the work of discovering what reality is. If you do not work through your emotional problems your mind will be filled with them. Your mind needs to be somewhat unburdened from these issues before you can even be interested in looking deeper.

It is important to remember that our emotional issues, our difficulties in life, are not our basic focus in the Work. You can come into a group and see that sometimes these things are addressed; they arise in your process, and you think that is what you need to be working on. You believe that you need to work on your problems with your wife, your husband, your job, your inner critic. That is only the initial part of the Work. Our Work is oriented towards a much deeper dimension, and we deal with the emotional level because we have to, because the content of the mind is what the person is aware of. In the Diamond Approach, we use these emotional problems as stepping stones towards the more fundamental reality. We work to understand and resolve them, in order to be free from them. But the point is not only to be free from them; it is to enable us to look deeper, into what is not apparent.

We use the appearance to go beyond it. This is what distinguishes the Diamond Approach from other approaches to spiritual work. Some methods try to go to reality directly. Some just try to push you to the other side. In our approach, we have a systematic teaching of understanding and a methodology which uses the appearance—its issues and conflicts and misunderstandings—as a stepping stone to go deeper towards the fundamental reality. This approach works well in this particular culture at this time.

But the problems and issues will never disappear if you stay on the level of issues. The fundamental problem is an issue of identity. The basis of these problems is that we have a certain way of looking at reality. We are the elephant taking itself to be a mosquito. That's the main problem. The mosquito might think it does not have enough food or the right mate, or it still hasn't found its work in life. But the mosquito will not know what its right work is until it realizes that it is an elephant. Only then might it stop trying to accomplish jobs that require flying!

I have not yet talked about the relationship of fundamental reality to appearance, and I will not say what fundamental reality is, since it is not easy to describe. Here, it is simply important to remember, and eventually to directly perceive, that what we see is not how things are. We take ourselves, and the world we live in, as our real selves, the real world. But this is not true; things are not actually like that. Our perception is not completely false; it is just that it is only part of the picture.

Taking the appearance of what you see in the mirror to be who you are would be the same as taking your clothes to be you. If you took your clothes to be you, then it would be very difficult to change clothes! Imagine how much trouble you would have if you took your clothes to be you. This might sound weird, but what most people believe about who they are, relative to what is real, is even weirder.

The suffering that we all experience comes ultimately from a mistaken point of view, a mistaken perception. Your suffering is not only because your mother didn't love you, or because your father punished you, or because you were abandoned in your childhood. It is something much more fundamental. Your suffering about the fact that your mother didn't love you enough or that your father abandoned you, persists only as long as you take reality to be the way you think it is. Suffering persists as long as you take yourself to be a person who was a child, who is now a man or a woman, with this occupation, and this name, and so on. Your past affects you and determines your joy or your pain only if you take yourself to be the person that you have always thought you are. If you believe that you are your parents' child, then obviously, everything that happened will affect your life and will continue affecting you until the end of your life. When you take yourself to be the child of your parents, you have already determined the character that you are; it cannot be changed.

You can be free from that character only if you eliminate that history, and you can eliminate that history only if you realize that it is not *your* history, only if you begin to perceive beyond the appearance of things. As long as you continue to be the child of your parents, your history will continue to determine your experience. You will continue to be the particular child of your parents, with a particular history and character, and with particular traits, patterns, and problems.

In our Work, we do many explorations to help you understand your childhood, and how your childhood has determined who you are. This helps the world of the personality—the appearance of things—to loosen up a little, so you are not so controlled by it. You are more relaxed. The less repression you have to hold on to, the easier it is for you to just be, to let go. When you can do what you are doing in a relaxed way, it is possible to just be. When you can just be, then it is possible to see the reality of things.

The world of appearance has a certain pattern or flavor for each of us. If you look at yourself over the span of your whole lifetime, you realize that although there have been changes, there are things that do not change. Certain patterns in the way you do things are always repeated; the same kinds of thoughts and preferences persist. You live in a certain groove, determined by your history, and that groove—your personal groove—does not change until its basis is gone. Its basis is the belief that appearance is reality. This belief is the ultimate basis of the existence of the personality and all its problems.

You actually walk around believing that you are what you think you are; the only time you do not do this is in deep sleep. This belief has many levels. On the psychological level, whenever you are talking with someone, you behave towards that person as if he or she is your mother. This transference is a distortion; it is not true. But even when you see through the transference, you are assuming something else that might not be true: You are assuming that the other person is a person. You believe you are a person, you believe this is a chair, and this is a rug. You do not question these things. You assume that this is the real truth, the basic truth. But it is only the appearance. A house appears to you as a house. You appear to yourself as a person—as a body with personal energies and feelings, talking to another person with feelings and a history. You appear to yourself as someone who sometimes experiences essence. That is part of the appearance of reality, and in general, we are thoroughly convinced of the fundamental truth of it.

But what if this appearance is not true? It is not only that the elephant believes it is a mosquito; the elephant thinks that it is a mosquito flying around in space. It does not even know where it is. Then the mosquito wakes up and realizes that it is on earth; but until it does, it thinks that it is flying around. So we see more about our situation: not only do we not see who we really are, we also do not see our actual environment.

You might think that you need to work on not being identified as a little child: You need to wake up and notice that you are an adult. That's part of the psychological work we do. A person feels and thinks like he is a little boy— being rejected, for instance—and he works on that and realizes that it is not true, that he's an adult now, and eventually the pattern falls away. Some of the falsehood has been seen through. But there is eventually a bigger, more fundamental falsehood. Even when you work through these things, you realize that there is still something you believe that might not be true. There are things you believe about yourself that are not dependent on your personal history. It is global conditioning; it is part of your human inheritance. This inheritance is that we believe that we are the persons we think we are. We are elephants who think we are mosquitoes. This fundamental delusion is the reason our personal history affects us in the way it does. It is the main support for the emotional personality.

There are many assumptions and beliefs that keep the personality in power over you. You assume that there is time, and that there is space. You assume that you are an entity separate from other entities. You assume that you were born. You assume that you are going to die. You assume that you will change. But these assumptions are only the appearance, and are true only from the perspective of the apparent reality. They are not true from the perspective of true reality.

Again, we are not saying that the way things appear is completely untrue. We are just taking the appearance to be the reality and thus, we are not paying attention to the much more fundamental, basic reality that is actually there.

The primary and ultimate objective of the Work is for us to see that there is another, deeper, reality, that the appearance is not all of it. This does not mean that you need to leave the world of appearance, the world of the senses; it means that you need to see that there is something else without which even the appearance cannot exist. The world we see could not exist without the true reality.

It is better not to try to imagine what the true reality is because it cannot be imagined. You can try to imagine it only by using what you know from appearance, and that just does not apply.

True reality is what appearance is not. So one way of knowing the true reality is to know that everything you see and experience, everything you think about, is not true. Just eliminate one thing after another: Not this, not that. Everything goes. It all goes: everything you have experienced, everything you can experience, everything you can think, anything that can enter your mind. When all that goes, that, then, is the true reality. You cannot think of it, you cannot conceptualize it.

True reality is how things are before you think about anything, before you conceptualize. Reality is not necessarily different from how things appear. For instance, you think that if you leave this house, the house will exist the way it is. But the fact is that the moment you stop thinking about this house, it does not exist in the way you think about it. The reality of this house is the reality of it when you are not thinking of it. What is that? When you think of the house, it will appear in the way that you think about it.

We are so involved in that process of thinking and conceptualization that we never stop to question it. You are sitting there in a chair, and you think that you are there, sitting in the chair. Many times that is not what I experience. I do not experience that there is a chair, and I do not experience someone sitting in a chair. The chair, me, and everything else are the same thing, and the whole thing does not have a name, and I cannot say what it is. I can look, and see that there is my body, there is the chair. But it is very clear to me that that's how things appear, not how things are.

When we believe so completely in what appears, we do not see that we are somewhat responsible for the way we see things. We think that everything is thrust upon us, everything is given. But reality is not like that. You are the one who is projecting the whole universe outside of you. You are saying, "This is the universe." When you begin to see this, it is possible to let go, to go beyond mind and the conceptual way of looking at things. Then it is possible to see the true reality of what is here. Only when that happens does the support for, the ground of, the world of the personality, begin to crumble. The personality begins to lose its supports and its substantiality. You realize that how you think of things is incomplete and erroneous. Things do not exist in the way you think of them, but in a different way.

Many people here experience essential states, states of being, but clearly do not believe them. You do not take essential reality to be the fundamental reality; you take your body to be more important, more real, and you think that essence comes and goes. Your essence is some kind of goody that comes once in a while. But from the perspective of fundamental reality, it is the other way around. Your body is something that comes and goes, and the essence is actually what is always there. So we see things in the opposite way from the truth.

The shift of perspective from conventional reality to fundamental reality is a huge, quantum jump from one universe to another. No wonder this Work is difficult! When we see just how difficult, we understand more why we need to be patient and compassionate with ourselves. We are not here simply to become free of the inner critic, or free from the emotional conditioning, nor simply to be successful. These things—the content of the world of appearance—are all part of life. Without appearance, there would be no life. But we want to move towards something more fundamental, which is to work with the ultimate basis of suffering, not the relative suffering that comes from our history.

We are beings who exist in two worlds at the same time, while believing that we exist in one world, the world we know. But the way we need to live is with one foot in each world all the time. With one foot in the appearance and the other in the reality, we will never forget one or the other. In the world of appearance there is suffering, strife, success and failure, pain and pleasure, life and death. The true reality of things is the absence of all these. There is no birth, no death, no you, no not-you, neither pleasure nor pain. There is complete freedom, complete release.

However, when we realize the reality and see that it is actually the ground without which the appearance could not exist, then the world of appearance transforms. It becomes more harmonious. It becomes the world of appearance rather than the world of suffering, success, and failure. It becomes a world which is an expression of love and compassion and goodness and value. The appearance then is an expression of the beauty of reality.

When this happens, the two worlds are connected, and the connection is a human being. Who we actually are is the bridge between the two worlds. We are both worlds and we are also the connection. But we cannot be this connection when we take one of the worlds to be reality, and forget about the other.

Reality is one. The reality of who we are is the reality of everyone else, of all beings, all that exists. There are no people in reality, there is just reality. The fundamental reality is a complete, unconditional state of oneness, which is a completely nonconceptual way of perceiving and being. If we do not believe anything, if we become completely separate from the mind which is the product of the past, if we become truly alone, then we see how reality is. Then you do not experience yourself as the person who was born to these particular parents. You experience yourself as never being born. You see yourself as undying. You see everything as undying. There is only one reality, and there is no one there to say it is one.

Appearance is an expression of this one reality. This reality expresses itself through appearances, which are nothing but the body of the one reality. Your body is not your body; it is part of the one body. This body that I usually think is mine does not belong to me, really. It is incorrect to say that this is my body. Everything that I see is my body, everything that is perceivable. The whole universe, everything that exists in it and does not exist in it, are all the body which is the appearance of the reality.

Most of the time you take yourself to be your body. This is a big mistake, thinking that this one body, this separate body, is my body; that's where the trouble starts. The biggest barrier to knowing who you are is taking your physical, separate body to be who you are. You think you end at your skin; what is inside your skin is yours, what is outside is not yours. If you just follow this logic, you end up in short order with all the wars and trouble in the whole world.

Physical reality is the appearance of things, and by its nature it appears as separate things with boundaries. There is a pole, there is a fireplace, there is a chair. We take that perception of physical reality and apply it at all levels of reality. But on the level of Being, these partitions do not exist. On the level of energy, they do not exist. My energy does not stop at my hand; it goes further. Why don't I take my energy to be me? My energy might be filling the whole room. Why don't I say that I am the whole room? Why do I say that I am something sitting here? You say, "I am sitting in this chair," because you take the body to be you. Why not take your energy to be you? Your energy could be smaller than your body or bigger than your body. When you are your essence, it is much more expanded yet. When you reach the depth of your essence, which is the fundamental reality, you see that no boundaries at all are there; the boundaries exist on the surface only.

When you apply the perception of physical separation to everything, then that body that is you has its own desires and needs and rights, issues about whether you are going to contact someone else or not, or whether you like someone else or not. It is all ridiculous; there actually is not anything like this separated appearance. It is only the way things appear.

When you see reality, you realize that your skin does not define or bound you. When your action is different from others, it is not in opposition to other people. Other people are seen as part of the whole reality, just as the arm and the leg are part of the whole reality of the body. The leg does not say to the arm, "Now do not take this, this is mine!" with the arm arguing, "No, it is mine. I'll punch you if you take my thing!" If your arms and legs had such conflicts, it would be very hard to walk around. It is the same way with the whole human race. A lot of trouble comes from each one saying, "This is mine, this is yours."

All the philosophies, all the ideological, political, and economic systems designed to do something about this trouble, are based on the same assumption that causes the trouble, the assumption that we are bounded by our skin. So these philosophies cannot resolve human problems. There might be improvements or transitory changes, but only realizing and resolving the fundamental problem can lead to any fundamental change. This is why people who know the fundamental reality generally do not care about ideology and political systems.

The conventional world view is a big mistake, and it is a mistake that creates trouble. We take things to be completely different from what they are, and this happens in a way that creates opposition, separateness, conflict, and war. The moment "me" and "you" are created, conflict begins, even if there is love there as well. The only way that conflict will cease is to see that "me" and "you" are part of the appearance of the total reality. We are fundamentally not separate; we are the same thing. We are so deeply the same thing that our oneness is much more of a unity than my arm and my leg. The arms and legs have different structures, different appearances. But when we know reality, we know that you and I are completely the same thing: We are made out of the same substance, we are the same consciousness exactly. No difference at all! The difference is only what appears on the surface, and to see this is to see that the difference is good; it is beautiful to see that appearance is a multi-faceted expression of reality, of love and joy.

Now, things become more colorful. The different appearances—manifestations, differentiations—are all beautiful. Ultimate reality does not have a color. You cannot say it is beautiful, and you cannot say it is ugly. You cannot say anything about it because there is no differentiation. But appearance is full of colors and all kinds of amazing things. These different appearances are what we see; they are the content of life. When you see the appearances from the perspective of fundamental reality, you know that you were never born, that the appearance merely changed—the ocean has another wave of a different color. You know then that each person will never die, not because we as individual entities are eternal or immortal, but because we are not something that can die.

Time has nothing to do with who you are. Time has to do with appearances, which come and go. Your body, your senses, the appearances of things, are like your clothes; they come and go. You could say that your shirt was born when you first put it on, and it died when you took it off. You put it back on—a rebirth! When you know the fundamental reality, you see that you can put things on and take them off, but there has never been a death, a birth, a rebirth. All that is only appearance.

I am not saying that the appearance is not there, or is completely nonexistent. It is just not actually happening, from the perspective of fundamental reality. Things certainly do happen from the perspective of appearance. You are born, you see a world, you have parents, you grow up, you live, you die. But from the perspective of how things actually are, these things are not actually happening.

To live in the world and to know yourself, you have to take both worlds into consideration: reality and the appearance of reality. When you believe only the apparent world, you create all kinds of ideas about how things should happen. Sickness comes and you push it away; health comes and you hold on to it. Misery comes, you try to push it away; happiness comes and you try to hold on to it, and you increase your suffering even more.

When you realize how things actually are, you know that things simply change; appearance changes, but it is not actually death, rebirth, sickness, health. Never has it been different, never since the dawn of consciousness has anything actually changed. We see something coming out of something, we call it birth. We see something that used to move, stops moving, we call it death. We have created these words to describe certain changes of appearance.

But if you forget about these words, if you forget everything you have learned, if you see appearance without all these thoughts, if you are mentally alone, you simply see things arising and disappearing. You do not need to call them anything. You do not need to react. You do not need to call yourself by a name. These names are conventions; this is why that reality is called conventional reality. That reality is created through language. But who we are exists without language, prior to language.

The reality we see is usually the reality of names, of words. Death is a word, life is a word. Birth, body, happiness, suffering—all words. Without the words, all this is neither life nor death; it is simply what is, and that's all you can say about it. The ultimate reality is how things are, not how we think they are. It is not easy to see this, because your life is so pervaded by words and concepts, which you take to be reality. The reality we see, the creation, is nothing but words. The Bible says, "In the beginning was the Word." God is the ultimate reality, and the beginning of creation is a word, and the world of appearance is with God, and it is not separate from the reality.

Human reality is completely linked to language. Our world exists through the language we use. The less we are caught by this language, the less we are attached to our beliefs about how things are, the more we see the whole of reality as one solid, immense clarity, pervading everything through and through. We see that words appear and create appearance, a very thin layer over reality. When we take that layer to be the whole thing or the real thing, there is trouble. That trouble will not disappear as long as we take our skin to be the whole thing.

You can see that the Work we do is a very deep, fundamental process. We are dealing with the basic, rock-bottom nature of reality. It is such a huge flip from the normal way we see things to seeing this reality; it is not easy. It is not easy to be free from one's concepts, from one's mind. We cannot even conceive of ourselves apart from them. We are in fact creating who we are with concepts at every moment. We do not know we're doing it; it is unconscious. In our Work, we gradually become free from this way of looking at reality. We work on the emotional patterns that make us hold on to this reality, on the reactions based on our concepts of ourselves and the world. We work on these issues to relax them. These issues will not be eliminated by working on them, but they will become lighter, and we will have more space and more capacity to look deeply. And when we have a glimpse of actual reality, we understand the two truths. Then it is possible to live the life of appearance in harmony, as a life of beauty that is the expression of love.

Perhaps this perspective will help us not to get stuck in emotional issues, not to take them too seriously, but to understand them as stepping stones to something deeper. You are not looking at your issues with your boyfriend or your girlfriend so that you will have a good relationship. That is worth doing, but it is not the fundamental reason we do this Work. Your relationships are not fundamentally important; your career is not fundamentally important; these are important only from the perspective of appearance. The Work uses this appearance to help you move towards what is real.

In this sense, we are trying to leave this world. We are trying to go to another world. But the other world is not somewhere else, it is right here. The reality is not separate from the appearances we see. If we have that perspective, perhaps we can take things more lightly. We will understand our issues and difficulties as part of the path, without attributing ultimate significance to them.

Issues and difficulties are not the only stepping stones towards reality. You need also your interest, your curiosity, your appreciation of, and love for, the truth. Your essential experience will help counteract your emotional identifications. However, such experience is not an end in itself. It is not something you get. It is a tool you use to keep seeing deeper truth. Essence is the direct expression of the fundamental truth; it is what is between appearance and fundamental reality. Essence crosses the boundary between the two truths, the two worlds.

The qualities of Essence are the first words. The aspects are the first concepts; they are universal concepts, the archetypal states of being. They are more connected to fundamental reality than the world of appearance, but they are part of the world of appearance; Essence appears to us. Or, more accurately, experiences of Essence are glimpses of fundamental reality, viewed from the world of appearance.

The work on the personality and the realization of essential aspects is the method of the Diamond Approach, whose purpose is to take us to the fundamental reality. The life of Essence becomes the beauty of that reality, as it appears in and through human beings. It is the fulfillment of the human life.

ELEVEN

The Courageous Heart

Today I will talk about a question that is difficult to talk about, something most people look for without knowing exactly what it is they are seeking. It is something normal, nothing out of the ordinary for human beings. The question is: What is a real relationship? What is a real relationship between one human being and another? The exact answer is very simple and straightforward: The real relationship you have between you and another human being is exactly the relationship you have between you and that human being. The real relationship is the relationship that is actually there. Now, saying that the real relationship is the relationship that is really there is not necessarily the same thing as saying it is the relationship that you perceive to be there. That is the crux of the problem. The relationship that is actually there is very rarely perceived as it is. In fact, most people tend to do everything possible not to perceive or acknowledge the real relationship. We always try to make it something that fits with our mind or our ideas.

The difficulty is that we do not see the relationship that is actually there, and we do not even experience ourselves to be engaged in the relationship that we are actually engaged in. We are engaged in many kinds of other relationships that are not actually there, which exist only in our minds. We could call these mental relationships. So we are distinguishing a real relationship from the relationship that a human being usually perceives.

So far, it is simple but not easy to understand or to actualize. Rarely will you acknowledge the relationship that really exists. What you acknowledge is usually something in your mind, a mental relationship and the feelings that go along with that concept of the relationship. For some time, part of our work will focus on clarifying our relationships, all relationships. For instance, the relationship you have with me is the relationship that actually exists. In your relationships with me, with each other, with everyone in your life, you need to see what is happening, what the relationships are. If we do not clarify, perceive, and live according to the true relationship that is actually happening, there will be no contact. There will be no real relating. There will be only mental interaction, one image interacting with another image. There will not be a real human being relating to another human being; there will be your past interacting with someone else's past. It is obvious how complicated that can be. If your personal history is interacting with someone else's personal history, but you are not interacting with the other person, you are not really relating.

Now, saying that the real relationship is the relationship that is actually present does not say what it is yet, because we do not perceive the relationship that is really there. We can only perceive what our mind tells us is there. When I say the real relationship, I do not necessarily mean a purely positive relationship, although some people might assume that. The purely positive relationship is one of mental relationships because the true relationship is rarely purely positive. If you really experience and examine any relationship you have with any human being, you will notice that it is never purely positive. In fact, that is where the problem starts: We want it to be purely positive, whatever that means to us. The drive towards a purely positive relationship is the main reason our relationships are not real; this is why we do not perceive the true or real relationship that is actually there.

The mind tends to see relationships in black and white—a relationship is either purely good or purely bad. If you look, any moment, at what you feel your relationship to another human being is, you will usually realize that it is either purely good or purely bad. You do not allow yourself to have both at the same time. On the one hand, you either feel that you like the person, it is wonderful, it is great, they love you and you love them, no problem. If there is any problem, you do not want to see it or consider it. You do not want to take it into consideration in the relationship. On the other hand, the moment you start to become aware of problems, you want to make the whole relationship purely bad. Then the person is bad, you are bad, you are angry and hurt, and the person is this or that.

We look at most relationships in these absolute terms: Either the other person is good or the other person is bad. When we believe that the other person is good, we believe we have a good relationship, a purely positive relationship, with the hope that it will continue to become more and more positive. This negative hope will make you want to exclude, not allow, not recognize, not acknowledge the negative aspects of it. When you see the other person as bad, you tend to see them as purely bad, and you react in a way that makes the whole relationship frustrating, hostile, or bad. That is the tendency of the mind.

This is a simplification, but it highlights a primary tendency in human relationships. There is the tendency to want to make relationships either all good or all bad, although we know that a relationship is never one or the other; it is always a mixture. In our minds, we do not think of it as a mixture; we think of it as either good or bad, as black or white. The moment we begin to perceive the good, we want it to be all good. The moment we perceive the bad, we feel disappointed and hurt, and the tendency is to make it all bad, to react in a negative way. In a real relationship, what actually happens, the interaction that actually occurs, is rarely purely one way or the other. Interactions are mixtures of various proportions. Our mind does not let us acknowledge and live according to the actual reality of what transpires in the relationship, but is always thinking in terms of absolutes. When your friend is bad, you respond in a completely reactive way.

This might seem an extreme way of viewing normal relationships—we are not usually absolute in our responses to pleasant or unpleasant interactions. But it is true that we tend to make things one way or the other. This tendency is much more pervasive, ubiquitous, and powerful than we are usually conscious of. While the tendency might be mostly unconscious, it is a major force in determining our responses. If a person frustrates you or rejects you, you react by being hurt and angry, even hateful. All negative. If you believe that the other person loves you, that they are good and are satisfying you, you want to respond with positive, wonderful feelings, and you do not want to have any negative feelings. If you have negative feelings in those situations, you feel they are disturbing and interfering, that it shouldn't be that way. So that is the situation. The tendency of the human mind is to look at relationships in terms of splitting the all-good from the all-bad, while in reality, it is rarely ever all good or all bad. It is always a mixture.

When you see a relationship in absolute terms of all good or all bad, it cannot be a real relationship. It is a mental relationship—something in your mind. It is not what is actually happening. A true relationship is not like that. When you look at and perceive things from that absolute perspective, obviously you are not involved in the real relationship. You are reacting and being involved in a mental relationship that is not actually there. Don't you notice, for instance, if you are having a good time with your friend or your spouse and something happens that disappoints you, you tend to get disappointed or hurt or angry as if all of the good is gone? It is as if whatever happened destroyed the whole thing. Of course, in time, after a few minutes, hours, or a few days, you might become more realistic. You might say, "Oh, it wasn't true," but in the moment you react, as if the relationship is all bad.

As long as we are engaged in a relationship in that way, having to be absolute in it, we are not able to engage in true and real relationships. We cannot relate to another human being in a real way. Our relationships remain mental, based on past relationships. When you split your relationship and see it as all wonderful or as all bad, it is not only that you are taking the good part and seeing it by itself or the bad part and seeing it by itself, but the bad part is not necessarily what is even happening. It might be some part of what is happening, but most of it is the result of all the bad relationships you have had before. All your negative history comes into it. You start seeing and experiencing and feeling things, reacting to things, projecting things, that are mostly not there. When you see it as all wonderful, positive, purely good, that is also not what is there: You are feeling, projecting, responding with reactions based on past experiences.

Rather than being aware of what is really there, you are seeing your projections and reacting to those projections. This means that you are bringing a part of your mind to bear upon the present situation. You are engaged in, and activating, a certain one-sided relationship that you have in your mind all the time anyway. You might notice, for instance, that the moment your relationship with someone becomes good, something curious occurs. It feels similar to all positive relationships you have had in your life: There are the same feelings, the same way of seeing the other person. There is very little variation in how you see yourself, how you see the other person, the kinds of feelings that arise, things you hope for, your plans and dreams. They are always the same. And when it becomes negative, isn't it the same kind of negative feeling that you have always had before in relationships? If you see the person as rejecting you, it is the same way you always feel whenever a relationship gets bad. It is rarely different. Some people are perpetually engaged in negative relationships where they feel rejected. Some people are always the rejecting and angry one. Some people engage in negative relationships where they are continually frustrated. They want someone, and that person is not giving them what they want. It is always the same flavor; there is little variation. Now, that same flavor is a little suspicious, to say the least. Obviously it cannot always be what is happening. That same old flavor must be something you bring with you from the past.

If we delineate these mental relationships, we can distinguish three kinds that our mind is engaged in all or most of the time. There is the positive one, which is usually an idealized relationship. The other person is an idealized other—all wonderful, powerful, good, perfect, whatever the idealization is. You feel when you are with that person, everything will be wonderful, and you will be taken care of, loving, melted, and so on. That is what we call the all-good, idealized relationship. The moment you know you are feeling that way in a relationship, you can take it for granted that it is a mental one, not a real one. Also, when people are in that kind of relationship, they feel that they are completely in love. But you can be sure that your feeling of being in love is in your mind and not real, because it is not taking into consideration the real relationship.

The second kind of mental relationship is where the other person is what we call the frustrating other. The other is the yummy one that you always want but you cannot have. That's why we call the other the frustrating object—exciting, wonderful, but unavailable. I think many people are aware of that relationship. They spend much of their life wanting somebody they cannot have, either in reality or in their dreams. But there is a hope and belief that one of these days you are going to get that thing or that person. You do not understand that that is only the relationship your mind is actualizing all of the time, that you are invested in that kind of relationship. You do not want the satisfaction to become actuality. If you make it become an actuality, you will lose that mental relationship. Then all kinds of new things will happen. So, if you are one who is always involved in the frustrating relationship, you will find that it is important that that relationship continues to be frustrating even though you are always complaining about it. You do not want your hope to become an actuality. If it became an actuality, you would have to become real. So it stays like that: pie in the sky. You pine for something year after year, you are always excited about it, but you cannot have it. That is the frustrating kind of relationship.

The third kind of mental relationship is the hostile relationship, where you feel unwanted, rejected, or hated; or vice versa, where you are the one who is not wanting, rejecting, hateful, and hostile. Although you might think you do not like it or want it, if you keep being engaged in that relationship, you will notice that in reality your mind is attached to that relationship. You are engaged with it either with the other person or in your mind. Your mind needs the relationship for its own equilibrium. That is why some people feel rejected in most of their relationships with other people; whatever happens, they take it as rejection. If someone turns his head away, they feel rejected. If someone says something, they feel rejected. If someone does not say something, they feel rejected. It would be very difficult to convince them that the rejection is not true. It is difficult because they do not want it to not be true. It is important for them for it to be true. If it becomes clear that the rejection is not true, then the person's mind will lose its equilibrium.

These are the basic mental relationships, and they are dependent on the basic perception of the other. Depending on what kind of object the other is, you become the corresponding person relating to that object. Most human relationships that are conflictual, that cause suffering, fall into one of these three categories of mental relationships. Also, if you investigate this issue of your relationships, you realize that those mental relationships are the source and the site of most of your emotional suffering. Most human suffering comes as a result of these mental relationships. There are other sources of suffering, but the primary source of emotional suffering is engaging in those mental relationships.

The real relationship usually contains elements of all three kinds of mental relationships. With any human being there is satisfaction, fulfillment, and love, there is some negativity, anger, and hatred, and there is frustration. The real relationship is the relationship where these three are acknowledged, where the person realizes, "Yes, of course, I love this person, but I know he is angry at me," or "I do not like this or that, but I still like her anyway." Even when we are feeling rejected or hated or hateful, it does not make us forget that we love each other. But in the moment that the other person hates us, our normal tendency is to forget that he or she loves us. The moment that we are hurt, we forget that we love the other person. It is difficult to keep the whole thing together. The mind does not allow us to keep the totality of the relationship in perspective. The mind is always trying to protect itself by splitting relationships into purely good or purely bad components. It is very difficult for the mind to allow the perception of the complete, real relationship that exists.

Because we usually engage in mental relationships instead of real relationships, we are not present and we are not in contact. Contact requires real relationship. Contact means contact with what is actually there, with the actual relationship. The moment you split it, make it all positive or all frustrating or all hostile, you are not in contact. You are in your mind then. You are operating through your thoughts, and emotional reactions which are reacting to your thoughts. You think you are reacting to the other person. No, you are reacting to your thoughts. I am not talking only about couples or love relationships, but any relationships you have with any other human being, or with any other object. It could be a work relationship, a business relationship, a friendship, a love relationship, or a marriage. We see that one major reason we are not present, why we are not in contact with ourselves or with the other, with reality, is that we are engaged in these mental relationships. And we are very attached to these mental relationships because we do not want to see the totality of the situation. We do not want to be in contact with the real relationship. That would be devastating for a part of our mind that is based on that splitting.

It would be good for everyone here to spend some time observing your relationships. How do you experience your relationships? We have to perceive our tendency to divide into absolutes to be able to work with it. It is not enough to just hear about it. You have to see your minute-to-minute interactions with people. You have to see how at each minute, interaction is either all positive or all negative and rarely a mixture. But when we step back and look at our interactions, we realize that they are usually a mixture. It is extremely rare that when you are with another human being, the relationship itself is all purely wonderful or purely negative. You might *feel* all-wonderful, but the relationship is always mixed. The person may not be doing exactly what you want them to do, or whatever. So, although you might feel all-wonderful, the relationship itself is not all-wonderful. And of course, engaging in the mental relationships involves all the judging and blaming of the other or oneself, or the idealization of the other, or grandiosity about oneself. This splitting is a protective mechanism that the ego employs to continue existing. The ego cannot exist if there is true relationship. The ego's continued survival depends on this separation of relationship into black and white.

What is the resolution of this situation? The resolution is to be aware, and to allow, accept, and acknowledge the real relationship that is actually happening, instead of trying to make it something different from what it is. But to be able to do that you need to manifest what I call the courageous heart. The real relationship is the relationship of the courageous heart. If you look at the reason you split your relationships, the reason you do not see them as they are, you will see it is because you are a coward in your heart. You are scared. Why do I say that? Because when you are splitting relationships, making them black or white, good or bad, what you are doing is separating love from hatred. You are separating what you see as the good feelings in your heart from what you call the negative feelings. You either feel love, by itself, or you feel a negative feeling by itself. You do not let them co-exist. You do that mainly to protect your love. You are afraid of the negative feelings. If the other person is good, the relationship is good, you are loving, and you allow your heart to be there. The moment something negative comes in, it brings in the negative mental relationship. "It is fine to feel all angry and frustrated, it is fine to feel all loving, but I do not know if I can do both. What will happen to my love? It will be contaminated. It will be destroyed by the hatred, by the negativity."

Now a courageous heart is a heart willing to love regardless of the negativity. The courageous heart is the heart that will love in spite of the badness that is there. The courageous heart is not just the heart that only loves and nothing else; it is the heart that loves regardless of what happens. The courageous heart is the heart of unconditional love: whether the other is good or bad, you continue loving them. Usually, with your friend or your spouse it is easy for you to be loving if the other is loving. But if the other is frustrating or mad, angry or rejecting, right away you shift, and close your love and bring in another reaction. You are hurt, you are angry, hateful, or frustrated, and if you are angry, frustrated, or hurt, you do not let yourself feel your love, at least not at the time of your initial reaction. What splitting does, more than anything else, is close the heart. Whether you are all bad or all good, whether you are all loving or all hateful, what you are doing more than anything else is covering up your courageous heart. You are not allowing yourself to have your courageous heart, to be your courageous heart. You are not allowing your love to be unconditional. Your love becomes conditional. You respond lovingly only under certain conditions, or with certain manifestations of the other.

So true relationship, real relationship is based ultimately on love, and does not exclude anything else. The courageous heart does not exclude negativity. If your heart is loving, you do not have to exclude the negative. You do not have to forget what you know about the situation, about yourself, about the other person. If you have to make the situation unreal, then your love is not real yet. It is conditioned by the beliefs in your mind. Your heart is not spontaneous yet, not real, not courageous yet.

For instance, if you notice you like or love someone and have a relationship with this person, and then when something happens, you feel hurt, attacked, scared, or jealous, you will realize that your tendency is to not want to love at that time. It is not only that you do not want to love; in your mind you say that you shouldn't love that person. You feel that if you love that person even though they are doing that, you are going to lose. You feel that you are going to lose your pride. What is your pride? It is your ego. So if the other person responds or manifests anything that you take to be unacceptable, negative, or bad, most of the time your tendency is to not want to be in contact. So you react—you feel hurt, betrayed, angry, hateful, or you want to get even.

But why not continue loving? Yes, you might even feel angry, you might feel frustrated in the situation, but why does that have to close off the love? Why not continue loving, continue being open, and let that love, that openness, contain whatever else is there? Why not let it be bigger and stronger than any negativity that is there—whether the negativity is yours or the other person's? The moment we see the other person as the bad object, the bad person, right away we want to react by closing our heart. That's it. A desire for revenge comes. Not only does vengefulness or hatred come; when it comes, it is the only thing we want to feel. We do not want to remember the love.

When there is frustration, it is natural that there will be hatred and anger. That is not bad. But it is destructive to allow that anger or hatred to eliminate everything else. The courageous heart does not allow that. The courageous heart wins all the time, by continuing to love regardless of what is happening. You do not love the other because he is good; you do not stop loving him because he is bad. You love because it is your nature to love. Your nature, part of being a human being, is to have a heart; and the heart loves and appreciates and understands and forgives and accepts. Part of that acceptance and understanding is to have room, space, for the other parts of the relationship. You realize that yes, there is frustration, there is difficulty sometimes, sometimes the other person does not like me or I do not like him. But that does not eliminate the courageous heart. It all becomes contained within and absorbed by it. If we allow that to happen, then the relationship is real. We see it as it is. We are not making it something that it is not. We are not looking at it in a purified, artificial way. We are being total, all of ourselves.

If you take just one reaction and be that, and that's it, you are not a complete human being. You are not seeing the other person as a complete human being. You are seeing a mental relationship that has been extracted from other situations. The fact that there is always love for the other person regardless of what else you feel comes from the fact that it is your nature to love. Your heart is always there. You might not be aware of it, but it is there. Although you might not hear the beating of your heart, it does not mean that your heart is not there. Having a heart is part of being a human being. You cannot lose it. Never. If you lose your heart you cannot live any more. It is just like saying to someone, "Well, I do not love this person and that's it." What does that mean? Does that mean that you lost your heart? There is no such thing. You can never purely hate a human being without love being there; it is not possible. You might not be aware of the love, you might be blocking it, but it is there.

It is our nature to love. We are the source of love. We cannot help but have love somewhere; love always underlies any relationship. If there is no love, there is ultimately no relationship. The fact that there is love is absolute—whether you feel the love or not, it is there. When we take one side of the relationship and focus our attention on it and fail to see the other part we are not allowing love. Sometimes there is love and there is no hatred and no negativity, but there is never hatred with no love, because hatred is a reaction, while love is being; it is not a reaction. Love is the flow of your nature. Hatred is the reaction to that flow being blocked, that's all. Whenever there is hatred, whenever there is negativity, there is love somewhere. If there was no love, there would be no hatred.

A person who does not have a heart cannot hate, cannot be angry, cannot be hurt, cannot be jealous. Without love there is no such thing as jealousy, hurt, fear, hatred, or anger. All of these things are reactions to the absence of love, to the blockage of it, to the non-perceiving of it. To be aware of the real relationship means that there is always awareness of love. This never goes, in any relationship. There is always the lovingness, and love has understanding in it. Love has forgiveness and acceptance in it. Love has compassion, appreciation, pleasure, happiness, strength, and gratitude. All these are elements of love, and it is there all the time; it is part of our nature. The courageous heart is the heart that is always present, regardless of what happens. If your heart is present only if good things happen, your heart is not yet free, not actualized. You are still a coward, still afraid. You have a heart, but not yet a courageous heart. So to have a true relationship, a real relationship, means to manifest the courageous heart.

To manifest the courageous heart means to continue loving regardless of the situation. It does not mean seeing or not seeing the situation. The moment you make the situation all wonderful, all positive, with no negativity, no difficulty, no frustration, the courageous heart is no longer present. It is an idealized relationship. It is a mental, unreal relationship. There is ultimately no such thing as an all-good relationship. As long as we are embodied in a physical body, there will be difficulty and frustration. If you hope that one day you are going to have a relationship that is all wonderful, all satisfying, never frustrating, you are dreaming. There is no such thing here.

And because there is heart and there is love, we can live, we can take in that difficulty, that frustration. We can tolerate it and continue loving and continue being happy. Love is not here just for enjoyment, for happiness. Love is also here to help you tolerate and accept and understand the difficulties. Love is here to help you continue being happy regardless of the difficulty. Love does not reject difficulty. It is not in the nature of love to reject hatred. Love loves. It does not stop loving when there is hatred or frustration or pain. So when something negative happens in a relationship, whether you feel hurt or anger or frustration, and that event makes you forget about love, then you know you are engaged in a relationship that is not real. You are involved in your mind and not in the actuality of the situation. You are not perceiving the real situation. You are not perceiving yourself in a real way. You are not perceiving the other in a real way. You are not seeing the relationship in a real way. And you are not in contact with the other person. You are only in contact with that part of your mind, but not with reality.

If we allow ourselves to be in contact, to acknowledge the relationship that actually exists, for a while there will be hurt, there will be frustration and hatred, there will be fear and vulnerability. You might feel a lot of negativity for some time. But if you do not withdraw out of fear, and you allow your heart to be courageous and let yourself be present, in time, love will triumph, and there will be mostly love in the relationship. That does not mean that the frustration and difficulty will go away, but they will not be as powerful. They are never really as powerful. Difficulties are powerful only because we are identified with the negative relationship. Our nature is love. We are, in fact, the source of love. So the most powerful force within us is the loving force. That is the reality. We do not see it and we do not allow it to happen because we are identified with another part of ourselves that is not real. We are engaged in something mental, not something real. The more we allow ourselves to be, and to be in contact, the more we are able to perceive the difficulties, the frustrations, the painful feelings and emotions, the more we are able to accept them and tolerate them. We are more able to absorb them, contain them, assimilate them into something larger, bigger, something indestructible, which is the heart. It is important to see that the courageous heart does not reject the bad, does not judge the bad, does not withdraw from the bad, does not exclude the bad. The bad is contained, perceived, felt, acknowledged, accepted, and understood. And the heart continues to love, regardless. When the heart is courageous, then love is unconditional. When the heart is afraid, then love is conditional.

Originally, to start with, human beings create all these mind relationships, these mental relationships, these splittings in relationships, to protect the love, to protect the heart from hurt. That protection comes from ignorance. We do not know that our heart is indestructible. The heart cannot be destroyed. Your heart is more permanent than your body. Even when you feel hurt, it is not ultimately your heart that is hurt. What is hurt are your identifications, your self-image, your pride. So to continue loving regardless of what happens is not giving in to the other person; it is giving in to your heart, to your nature. Sometimes we do not allow ourselves to feel loving, and to be loving, and to act loving. This is because we think that loving means we are going to be weak, or that we are going to be taken advantage of, or exploited, or that we are being stupid, or that we are going to lose something.

The fact is that the moment you close your heart, you are the one who loses. If you give in to your heart, it does not mean that you are giving in to the other person. It does not mean you are giving in to negativity. You are giving in to your nature. You are surrendering to who you are. To be always loving does not mean that you do not defend yourself. The courageous heart perceives and acknowledges what is there—good or bad. It does not pretend that there is no negativity. It perceives the negativity and deals with it with love. So to continue to be loving does not mean that you are weak. It does not mean that you are going to be dominated by someone. In fact, to have a courageous heart means you are able to be inwardly alone and independent. There is no true autonomy without a courageous heart. And there is no courageous heart without true autonomy. To have a courageous heart means to continue loving in spite of the situation, which means your heart is really autonomous. You have achieved the aloneness of the heart. It does not mean you are weak or relinquishing anything. It does not mean you are being exploited. It does not mean you are a dupe. I am saying all this because that is how most people see it: If someone has done something bad to you, you feel that you shouldn't love them, that you are dumb if you do. No, you are being courageous.

I am not talking about continuing to love someone and letting them walk all over you. No, that is not what I am talking about. That is not love. That is dependency. That is need. I'm talking about real understanding, forgiveness, appreciation, joy, and pleasure. That's the love I'm talking about. I'm not talking about a situation where there is negativity, the person hates you and exploits you, and you still stick around—that's not love. You are probably just engaged in the frustrating relationship then, the mental relationship.

Real love is courageous, it is strong, it is no bullshit. If someone does something hateful to you, you deal with it with strength, but you do not stop loving. You do not eliminate the good just because there is bad. You do not eliminate what is really there just because there is also something you do not like. So your courage is in being real, and in being real, you are truly courageous to see the other person as who they are, the whole package.

You can be angry sometimes and still have the courageous heart. You can even hate, and still the courageous heart is there. Hate does not contradict love because it can coexist with it. If you are really courageous, sometimes there will be hate, sometimes there will be anger, sometimes frustration, but these are passing reactions. They are not real. What exists, what is permanent, is the heart itself. The heart is beingness, an expression of Being. Being is indestructible. It is independent of your mind. A human being is not truly realized unless he can be the courageous heart. No matter how much you are realized, if your heart is conditional, it is dependent on the situation and frightened; it is cowardly. You are still not yet real, not complete, regardless of how you experience yourself or how you experience the other. This means that your relationships are not yet real. The real person has real relationships.

The courageous heart is independent of what the other person does and what the other person thinks of you. To have a courageous heart, you need to accept a certain kind of aloneness, a certain kind of independence. With the courageous heart, you are so independent that the person can do all kinds of unpleasant things but you can still see the reality. In that independence, the feeling is that you have to give constantly, regardless of what the other person does or what the situation is. That is where many people balk. If the person is being a jerk, why should I give? Right? Why should I give in to a jerk? Why should I be understanding?

Why should I be accepting? You are understanding, accepting, and forgiving not because of who the other person is, but because of who you are. That is independence, that is autonomy, and that is aloneness. So you have a real relationship with yourself. Having a real relationship with yourself allows you to have real relationships with others.

You understand and accept that in human relationships all kinds of negative things happen. There are difficulties, frustrations, and disappointments, but that is part of life that can be tolerated, accepted and learned from. As a matter of fact, we cannot really learn and grow from those interactions unless love is there. If we eliminate love from the scene, it is not possible to learn; we are completely reactive. If you become completely reactive, then there is no learning. You just bring something from the past to bear on the present, and that's it. You are just repeating the reaction, an automatic habit. But if love is there, it is possible to understand the situation. It is possible to use the experience as some kind of food for your soul.

I am not talking about something easy; it is not easy for most of us. It is very difficult. It is not easy, but at the same time, it is what is there. I am not saying you should do anything about your relationships, that you should make yourself change them. Just see what is. Just acknowledge the facts. What is the actual relationship? Acknowledge all of the feelings, not just some of them. We tend to see just some of the feelings; we do not want to see all of them. So to have a real relationship means to really acknowledge, perceive, feel, and be the whole thing. This is courageous. You are willing to take on the totality of who you are and the totality of the relationship.

The totality is already present; it is not something to be created. All the time you are creating something that is not there. You need to see through your creation and see what really is there. If you see what is really there, you are bound to see that love is the governing force, and that everything else is a reaction to it, or about it. So we are not trying to create something that is not there. What I am saying is: See what actually is there. Your ego self will not let you see what is there. It does not want to see what is actually there. It wants to maintain its distorted vision of one color or another. To see the totality of the relationship means to experience the totality of who you are. This means to become a real human being, a real person, and to see the other person as a real human being. Then you know that both of those persons are grounded in, and are manifestations of, awareness, a larger ground. The other person, and you, and all persons, are nothing but the manifestation, the expression, of the love of that ground. That love is not only in our hearts, that is, something we feel in a relationship; love is what creates us. We are the manifestations of the heart. The human being is the manifestation of the heart.

The human being is nothing but the manifestation of the heart of God. So if there were no love we would not exist. Love is that basic. The heart is that basic. All that you see is a manifestation of love. When you actually, finally, let yourself see it, you see that you are a particularization of loving energy. Your atoms are made out of love. Your body is made out of love. Your mind is made out of love. Your surroundings are made out of love. Everything is made out of love. If there were no love, you would see nothing. Beyond love there is just God. Out of that love that manifests from the God state, or from the supreme reality, emerge all of the particularizations. We are the final fruit of that particularization, and because we are the final fruit, we have the microcosmic heart that reflects the universal heart.

Just as the universal heart does not judge or reject negative things in the world, the personal heart, the human heart, also has the capacity to do that, not to reject, not to judge, to continue loving, to continue enjoying, regardless of what happens. So in the usual mental relationship—which is avoiding contact—you will notice that you avoid contact if there is no experience of love. If you are in complete contact, you will perceive some love there. Being in contact does not mean you will experience only love. To be really in contact means to be in contact with whatever is there, all of it in all of its dimensions. If you feel that you are in contact, but you feel only pure frustration or anger or hurt or hatred, you realize that there is something there that you are not in contact with. You are avoiding something: your heart. Your heart is always there; you cannot lose your heart. So where does it go? Sometimes you do not see it, do not perceive it; you do not feel it, but it is there. It cannot go. How could it go? There is no such thing as your heart being gone, or your being will disappear. To say that your heart will go is like saying that you can continue living without a brain. If the heart completely goes, you will not be able to live. There is no life. You will not be able to feel anything.

Questions?

Student: Do you mean to have contact, it has to be between a heart and another heart?

AHA: Contact is the totality of who you are, and the totality of the other. Heart is part of who we are, but not the totality.

S: So when you are actually having contact, you are angry, you are hating, there is joy or pleasure, whatever?

AHA: Yes. If you are really in contact, there is all of that. When you can experience and be in contact with the totality of what is there, then you can be the totality of your essence. And the totality of Essence is the courageous heart, what I call the Crystal Heart.

S: Is the ego based on separation because of love and negative emotions?

AHA: The beginning of ego is really the splitting between positive and negative, between love and hatred, between pain and pleasure. That is how ego starts. Without the need to protect oneself from the negative, or to protect the positive part from the negative parts, ego would not arise. So ego is based ultimately on splitting. We see it manifest in relationships. These split relationships are the basis of ego. Without split relationships there would be no ego.

At the beginning, in childhood, there is a relationship between the child and the mother, the parents, the environment. When the relationship is difficult or painful, the child deals with it by splitting the difficult from the easy, the love from the hatred. But to do that, you have to do it with your mind, because it is not real. You have to split your perception. You have to split your mind. You have to believe something that is not there. That is the beginning of mental structure. You have to split the reality into this and that, split mother into good mother and bad mother. Well, your mother is never all good or all bad. She is a mixture. So if you split her into good mother and bad mother, and you have to remember this and that, you are creating something in your mind that is not really there. In time, that becomes the mental relationship that you reenact in your life relationships. So there is the idealized mother, there is the frustrating mother, and there is the attacking mother. And your relationships with those three parts are what become reenacted in your life as mental relationships.

We usually look at ego from the perspective of self-image. I am looking at it now in terms of relationship, instead of only from self-image: That includes both the self-image and the object image, both you and your mother. I am looking at the totality of the relationship, within which the self-image and the ego developed. We are seeing how we split those relationships, and how that splitting led to the ego and the identifications of the ego. At the beginning, there may have been a need for that splitting, because the child actually could not tolerate the whole thing, didn't have enough understanding, didn't know. The system was not developed, the perception was not developed enough to see the totality, to understand it, and tolerate it. The child had to split the different parts. But for us now, this splitting is no longer needed. We can tolerate reality now. The child, we could say, could not tolerate reality completely.

The ego is based on not wanting to see all of reality. The ego is always based on dissociation and splitting. If the ego sees all of reality, it won't exist any more. Ego continues to exist because it believes its own perception. Ego is part of the mind, and the mind has a great capacity for self-deception. The mind can be lied to; Being cannot be deceived. So in the beginning the mind deceives itself, and it continues to believe that deception, taking it to be reality. But the moment it recognizes that something is not the truth, it cannot hold on to it. In a sense, the mind is very honest, very sincere. It is honest and sincere, but it is not completely knowledgeable or intelligent. But the moment it sees the truth, it cannot pretend that things are any other way. The mind continues to believe the false only because it thinks that it is the truth. The moment you show it that something is false, the mind will let go of it. So the moment the mind sees the whole totality of the truth, it will let go of the false, and the ego will go. One way of going about this is seeing the complete relationship. If you really see, acknowledge, and live a complete relationship, you will have to live as a real human being, not as an ego, not as a mental structure. A mental structure—which is a self-image—persists because you keep engaging in mental relationships, which are split relationships, unreal relationships. When a relationship is complete and real, you have to be complete and real.

I am the heart, the courageous heart, not the unconditional heart. People use the word unconditional to mean subservient, staying in a situation regardless of what someone does to you. I am not talking about that. Yes, you love regardless of what someone does to you, but you also love yourself. You do not just sit there and let people abuse you. You are courageous. You are willing to see the truth. So the love here is real, it is a mature kind of love, objective love. I call it Crystal Love. The crystalline clarity that is love.

S: When one is involved in one of those three different relationships, is it usually one of them that you involve yourself in, or can you involve yourself in several of them, in different stages of relationship?

AHA: Usually you shift back and forth between the different kinds of mental relationships. Sometimes a person's overall or general pattern is to be involved in one of them, but from moment to moment, the person shifts back and forth between them. People have their own patterns. When you are engaged in a relationship, you go back and forth between the three, or you see the totality of it which has all of them in various proportions.

S: So isn't there one that is predominantly the way you are?

AHA: Usually there is. Some people have one, or they might have one that is predominant for a month or two, or a few years, and then another one predominates.

S: If you are rejecting your hatred, you are also rejecting your love?

AHA: Yes. If you reject your hatred, split away from your hatred, your love becomes unreal, because it is based on an idealization, an unreality. Usually you will be disappointed at some point. So this is what happens: There is love, it is an idealized relationship, all loving, all wonderful. Everything you see is wonderful: the way your love moves, her eyes, the color of her hair. You can stare at your love for hours and hours. Then one day something happens—the other person does something and you become really hurt and disappointed. You are hurt and disappointed not because of how bad it is that the other person did something, but because that idealized image is destroyed. The other person is not perfect. Then the relationship turns sour.

But if you are mature and you have learned how to have a real relationship, you will accept that imperfection. You see that it cannot be wonderful all the time. It was never that way anyway. The person has not really changed. You realize how the capacity for a real relationship is necessary for a long-lasting relationship. There is no long-lasting, satisfying relationship if you can't have a real relationship. Those mental relationships cannot last very long. They are not real. With the idealized relationship, at some point you will be disappointed. With the negative relationship, at some point it will be too negative and you will have to get out of it. The frustrating one means there is no relationship there anyway; it is just something that you want and cannot have.

Many people who are not in a relationship but are always wanting one, tend to engage in the frustrating relationship. They have an idea in their mind that they should have a good relationship, but they are destined to not get it. If they got it, they would have to deal with the splitting in their relationships, and the feeling of aloneness that arises, the absence of relationship, the absence of contact. Every time you see through a mental relationship, you have to deal with some kind of absence of relationship because the fake relationship is a substitute, filling the hole of real relationship.

If there is no real contact, there is no real relationship. So you have to constantly activate one of those mental relationships because you cannot tolerate being with no relationship in your mind. You cannot live without relationship, so there is always an activation of some kind of mental relationship. That is why most of the time people are thinking about other people. If you examine your thoughts about other people, you will see that you categorize them into these three groups. You are always engaged in some kind of relationship in your mind. You do not allow yourself to be alone. You do not allow yourself to feel the absence of the real relationship.

But you have to allow yourself to feel that absence, feel the aloneness—which is the hole of the real relationship—before you will be able to experience the real relationship. You have to experience the absence of it completely—no relationship, I'm empty, nothing there, no contact. When you feel that way, you may also feel that you are not real, that you do not exist, because you cannot exist without relationship. The moment you allow the negative relationship to go, the mental relationship to go, the ego starts freaking out, starts disintegrating, disappearing, and the aloneness will be felt as some sort of emptiness, some kind of absence of self. So when the mental relationship goes, the part of you that is relating to it goes, too, and you start feeling the absence of self, an emptiness which will be felt as an aloneness. When the aloneness is accepted and tolerated, it is then possible for real contact to happen, and not before that.

When the relationship is in the present, you can see when there is negativity in it, what is really negative in it, not what your mind says. If the other person does not understand you, you know that it really is because the other person does not understand, not only because you believe that they do not understand you. If the person loves you, it is because he really loves you, not because you want him to love you.

This is all part of the new perspective that we are exploring. Real relationship is a way that true digestion of experience happens. That is how we grow. It is the context in which a real human being grows and develops. Because we split our relationships, making them all good or all bad, we cannot digest and metabolize them. We cannot digest something that is not real. We have to see the truth in order to learn.

TWELVE

Our Knowledge is the World We Live

Today we will explore a certain understanding: the perspective that our world is our knowledge. What does this mean? I will explain it gradually.

By the time in our mental development that we become aware of ourselves, we feel that we live in the world, and that we know the world as it is. We look around us and see the world extending endlessly. We believe that we know our bedroom, our clothes, our pets, our parents, our siblings, our friends, the street we live on, cars passing by, airplanes in the sky, birds in the trees, trees and the ground, water in the rivers, oceans and clouds, sky and stars and moon. The whole world. From the time we can be aware of such things, we believe we are learning to know about the world. We never question that belief. Our parents and the people

around us tell us, "Yes, this is the world." We are now part
of the world. We live in this world and we feel we could
learn to live happily in it.

We don't normally question this perception of the world.
It is just assumed—this is a world. We come into this world,
we grow, and we learn about the world. We experience
whatever we experience as we participate in this world. Our
world-as-it-exists can be shaken by simply contemplating
the historical changes in our knowledge of what the physical world is. We believe now that our world is a planet
which is rotating around the sun, which is at the edge of
the Milky Way, which is one galaxy among millions and
millions of galaxies scattered throughout space. However,
according to everyone who lived two hundred years ago it
wasn't like that. And a thousand years ago or so we were
actually in a flat world, or our world was riding on the back
of a turtle. Nearly everyone believed the prevailing notions
of the physical world, just as we now believe we are on the
edge of the galaxy. So it shakes our world a little when we
know that the world that people assume is a fixed given has
changed so many times. What is it going to be a hundred
years from now?

We grow up in this world, and we get a little bit older.
That's one thing we know about being in this world: We
get older, we grow, we get bigger. First you are a baby, then
a little kid. Then you are a big kid. Every kid wants to be a
grownup. Grownups want to be little kids. Now that's part
of the world.

So far I haven't said anything mysterious; I am just pointing out the picture of ourselves in the world that we hold in
our minds. In the beginning we might know our bedroom,
our house, and the surrounding area. These things constitute
our world. In time we learn more, and our world grows bigger. As you get older, you see more things; at age six or seven
you see the sky and realize, "This is the real world: Earth!

There are big things here!" Before that, when you are a little kid you look at the bright things you see when you look up—mountains, sky, the moon—and you think they are nice ornaments like what you have on the ceiling in your room. Then you learn that there are real planets and stars, and you feel that your world has expanded. What is interesting is that nothing has changed about the planets and the stars—something in you changed and expanded the world.

As you grow bigger and older, and become a man or woman, you experience life the way everyone collectively knows it. Depending on where you live, the culture you live in, your background, your family and friends, and your education, you have a certain experience, a certain life; you find yourself either happy or unhappy, thinking in terms of getting what you want, or not getting what you want. So part of living in the world is to get what you want or not get what you want. Part of the world is to be happy or not to be happy. Everyone knows that.

Part of what you know as the world is that when someone is born everyone is happy, and when someone dies everyone is sad. People get sick, and they get healthy again. When people like you, you are happy. If you become famous, that is something to be happy about. Failure is something that you are supposed to feel bad about. All these things are elements of the world you learn.

At some point, when you are older, you realize that something is not quite right. You are having some problems with your life, perhaps with work or with a relationship. So you might begin to become psychologically sophisticated, and try to understand your mind and your personality. You do therapy, study psychology or philosophy, and understand your problems. Why do you have problems? You might want to know what it is about your perceptions of things that makes you unhappy. You might realize that there is more to life that just growing up, living, and eating.

You realize that you might not really understand what's going on here. Most people don't begin to wonder about these things until later in life. When you are ten years old, you do not ask such questions. It doesn't occur to you that your misconceptions can cause you trouble. To begin to question your notions about the world takes a lot of living, until you are sixteen or seventeen if you are lucky, or maybe until you are thirty. You begin to realize that part of your difficulty is that there are certain things you don't understand, or certain things you have assumed that are actually not true. You begin to realize that your mind has some influence on how you experience the world.

At some point you might become spiritually sophisticated, and wonder about experiencing deeper things in your life, in yourself, in the world. So you become interested in the spirit, in spirituality, in the subject of God, or Essence, or Being. You begin to consider that maybe you have a soul, maybe you have spirit, maybe you have Essence. You feel something new in your inner experience. People talk to you about the God or Goddess within, and other people talk about the God that's outside, up there, or the Goddess down there. So you develop the notion that there are things in the world that are not seen by the eyes, not perceived by the senses. You are becoming very sophisticated. The world is not just the way you knew it when you were fifteen, when you had your boyfriends and girlfriends, and cars you rode in, and movies you went to. Now you are aware that there are spirits and minds. It seems to you as if the world has taken on more dimensions. You are aware of mind and heart and spirit, of thinking, mental experiences, emotional experiences, spiritual experiences. You are further constructing yourself, building your life in the world.

But basically the world you live in remains the same. The trees continue being trees, the mountains are still mountains; they are the way they are, located where they are.

People are people. Men are men. Women are women. Once in a while there is a little confusion, but most of the time it's definite. Basically everyone knows what rivers are, what oceans are, and that does not change. Even when we understand ourselves psychologically or realize ourselves spiritually, our experience remains within the context of the world we began to know when we were two, three, four, five years old. The world doesn't change in any fundamental way. There are just more things in it. We are aware of more things, just as we come to know that there are other countries. Now, you realize you have a mind and a spirit, or soul, or Essence. These are new things, that you hadn't seen before. And knowledge of these things is simply added to what you already know; it usually doesn't shake up your previously known world.

We believe that in our realization or our understanding, or with more experience or more maturity, something new is happening, but it is actually a matter of adding content to the same given world. We are seeing more of what is already there that we have not yet seen. The basic notion of the world is not questioned. Tables continue to be tables. Houses continue to be houses. That is never questioned. We do not question whether we are a man or a woman. These basic things continue to constitute our world.

What do I mean when I say, "Our world is our knowledge"? We can explore it experientially, bringing ourselves to the moment and contemplating the world that we perceive now. We can contemplate the people here in this room, the bright lights, the rugs, the chairs, the walls. We can experience the part of the world that we perceive right now. As we work with our contemplation we think that this work is happening in *this* world that we see. We can work on ourselves psychologically, or spiritually, in the context of this world or in the context of this situation, contemplating and exploring ourselves. As I said before, we might be psychologically sophisticated, and see how the mind determines what we experience and what we feel. One of the first things we realize when we become more knowledgeable about ourselves is that our emotional state depends a lot on the memory content of our minds, on what we have experienced in the past.

You might realize then that how you feel about different situations has a lot to do with the past and not necessarily with what is going on now. This is common psychological knowledge. Or you might do some kind of spiritual work, such as a meditation practice, and begin to have certain experiences. Perhaps your chakras open, your heart opens, your mind becomes clear, or you see certain lights, or talk to angels. You will continue to believe that all these experiences are happening within the world that we already know, the world that we never question.

For instance, you might realize that in this moment you are feeling anxious or uncomfortable because of a certain situation. Then you might see that the situation reminds you of an occasion in your childhood when you were afraid. Now you are aware that you are afraid when there is nothing to be afraid of, because this situation contains an element similar to that previous time. When you have this insight, you are gaining knowledge, but you are still living in the same world in the sense that you are saying that you are afraid now in the way you were afraid then. You are saying, in effect, that one thing that hasn't changed about the world is your fear. There is fear now that is similar to fear in childhood, so that is a definite part of the world.

So, you are afraid in this situation that reminds you of other situations in childhood. Well, what's the situation? Perhaps there is another person here, of a certain shape or age or a certain demeanor, whom you are reacting to. So your knowledge is that there is a person here, now, just as there was a person then who looked or acted in a certain way. The world hasn't changed—there are persons, and persons behave in certain ways, you are a person who reacts, there is fear, and so on. That's the world. Nothing about the world has changed; the elements of the world are simply interacting in certain ways, rearranging themselves in certain configurations.

So we see that even when we learn about ourselves psychologically, although we believe we have gained in knowledge, the kind of knowledge we have gained is simply seeing new connections in the world that we already know. In some sense, although there is an increase in knowledge, there is no change in the depth of knowledge. You know about fear, you know about people, about behaviors, but these are not different from the categories of experiences you had as a child. The same kinds of experiences you had then, you are having now. They are happening within a similar context, in the same world.

You know about light and darkness, and at some point you learn that you can make things dark or light with the switches on the wall. Before you learned this, you had seen the switches, you knew about lights, you knew that you need light to see things, you knew that darkness is good for sleep. In learning about how the switch works, there is nothing new except the connection between these elements.

Most of us believe that education, psychological understanding, and spiritual realization are the same sort of thing. You just learn more of what is there, of what you already know. You are a person, a man or a woman, who has a child, who lives in a particular house with particular people, who has certain connections with these people. You believe that it is that person who is connected to those people who are living in that house who is going to know something about himself or herself with regard to those people. What you know is still about the same world, the same realm.

Seeing new connections might make you feel you have more self-knowledge, but what you know is more about the same dimension, about the same kinds of entities. You might, for instance, have known about rocks and crystals, and then learn about different kinds of gemstones, like diamonds and emeralds, and say that your knowledge of minerals has increased. But in some sense you haven't learned anything new. It's all about minerals, and minerals are all the same kind of thing. They simply have different colors and different structures, and you see more about them and learn more names for them. But they are all composed of crystalline structures, they all have certain colors and certain characteristic shapes, they all have a certain hardness. These qualities are all the same. You are just seeing them in different combinations and calling that "new knowledge." The more we experience the world the more knowledge we have. The more we see the world, the more our knowledge expands; the more our knowledge expands, the more our world expands.

So far I haven't said anything mysterious or unusual. I'm just pointing to something that we all take for granted. It is common sense, but we usually don't consider things this way. I'm thinking about things in a kind of childish way.

Basically then, the world we live in is composed of the same things, which don't change. There are rocks, wolves, and trees; there are plants, animals, machines, people, rivers, oceans. There is water, clouds, weather, stars, galaxies; and there's blood, urine, and bones. There is light, darkness, sadness, fear, anger, happiness, and there's freedom. There is work, failure, success, fame, and there are televisions. There are actions, lying, and telling the truth, and all these things have been the same since we were five years old. And we believe that growing and learning involve simply becoming aware of the juxtaposition of these things. That's what life means. We see more of the same things that we learned by age five.

In the normal course of events, knowledge and expansion involve continuing to walk on the same surface. We haven't taken steps up or down to different levels. We just go on along on the same terrain from one place to another, but it is the same kind of terrain. Increased maturity, knowledge, or growth means basically being aware of more complexity in the juxtaposition of the elements that we take to compose the world. There are more interconnections— how this connects to that, how this is here and that is there in time and space.

We still haven't explained why I say that our knowledge is the world we live. We see how our world expands as our knowledge expands, or how our knowledge expands as we seem to know more of our world. Of course our world includes us—our bodies, our minds, our spirits. We don't question those kinds of things. Whatever we do, or whatever plans we have, however we think in terms of learning, growing, expanding psychologically, spiritually, emotionally, our perspective remains within that world. Even when we begin to experience deeper things like truth, or Essence, we relate them to what we already know, and sense them in ways similar to how we sense things we already know. "I feel sweet, or hard, or soft, bright, or dark, happy or sad." These are still elements of the same experiential world we already know.

In some sense, our knowledge never increases. It is like the alphabet. Knowledge is made up of bits like the alphabet is made up of letters. We all have the same alphabet of knowledge, and then we combine our knowledge alphabet in myriad ways. It is like our language. How many letters are there, twenty-six? With twenty-six letters we have hundreds of thousands of words. We can speak and write forever, but all our words are still made up of the same alphabet. So all the books, all the written knowledge we have, is composed of those twenty-six letters, regardless of how advanced, how developed, and how profound the language gets.

Our knowledge of the world is composed of an alphabet like that. This alphabet consists of all the elements of the given world—the rocks, the oxygen, the flesh, the bones, freedom, and sadness. Our world is composed of the categories of what we think the world is made of, which affects how we recognize things, which determines how we perceive. Tables, wood, notebook, water, glass, microphone, television, lights, sun, box, thoughts, ideas, feelings, sensations, and so on. These are the things that constitute the alphabet of our world. The categories never change, we just see different relationships between them.

What I want to explore today are those elements. What are they? I want to explore rocks, mountains, people, water, noses, eyes, livers, pigs, and pigeons. Snakes and stars and dust. Evaporation, consolidation, processes, freedom, choice. The whole dictionary. The world that we know is the dictionary that you have on your shelf. All your perceptions occur in terms that you can find in your dictionary. The moment you wake up, you go to the dictionary. *Wake up.* You can find exactly what "wake up" means. You wake up, you see your mom. "Mom" means such and such, and is explained by other words that you can find in the dictionary. Those words are in turn explained by other words in it. So everything that we experience is in the dictionary.

We believe that the dictionary categorizes our world. We don't believe that the dictionary *is* our world. That makes us sane. If we really believed that the dictionary is our world, we could be considered cuckoo. So we say the dictionary is just an attempt at categorizing and describing elements of our world. But those elements of our world really constitute our world. The world is really there. There are rocks; there are birds. I do have a nose. It is true, the dictionary describes what it is. There is a nose, and there actually are eyes. Your eyes have certain shapes, and the dictionary may be what describes and gives the understanding of what the word "eye" is, but there is an eye. From the beginning we never question that there are eyes, noses, knees, hair, flesh, blood, and all the rest. The words in the dictionary are finite. But we can create an infinite variety of relationships between the different words, just as the juxtaposition of letters can make innumerable words.

So the alphabet of the world is made up of the elements that constitute our known world. We believe that these things actually exist, that they are solid entities. There are actual things, like a rock. There is no doubt about it. We might doubt whether freedom exists or not, but a rock? A rock is there. If you don't believe it exists, you kick it, and then you know it exists. That is the famous final proof that the rock, and this physical reality, really exist.

But philosophically, that is not the final proof. A philosopher will question your interpretation of your sensation. How do you know, how can you assume there is a rock, just based on the sensation in your foot? People can hallucinate the existence of things because of pains in the foot. So logically, philosophically, it doesn't follow, but we believe the rock exists anyway. If you did not believe that the rock exists, your mental stability would be in question, regardless of how philosophically and logically you could frame your question about it.

What are these elements that compose our world? Were they there before we were born? Were they there when we were two, three months old, before we knew about them, and then as we grew up we just learned about them? That is what we generally assume—that they were there when we first arrived in this world. Everything was already here. Mountains and trees and people and flies, freedom and justice, Essence, spirit, everything. But I am asking, do trees actually exist before you have learned about them?

Let's take a certain element of the world that we could explore this question with. Let's take the element of freedom.

We say you are either free or not free. Is there such a thing as freedom? If you are a child two years old, freedom doesn't exist in the sense that you don't think in terms of whether you are free or not free. You begin to approach the notion of freedom through learning whether you are allowed to do what you want, for example. You learn, for instance, that you cannot make a mess without your parents interfering with you. After a while, having your way or not having your way becomes what we call freedom or lack of it. But at the beginning you don't think in terms of those categories. We look at a baby and the baby looks free, but is the baby free? We sense that babies are free because they feel just what they feel, they seem to have no mental restrictions on their experience, and we feel that that is a kind of freedom. But is it true from the perspective of the baby? Is there such a thing as freedom? The baby still doesn't know what is "not freedom." So the baby doesn't know what freedom is. We know freedom only because we know what is not freedom. If there is no such thing as "no freedom" there cannot be such a thing as "freedom." Could you know anything about freedom if you have never felt the lack of it? So freedom is actually known by its absence. If you are restricted then you can think about freedom, but if you are never restricted you never think that you are free, and in your world freedom doesn't exist.

Can you ever feel hot if you never get cold? There is no such thing as heat if there is no coldness. There is no such thing as tall if there is no short. There is nothing that is big if there is nothing that is small. All the things we know are known through contrasting them with other things. We know solid because we know fluid. We know good in contrast to bad. We know happy because we contrast it with unhappy. So one of the first things we observe about the elements that compose our world is that we know them by contrasting them with each other.

For us to assume that these elements of the world exist, and they compose our world—in fact for the world to be there at all—there must be contrast, differentiation between things.

Let me backtrack a little. Suppose you have an issue, a difficulty in your life because of something that happened in your childhood. Your experience of the difficulty is dependent on the categories of experience that you believe are real. If there were no such thing as fear, or sadness, or rejection and approval, or if there were no such things as persons, or if the passage of time were not an element of your experience, then it would not make sense to talk about a pattern that you have now that is dependent on something in childhood. On the level of the given elements, you can work on the interconnections and patterns, see through them and free yourself from some constriction in those patterns.

However, we can approach this work of freeing ourselves in a different way, by questioning the elements of our experience. Without these elements there are no issues. To have a psychological issue that you can understand in terms of what has happened in the past, you have to assume the reality and existence of those elements.

As you develop, you have no choice but to assume the ultimate reality and existence of the elements that constitute the world. These are the basis of everything, not just your issues and difficulties. They are the basis of your activities, your decisions, the content of your life, and your communications—everything. Without these elements there is no life, no existence, no perception, no knowledge. For doing the work here, for knowing who you are, what your difficulties are, what it means to be free or not free, what it means to want to work on yourself, these elements are definitely important.

We can return to our understanding of the child whose mind is developing. The child sees shapes and forms moving around, lights and colors and movements, but the child doesn't think "black, green, movement, peace." The child doesn't know these things. The child might respond to the mother's face, for example, but does not think "face" or "mother." There are things happening, yet the child doesn't even think "things are happening." She doesn't know "things" and she doesn't know "happening" yet. There are impressions of all sorts, but the child doesn't know that there are impressions. There is some experience happening, but the child doesn't know there is an experience happening. There are simply sensations, impressions, experiences, perceptions, lights, colors, forms, changes, and movements. At the beginning we are aware of these things without being aware that we are aware of them.

The child sees the same things happening over and over again. Things like sounds and shapes and kinesthetic sensations are repeated until the memory develops to the extent that the child recognizes certain patterns. Of course she is more sensitive or attuned to certain patterns than others.

At the beginning, however, the world the child exists in is, in some sense, undefined, fluid, unstructured, and unknown. Things appear and disappear without her knowing what they are. It is not just because it's the first time she experiences these things; it is because she hasn't the vaguest idea what they are. She hasn't the vaguest idea that you could know what they are.

In this initial fluid, relatively unstructured experience, when you perceive movement you don't know whether the room moved or you moved. You do not have the idea that maybe someone is taking you from one room to another; all you know is that the picture has just changed. You don't even know yet that there is such a thing as movement in space. You don't yet have the idea that there could be two places.

Little by little, we begin to solidify the things we perceive: our inner sensations, perceptions, movements, changes, and shapes. What solidifies are repeated perceptions. We eventually become aware that people seem to make sounds about the things. You hear a sound coming from something over there that says "Laurie. Laurie." What's that? But you hear it a lot of times. "Laurie." After a while, you know that the voice comes from something familiar, something significant. You don't know exactly that it is your mother. And these sounds are like a song of sorts; you don't know what they are yet. You hear "Laurie" but you don't know what Laurie is. You also hear the song of the birds, which sounds rather similar.

In time, when you are maybe six or eight months old, your mother points to you and says "Laurie." You look at the finger. "Laurie." A pointing finger. Later you point to your mother's finger and say "Laurie." She says, "No, no, Laurie," and points in your direction. What does that mean? That means you have to point this way to mean Laurie, not that way. It takes a lot of repetition before you figure out that "Laurie" refers to you. At the beginning you don't know that Laurie is a name, or that you're Laurie. They keep pointing to you, and saying "Laurie," and finally you catch on. You say, "Yes, I'm Laurie."

What's a Laurie? You don't know yet. Hopefully your mommy knows. But you haven't got the vaguest idea. All you know is you're Laurie. And you're stuck with that for the rest of your life.

One of the first elements in the world that you learn about is your name, and your name is you. In time you begin to realize that you have a body, that this arm is actually connected to this shoulder, and it is not connected to your mother.

You are learning the sensations and movements and sights of your body at the same time you are learning your name; through your learning you come to refer both "Laurie" and the perception of the body to the idea that they are you.

So, body and Laurie are rather undifferentiable. Then you hear that "Laurie" is something that *has* a body. What is "Laurie" then? First you knew there was Laurie. Now Laurie has a body. What's this Laurie? It is a mystery.

But in your mind, one of the first things you learned was that Laurie and the body are somehow indistinguishable, inseparable. What does Mommy do with the baby at the beginning? She points to her nose and says "Nose. Nose." Finally, the baby says "Nose." The baby doesn't know what this looks like yet, you see. And then the mama points to her own nose and says "Nose. Here is a nose." You still don't see your nose. Finally, you figure out what "nose" is; finally, you look in the mirror and see a nose and say, "Nose!" "Laurie's nose!" You see? Now the world has a nose. Before that there were no noses. Before that there was no Laurie and no noses.

So Laurie exists, then a nose exists; besides the nose, there is a mouth, and eyes, and complexity increases. That's what parents do with their kids to teach them—you need to learn the elements of the world.

To say that the elements don't exist before they are mentally known doesn't mean that the child isn't seeing something. The child was seeing an ear, but hadn't the vaguest idea that it was called an ear, hadn't the vaguest idea that it existed separately from other things.

So for the child in the beginning the world doesn't include ears and noses, not to mention stars and galaxies, freedom and choice, God and all these things. In the world of the child, these things don't exist, in some very real sense. You say, "Well, they existed but you just didn't refer to them that way." What does that mean that they existed but you didn't call them that? If you didn't recognize them as such, didn't experience them as such, didn't call them anything, what does it mean to say that they existed?

On an abstract level, you could say that these elements of the world already existed. But in reality, in terms of your experience, in terms of the world that you knew, the world was not composed of these things. There is no world that can be experienced as constituted by these elements until you start naming things. So you name things—"nose, body, Laurie, Daddy, Mommy, give me, I want." This development happens little by little, and little by little the world becomes populated with its elements. But what is it that is constituting the world? It is nothing but an increase in your knowledge.

The world that you're learning about is nothing but words added to your mind. One day you learn, "tree." Mommy says "tree." You hear someone say, "I'm going to water the tree." And you say, "Water the tree? Water the tree? What do you mean, 'water the tree'?" You don't know. Water. Water. You drink water, but what does it mean 'water the tree'? The child says "Tree? Tree drinks water? I drink water. But what does it mean 'water the tree'?" And she is very surprised, and asks, "What is that?" First of all you have to learn a lot of things about this something called a tree, until when you see a tree you say "This is a tree." To begin with, you might look at a television and say "Tree!" And your Mom says, "No. Not tree. This is tree." And then she says "Look at that big one! Tree!" Oh, now these are looking the same. But that one over there doesn't look like this one. How come these are trees, but this one and that one are not trees? It takes a long time for you to learn that that huge thing over there and this little thing are both trees, and this thing is not a tree. So, at the beginning for the child, maybe two of these are trees and the other thing over there, who knows what it is?

That's the world of the child. But then as your knowledge increases, you slowly recognize the various elements. And after a while, the connection in your mind becomes more clear, and you recognize, "This is a tree. Tree means green leaves, and they all have branches." You have the idea of tree, and the concepts of branch and trunk and leaves. Before you were recognizing and naming trees, your world didn't have trees. When you begin to see trees and to recognize that there are trees in the world, all it means basically is that you have learned the idea, the notion, the concept of tree. Something was added to your knowledge. It's called a tree.

As your knowledge expands, you can differentiate more words, notions, ideas, and more connections, interconnections, juxtapositions between those first ideas and notions. These connections make up more of the world, which is simply more of your knowledge.

From this discussion, we see that from the beginning the world we live in is completely inseparable from our knowledge. I have compared knowledge to an alphabet, so that it refers not only to the knowledge of interconnection between things—like words, sentences, and more complex structures—but actually all the way down to the elementary notions, the beginning concepts, including the initial conceptual knowledge. They were not actually given in the world for you until you conceptualized them. No particular element existed. Look at this table, for instance. You have the notion of a table. This concept is something you learned. You came to know "table," then you could say "table top." What's a table top? At the beginning, "table top" doesn't exist for you until you understand the notion of a surface and that the surface is on the top, because the table top, at the beginning, is not separate from the side. You see something that's slightly different, right? But until there is an idea of "top," there is no top or side. There is no table top yet. There is a table top only when you conceptualize the notion of a table top. Before that there is a table, and it's a little mysterious what it is, because tables don't look the same.

At first, the child's concept of a table is very fluid and undefined. Over time you've learned about the sides, the legs, the tops, this and that, and the table becomes more and more fixed, and finally "table." Now you can actually describe it and write a whole paper on what the table is composed of—wood, metal, plastic, polish, tops and surface. We can discriminate something similar and call that a counter, but that counter is nothing but an increase in your knowledge. Your new notions didn't exist before you constructed them; and in fact, many of them don't actually exist. Is there such a thing as a top? Is there such a thing as a side? A top or a side is something we construct so that we can talk about the table.

Imagine that you had to communicate the notion "tables" to a bird. All the bird sees is that there is something there, something the bird could alight upon. That's all. It doesn't have a top, it doesn't have a side. The bird never thinks of these things. They are not necessary to the world of a bird. The bird's world doesn't consist of things like tables. It consists of things you can stand on.

So what constitutes the world we live in is the concepts that develop little by little. They don't exist in reality, they exist because we need them. We need to describe things in a certain way. We need to use things, to work with them, so we form concepts. Tables didn't exist until people needed them, you see. "Table" is basically an idea. Before that, people sat on rocks. They put their food on a rock, until that wasn't comfortable, and they made a flat rock. Later on it became a table. As tables came into being, the concept of table came into being. We can understand more easily that things created by human beings, like tables or airplanes or music or computers, did not exist before they were created as concepts in the mind. But it is much more difficult to see that our concept of star, for instance, actually *creates* the stars that we see, to see that before we discriminate them they don't exist. It is normal to assume that the existence of the star is independent of our conceptualizing of it; we think we know that they existed before human beings existed. We think of the stars as separate, independent, but we can't think of stars or recognize stars without the idea of stars. Without the idea we will see dots of light in the sky but we will not see stars. Without the notions of sky and stars, we will live in a world without stars or sky, a world with something above us that's light and blue, sometimes gray, sometimes dark, and sometimes dark with little dots of light.

We might differentiate, then, the dots of light from the part that is dark. We call these dots of light "stars." To live in a world with stars in it you need a concept of star. And the location of this concept of star is in your mind, not in the night sky. Without the concept, you can't say that you know what is in the night sky. Without the concept, you don't know what is there. Something is there that is independent of the concepts in your mind, and we can understand a lot about what concepts have to do with what is actually there. But here we need to see simply that our world is made of this constructed knowledge.

So we are seeing that the elements of the world don't exist in the way we assume they do—they exist only because we discriminate them from other things. As separate things, they don't really exist. This is a tricky point. As I said before, we differentiate our perceptions by perceiving contrast. And the contrast tends to actually separate the contrasting things from each other in our perception. Then we give names to these contrasting things. Then things exist. If you didn't think at all, would the world exist? Good question.

So the world we live in is composed of the concepts that constitute our knowledge. What we call the world is nothing but our concepts. What we call "the world" is simply ideas, concepts, notions.

We conceptualize a table, we conceptualize table legs, and we say table legs really exist. But does the leg of a table really exist outside of the mind, outside of our knowledge?

When the child forms the idea of a table, she doesn't yet think of table legs. There is just a table, as one thing. When the child becomes more sophisticated, she starts thinking of legs, a top, and so on. Before that there is just a table, and it's a little mysterious. The more we know it, the more we create concepts about it, more divisions, more separations, and fix them in our minds as actually existing on their own, the more the table becomes a fixed thing, less mysterious and more known.

By the time we are four or five or six years old, the world is quite fixed. Tables are tables, people are people, noses are noses, stars are stars. Laurie definitely knows who Laurie is, and everyone else knows who Laurie is. Before Laurie called herself "Laurie," she didn't really know. In some sense, there was no Laurie. There is something, God knows what. Maybe not even a something.

What we are seeing here is that the world we live in is so linked with our concepts that we cannot separate who we are and the world we live in from the content of our minds. The content of your mind has developed in the context of naming the world. The development of your mind progressed through your knowing the world. And you know the world by developing the mind. The two things happen at the same time, as one process.

These concepts quickly become specific and rigid. Along with that, what we are becomes fixed and rigid. The objects in the world are very fixed, just as the alphabet is very specific. An A is an A is an A. Laurie is Laurie is Laurie. In some sense, no changes can happen in this world.

In the process of conceptualizing and naming the world, we forget that these elements didn't exist for us until we differentiated them, separated them, isolated them, and named them. We don't remember what happened before that, because there wasn't enough conceptual capacity to remember things before that. What we remember is the notions we have developed. We cannot remember things that had no concepts associated with them.

Finally, we end up living in a world that is itself our own mind. What we call our world is nothing but the content of our knowledge. And our world becomes as fixed as the content of our knowledge. If that content is definite and set, then what you are is definite and set, people are definite and set, and life is definite and set. The more it is like that, the more your experience is fixed and unchangeable. And the more that happens, the more the world that you live in is the world of yesterday. It's no longer a fresh world. Life is not fresh. You are not fresh. The world is not fresh. You don't learn anything new. You don't grow or develop. There is no expansion, no deepening. Your world becomes more narrow, and increasing complexity is further narrowing, adding to the rigidity of the world you inhabit.

So what we call increasing knowledge is nothing but fixing the world, making it more rigid and making ourselves, our lives, increasingly fixed. Unchangeableness becomes our security then. To challenge the reality of these concepts makes us feel very insecure. It's all right to arrange them in different juxtapositions, in different relationships and categories. In fact, this gives us more security. As the weaving of our concepts becomes thicker and denser, so the fabric of our world becomes even more set, which gives us a firmer sense of security. At the same time, we lose the dynamic quality of who we are, and of what the world is.

Our world loses dynamism and becomes more mechanical, and we become more mechanical. We are not just living in our minds, we are living our minds. We are not just living in the past, we are living the past. We are living the person we became as a child. We are living our parents' daughter or son. We are living our idea of being a human being. We are not living in a house, we are living in our idea of a house. To be more precise, we are living the idea of a person living in the idea of a house. Our idea of a person is driving our idea of a car through our idea of city streets. The world we live in is old and dead. The freshness, the vitality, the spark is gone, because whenever you see something, you see it through the filter of a concept, and it has to fit a concept that you already know. So you never see it in its freshness. You look at the rug, and see red, blue and green already fixed. You already know what a rug is, you already know what red is, and what blue is. Nothing is new, these are just different arrangements. The more things are known, the more they are set, the more they lose the freshness, the dynamism, the brightness, the living quality.

Another factor that makes our world dead is our reactivity. We not only have old concepts of who we are and what the world is, we also have reactions and opinions about them that make our concepts even more rigid, opaque, and out of touch with the actual present alive world. Whenever something happens in your experience, you have to categorize it as happy or unhappy, as bringing pain or pleasure, as good or bad. You could have a favorite star, like Sirius, and every time you look up at night you look up and admire that star; you don't see the other stars or the sky, just this special star that brings you pleasure. Or you could believe that there are malevolent aliens in the sky and be afraid to ever look up and see it. You see the people you know as good or as bad, because you are seeing your idea of them. And your reaction makes it that much harder to see what is real in them; it solidifies your concept of them.

We see not what is there, but our concepts of what is there. You look outside, and you see trees, you don't see reality. You look up, and you see stars, you don't see reality. And what is "star"? Something in your mind. Not only do you perceive through the filters of your concepts, you have associations to those concepts. "Star" makes you feel a certain way. The word "mommy" makes you feel another way. The word "pet" brings different associations and reactions. These associations and reactions are all determined by your past. Basically, your parents teach you how to respond to things. You learn what to be afraid of and what to be happy about. When someone is born, everyone tells you that's a time to celebrate. If someone dies, everyone is supposed to be sad. So death is a concept—you don't know what it is—but you're already programmed how to respond to it. Birth is something we conceptualize, and your reaction to it is already determined. If you feel a certain sensation, it has already been given a name. Not only has it been given a name, you've been told how to react to it. So your world is set. Your life is set. Who you are is set. It's all the content of your mind.

The more we make the world concrete, the more dead our world is, and the more dead we become. But we usually don't think of spiritual freedom as confronting what we call our world, or our minds. We think of it as something that will happen within that world. We don't confront the whole question of what this world is. We don't confront the most obvious thing. We want to find some mysterious something that brings us freshness, freedom, a sense of dynamism, not realizing that the dynamism is right here. We have deadened the world by giving everything a name and believing that the name is the ultimate truth.

Just by calling yourself Michael, or Laurie, or Jean, or whatever, you are deadening yourself. You made yourself into an object, something unchanging, and ended up cut off from the dynamism that is your being.

The concepts arise to describe actual differentiations and contrasts in our perception. But the concepts become so concrete that they seem real. And because they determine how we experience ourselves and the world, our experience tends to continually reinforce the ideas we already have. So the concepts that constitute our knowledge become our reality. Even your idea of what God is, is a notion in your mind, which you learned from your parents. So you never really see what God is, because you already know.

The issue here is the belief that you know. You believe that you know who you are, you believe that you know the world, you believe that you know what existence is. What you actually know is your own mind. You don't know existence. You have lost the mystery that you live in. We all lose the mystery that we are, the mystery that surrounds us, the mystery that brings us wonder, freshness, and freedom. We have made our world into a fossil.

We have turned Being, mystery, God, into dead fossils. And we are looking for a new fossil that will make us feel alive and happy. We call these new fossils spiritual or psychological insights. Why not question all the fossils instead of running around looking for new ones?

We do not have to go anywhere to find reality. Freedom is not a matter of finding anything new. It is just questioning what we have always known, and recognizing that what we know is our own minds. The world that we know is composed of our knowledge, and we need to confront that knowledge at its foundation, and ask, "Is it true? Is this all there is? Isn't it possible that after all these years thinking a certain way, looking at the world from a certain perspective, reinforcing the conceptual structure in my mind—isn't it possible that in this process I have killed something? I have killed some subtlety, something alive, something that cannot be captured in an idea?"

We're always trying to capture our world in a word or an idea. This is fine, practically speaking, as we need to discriminate in order to function, to find our way around in the world. But when all our experience is filtered through concepts, we lose something. We lose aliveness and dynamism; we lose the mystery. We lose the living quality of existence.

So I think we have clarified our original statement, that our knowledge is the world we live. Our lived world—our feelings and actions, our sense of who we are—is the living out of the world of our conceptual knowledge. Wherever you go, whatever you experience, your world is nothing but the content of what you have known, what you have learned—the words, the concepts, and their interrelations. We call that the world. We don't really know the world. We don't know what exists. We don't know who we are. What we know are the ideas that we learn from our parents and the society around us, from the books we read, and stories we hear.

When we realize that different cultures conceptualize things differently, we might begin to confront and challenge our assumption that our known world is the actual world. We might become aware that another culture looks at the world in a different way, or has elements that we have never experienced. Cultural diversity makes our experience richer because it introduces new concepts.

When we first see a Japanese garden, for example, our perception is that it is alive and fresh, because we are seeing something novel. For an American, the Japanese garden is new and different, and perhaps it makes you a little uncomfortable, a little more awake, a little excited, to see it. But the more you see it, the more you get used to it; you end up seeing not the actual garden but "a Japanese garden," and after a while, it's just rocks over there.

So a new arrangement of things can bring us some aliveness and freshness because it jiggles our minds a little. Seeing things in a different frame makes us feel a little more dynamism. After a while, however, it becomes stale and uninteresting, so we have to invent new arrangements to try to feel alive again. It is the same with philosophy, with religion, with science. We have to keep changing things or we'll become completely dead.

I began by saying that the world we live in is nothing but the content of our knowledge, which is something we have absorbed from our parents and the society around us, which is a part of the history of humankind. So, the world we live in is the product of the history of humankind. All the concepts that have evolved, all the various combinations of ideas, the physical knowledge, social knowledge, religious knowledge, have become the world which is our knowledge.

A known world is a dead world. The actual world is in some deep sense unknowable, is a mystery, and is always changing. There is always change, there is always transformation.

The exploration we've begun today is the exploration of reality beyond mind. To know reality and to discover who we are beyond the ideas that we learned in childhood, we must confront those ideas.

On this level the Work is not a matter of exotic experiences, but of seeing the reality of the things we already know. When we see through the concepts that we already know, we can see the truth that is always there. To see through the concepts that have calcified our minds and our perceptions is to see reality freshly, immediately, to see it the way it is, not the way our minds have defined it. At the beginning, this might sound like an intellectual exploration, but actually we are confronting the intellectual. We're confronting the mind itself. We're challenging our mental notions so that we can see through them. So, in this phase of the Work, you might feel more mental than usual for a while. We will come to appreciate, however, that the mental knowledge is not just knowledge in our heads—it completely determines what we experience.

If we believe that we know reality, and we act and we react according to what we believe we know, there is no possibility of knowing or experiencing something new, something fresh. We will continue to rearrange our old world. What we want is to be able to live and participate in a world that is completely fresh, completely new, not determined by the past.

Penetrating the mental world is not easy. We will make this exploration more specific as we work with it, and deal with the various issues and perspectives relating to it. It is a big step to see that knowledge and the world it creates are not necessarily ultimately real but something we have learned.

To approach new knowledge, to become a new person, will happen through letting go of the old, not holding on to old concepts, which means not holding on to your mind. Our task, then, is not to take our knowledge as ultimate. This means to be willing to let go of our belief in the ultimate reality of the content the mind, of knowledge, at least for a while. This will feel like we are letting go of the mind itself, since we do not know the mind without content. But only this will allow us the possibility of seeing the world in its actuality and its truth. No matter how much psychological insight we have, how many inner spiritual experiences we have, how many times we see angels or talk with God, if our experience occurs still within the old concepts, no actual transformation of ourselves and our world will happen.

We are confronting our reality from its roots, from its basis. In time, hopefully, our experience will reveal the true reality that exists beyond the mind, beyond the ideas, the fresh awareness of how things actually are. The truth, or reality, or God, whatever we call it, is always here. Reality is not somewhere else, it is here, it is everything. It is the world when it is seen in its true nature, in its true light. When you can see the whole world, including yourself, without concepts, without these ways of knowing things you are accustomed to, you will see a completely fresh world, a new world. What is the truth that is actually here? Reality in its newness is beyond our personal history. What has happened or not happened in the past is irrelevant to what is now. What is now is just now and that's what really exists.

What is this something that we live in? What is it that exists? What is true existence? We need to be careful not to give this something that we are exploring a name right away because then we just turn it into another concept in our mental world. To be able to look with fresh eyes, we need to look without the mind that labels. When you label what your eyes see, the associations come with the label, and from that, all your reactions and emotions and identifications.

You want to be able to look without labeling, and thus to be free from having to react in the old ways. To see things without concepts, without the fixed elements of what we call the world, is the only way of knowing what is really here. As long as we see the world through old concepts, we will see our old concepts actualized again.

Our only hope of really seeing things as they are is to suspend the mind, to go through the mind. And, as we have seen today, to go through the mind means to suspend what we believe we know about the world, about ourselves, about reality, about everything. That is usually scary, and it will not be easy. It is quite a jump, but that is what we want to work on. Only when we can do this can we perceive what is called objective reality—what truly exists, what truly is. Only then do we know in a deep sense, in a real sense, what we are, what the world is, and what's really happening. This is the beginning of a real world, a real universe, a true living from the moment, from the now. Then true life happens. True existence is lived.

In a sense, what we are talking about today is something that cannot be talked about. How can you talk about something if you don't use concepts? When you are completely experiencing reality without concepts, you can't even say that something exists—existence is a concept. Ultimately, "experience" is a concept. We have tried to live according to these concepts; we have tried to know the world through them and fit our experience into them. What will happen if we don't do it that way? What will happen if our knowing is one hundred percent spontaneous?

THIRTEEN

Inside and Outside

This part of the teaching will be the deepest and finest level of our work so far. But working at this deep level has its price. I have observed that this level of the Work reveals which students truly love and want the truth, and which ones are seeking sensation or materialistic gain, or worshipping their own personal beliefs. I anticipate that many of you will not like this segment of the teaching, and that's fine. I won't mind if many of you decide that this endeavor is not for you and go somewhere else.

Most people tend to get into a rut, a slump, even in a Work school. Often students are inclined to twist the truth and the teaching around to fit their own personal beliefs or opinions or interests. This tendency basically protects and supports our little self and attempts to support our little life. But this is not the purpose of the Work. The purpose of this Work has always been and always will be the realization of the truth. To pursue this purpose means to put truth first and everything else second, until the time comes when you see that everything is truth. We will do this part of the Work in a way that will disturb everyone's comfort and everyone's inertia, so that each of you will either start doing the Work in a fresh, true way or you will go on your way somewhere else.

I would not like the school to be a place where people find comfort and a cozy support for the little self or the little life that they want to create. There are plenty of places in the world where people can do that. This Work is certainly not the place to make you comfortable and secure.

To truly do the Work and to live in the spirit of the Work means to sacrifice everything for it. If you do not have that spirit, you need to acquire it, because there is no other way. The Work is not for people to learn a career, to be successful in the world, to have more money. These things might happen as a result of doing the Work, but that is not its purpose. The Work might even take these things away from you. But if you really love the truth, you won't mind. The Work has always been like this, not only in this school. This part of the Work that we are embarking on will basically take things away from you. There is nothing for you to gain. We will continue to explore other elements of the Work in the weekends and other meetings, where we will deal more with some of the essential aspects and their related psychological issues. This element we're working with today, however, is important for helping us to remember the spirit of the truth.

You cannot do this Work if you are constantly arguing with it. If you are constantly questioning whether it is wrong or right, or whether it is for you or not, then it is better that you go somewhere else. This is friendly advice. It applies to each of you, regardless of how long you have been in the school, whether you have been here two days or twenty years. Truth has nothing to do with time. Some people believe that when they learn something, then they've got it, or they've got enough, or they can twist the truth for their own ends. It does not work that way. All that will happen for those who want to serve themselves rather than discovering or serving the truth, is that they will remain disconnected from the truth and continue the life of falsehood. You cannot use the Work for your personal aggrandizement, or for materialistic gains, or to get pleasure.

The Work requires us to give ourselves to the truth, always. It is true that the more you give yourself to the truth, the more your life will be full, but that is not the reason to do it. If you do the Work because you want your life to be full, you are already wanting materialistic gain, and because of that, you will disconnect yourself from the truth.

I hear remarks from many people such as, "I spend too much time on the Work, too many meetings, too many years." Bullshit! There is no such thing as spending too much time on the truth. It wouldn't be too much time if you spent a million years doing the Work. Spending a few hours a week for a few years in your life to actualize the truth and then complaining that you haven't actualized it—where is that coming from? You can complain forever to no avail. You do the Work sincerely, or you do not do it. You do it as long as you need to do it. You do it until it works.

The Work has always been like that. It is also true that different people will go to different levels of the Work; not everyone will go necessarily to the deepest dimensions. Some people will get to a certain level of understanding and realization, and that will feel like enough for them. They do not want more, or they feel that they do not need more. That is fine; then they can leave. Leaving is preferable to sticking around, pretending they're learning more, when they are just continuing the status quo. The Work is continuous growth, continuous change. It does not stay the same. Whenever it stays the same it is dead.

When the Work no longer makes you feel insecure and uncomfortable, it is either dead, or you do not need it. These are the only two alternatives. However, some people complain that they have a hard time. They complain that they are uncomfortable. They complain that they're not served enough food, or are not fed at the right time. Who said this is a nursery? Who said the Work is done according to the demands of the student? That applies for instance, in our physical work practice. Regardless of how much you have done it, regardless how much you have learned from it, you can still learn from it. And everyone, regardless of how much you have done it, how much you know about it, whatever else you have got to do, you need to continue doing it as if it is the first day of doing it. Always. Otherwise, it is better not to do it.

When you start approaching an aspect of the Work as if it is old for you, look at yourself; do not look at that aspect of the Work. What has happened to you that has prevented you from seeing the truth there, the freshness?

In my experience, the longer people learn from the Work, and the more they develop, the more they see the value and the necessity of doing the various tasks and practices of the Work, not the other way around. Some people think that the longer they do it, the more they learn, the less they need the various practices and activities. It does not work that way. The more you learn, the more you see how much you do not know. If the more you learn, the more you think you know, then that means you are not learning, you are believing. I remember some Zen masters saying that after enlightenment, what you need to do is to continue meditation. Just keep sitting. If the thought arises that you should stop sitting, you are deluding yourself.

The Work must continue until you cannot tell yourself apart from the truth, until you cannot tell yourself apart from the totality of all that exists, until you can experience yourself as the vastness of the universe, in all its purity and clarity and innocence. The Work does not stop even there. The work of realizing the truth is immense; the more you learn it, the more mysterious things become. The more you know, the less you feel you know. The bigger you get, the more you feel you need to work, and those who love the truth will love it by wanting to work. They will see that there is more truth to love. If you get into a rut where your small life is more important than the truth, that's the time to push on yourself ruthlessly, because then you are not really doing the Work.

I'm not saying that everyone should want the truth so completely; I'm saying that those who completely love the truth in that way will pursue it with this kind of dedication. Only these students can actually learn from the level of the Work that we are entering.

We tend to get lost in our mental concerns, our little preoccupations. Without intending it, we become focused, actually trapped, in a little corner of the universe. The more we are trapped, the darker our world gets, and the thicker and heavier it feels. It is the function of the Work to shake you off your position, until you realize that the Work is infinite—endless wonder, endless mystery, where security has no place. We need to establish our personal lives and our practical lives such that we can support ourselves and live somewhat comfortably. But from the perspective of the Work, supporting our lives should be done for the purpose of the Work, not the other way around. I know that many people do it the other way around—they want to use the Work so that they can support their little lives, their little selves. But if you do that, you just strengthen the ego, and make your little self more solid.

In our last meeting, we explored how the world we see is nothing but the knowledge we have accumulated—how our mind is our world. We will continue that exploration more specifically. This part of the teaching has to do with the nonconceptual dimension. Some of this material will be familiar to those of you with knowledge of spiritual traditions, and some of the material is unique to our Work. It requires an involvement, an interest peculiar to the reality we will be discussing. You need to be interested in the truth of this reality, not in what it will give you. If your concern is what it will do for you in your everyday life, you can forget it, because you will find out that from this perspective your personal life is a little bubble. As we go on, you'll probably be frightened, you'll feel insecure, you'll be angry sometimes. These reactions are natural. As long as you can explore your reactions rather than believing them and acting them out, you have the possibility of coming to know reality beyond your personal perspective.

So, our world is our knowledge. The world we live in is what we think we know. That brings us to the question: What does it mean to know? What is knowledge? What do we know and what don't we know? When we want to do the Work, when we want spiritual experience or spiritual insight, we tend to believe that spiritual work is an inward work. You look inside: Essence, spirit, Being, God, is inside you. This is true, but only in the lower levels of the Work. In the beginning, you have to look within, but finally, you have to look within not because the truth is inside you, but because the window that opens you to the truth is inside. The organ of perception through which we can see the truth is within.

Your own soul, your consciousness, is the organ of truth, the window to reality, and that's why you look inside. This does not mean that the truth of reality is inside; but for a long time the way we experience it is through the reality that's inside. We tend to believe that that's how things are—that essence is inside, spirit is inside, truth is inside.

At some point, we need to begin to see things more objectively. We need to question our assumptions about inside and outside. We need to wake up at a more fundamental level. We need to stop running after the illusion that truth is inside, and start waking up to the objective truth that is everywhere. For a long time, for many levels and dimensions, the Work of the truth has to do with experiencing things within you—Essence, essential aspects, spiritual experiences that are transforming, exciting, intriguing, and fulfilling. These experiences can bring a lot of excitement and joy into your life, which is very good.

If we allow this process to continue, and if we are truly interested in the truth, whatever the truth is, it won't stop there. Unfoldment won't just stop at any realization that remains internal, because internal experiences are limited. They take place within the mind, as part of your knowledge. Thus your experience remains governed by the perspective of personal mind, rather than by the perspective of the truth. So even though our inner experience might become more full and rich, without the perspective we are working on now, the world we look upon, our reality, will remain plain, ordinary, drab. We look around and see people, the sky, the trees, the cars, the street, and we feel, "I've known this for years and years. This is not the spiritual world. This is not what I want."

It is true that the method of the Work is to explore within your soul, within your psyche. This opens the window. But inner experience is not yet awakening. Inner experiences are not awakening; they are experiences of the path. They are helpful and necessary to continue the process. Without the openings and essential experiences, without the insights and openings to sweetness, value, and so on, most people will not have the stamina nor the motivation to continue. Such experiences are signs that you are moving. They encourage you, and indicate that, yes, you are getting in touch with something that you haven't seen, some part of the mystery, which can inspire you to go further and support you to continue.

Let's investigate this dichotomy that many people doing spiritual work experience, between the drab, ordinary, unexciting, old world around us—the physical world—and the spiritual. We think that it is spiritual to move away from the material world. To approach the Work this way presents us with a big problem. We want the Work to make us successful and secure in the physical world, and at the same time we want a spiritual life that has nothing to do with that, that is beyond it, that is inner, that is more spiritual, that is not physical. This is a split orientation. However, this split orientation contains a seed of truth that is not apparent to us. For instance, you believe that God is within, or God is over there, somewhere beyond the world. You feel as if this truth is something mysterious like a goody you'll find when you bite into one of your chocolates, or by doing strange things to your brain like ingesting some substance.

It is true that you can find a God in heaven, or you can find God inside your heart. But from the perspective of the teaching that we will work with here, these experiences happen within your mind, within your knowledge. They are not yet the objective truth, not yet the experience of awakening. To remain attached to your own mind is to be what I call the worshipper of personal beliefs. If you pursue inner experiences, you are what I call the seeker after sensation. If you want the Work to make you more comfortable in the world, more successful, famous, or rich, I call you then the one who wants materialistic gains. Ultimately, they are all the same. You remain the little self that wants something, that feels deficient, small, and empty, and wants some kind of reality to support it, whether that reality is God, Essence, truth, or whatever.

But this still does not come from the heart of truth. This heart will say to the truth, "Take me, get rid of me, I just want you to be there, whatever you are." The heart feels, "I really don't know what the truth is, but whatever it is, I wouldn't mind if it just takes over and only the truth remains. I do not even know what or where it is. Is it outside, inside, here, elsewhere—who knows? I love it, I love it so much I do not care what will happen, whatever it is."

If you do not feel this unconditional passion for the truth, if you are unwilling to submit completely to the truth, you remain a worshipper of belief, what was in the old days called the worshipper of idols, an infidel. If you are going to wake up, you will need to eliminate all your beliefs, all your ideas, all your needs, all your desires, so that you simply wake up and see the truth. You wake up as the truth. You need to go beyond looking at yourself from the perspective of deficiency versus fullness, from concerns about whether you are good or bad, weak or strong, small or large. All these things are just part of the self-centered perspective. What really matters? What does it matter, ultimately, whether you have a year or two of depression or misery, if ultimately you are the totality of the whole universe? What difference does it make whether you are living in a wonderful palace or a little cottage, if you realize that who you are, what you are, is the immensity from which the totality of the universe arises?

Some people tell me, "The way you talk about this makes me feel insecure. I do not even know how to be with people. I don't even have a secure job." Fine—go get your secure job. But that is not what I'm interested in. I am interested in the mystery of truth itself. From the perspective of the truth, the issues about whether you get your job or not, or whether you get married or not, are completely insignificant. Completely. It is insignificant whether you get what you want or not. From the perspective of the truth, everything is part of the expression of the beauty of the truth. It is the truth experiencing different things—whether happiness or misery. What difference does it make? You might say, "But that means I'm not important. You are saying my life is not important." Yes, that is exactly what I am saying. If you believe you are the little mental self, then your life is not important.

Your life is important only if you realize that you are the totality. If you want me to support the idea that your little life is important, you have come to the wrong place. I'm not going to support that attitude, because it is not the truth. Unless your little life is a little wave, a little expression, a little rain from the big truth, it does not have true support, is not real, and you might as well not live it. These words may seem harsh, but I see them as compassionate. To support the little point of view means supporting your little rock, the little corner you are stuck in, the view that makes you continuously feel depressed, small, and deficient.

We tend to look around at our world and feel, "This world is not spiritual. The spiritual world is inside, or in heaven, in paradise; it is somewhere else." The way I see it, God is nothing but what we perceive all the time, and the truth is nowhere else. There is no such thing as a truth that is somewhere else. Whenever we see truth, or God, or spirit, somewhere other than this actual world we are living in, it means we are still telling ourselves stories. They might be wonderful, sublime stories, but they are stories nonetheless.

The mind is very tricky, very subtle, very powerful. And to see the truth means to know the mind, to know it to the extent of being able to see beyond it, and of being able to use it instead of it using you. In some sense the mind is the most powerful thing there is, because it creates our world. What do I mean by that? Just look at the world you live in, the drab, ordinary world that you believe is not spiritual, the world you go around in from here to there, driving your car, meeting your friends, doing your job, and once in a while having a spiritual experience. You live in a world that you look at as made of physical things, moving around. You look at your car, for instance. What is your car? A Honda. Very good, now you know what you have—a Honda. Say you have a Honda, a Japanese car, and it is red. 1986. Automatic, with this and that extra equipment. You believe you know a lot about your car. Yes, you know a lot about your car, but you do not actually know the car directly. What do you know about your car? You say, "My car is Japanese." What do you know? You say your car is a Honda. What does that mean? What do you know? It is a name you have learned to call it. Someone else could call it something else. What does it say about the car? The name might help you distinguish it from a Chevrolet. But with all these labels, you still do not know anything intrinsic about the car yet. You could get more sophisticated—"I know what a car is, it is a vehicle made out of metal and rubber and things like that." You have become more sophisticated, but what do you know? What is metal for you? What is rubber for you? Is metal or rubber something you know? Or words you have learned? Do you perceive rubber or metal actually?

You might look at a tree, and say you know the tree. What do you know? How do you know? Do you know *about* the tree, or do you really know the tree? You think that because you can call it an apple tree, you really know the tree. Perhaps the closest thing you know about the apple tree is something about apples. Maybe you have eaten an apple. But you do not know an apple completely. What do you know about the apple? Perhaps eating its fruit is the closest you can come to knowing an apple tree. You know how it tastes. Sour. Sweet. You feel its texture. And you think you know. What is sourness? What is sweetness? Do you think that if you can say it is sour or sweet, you know it? What is it you know? Aren't sour and sweet just parts of your mind?

The sense of something being sour or sweet means nothing to you but a repetition of experiences you have had in the past, by which you differentiate taste. So you can tell a difference between sour and sweet. The words "sour" and "sweet" are applied to slightly different tastes or sensations in your mouth. So maybe you are getting closer now to finding out what it is you know about the tree, the apple tree. You have taken it to a sweet or sour taste maybe, or perhaps to texture. And you are still sanguine about knowing sour or sweet. "I've tasted sour and sweet before many times." Are you really knowing, now, what is sour and what is sweet?

We can take our exploration down to the next level of refinement; we can explore something like sweetness. What is sweetness? It is a taste that we've put a name on. It is a taste, a sensation in the mouth. We have put a label on it. We call this sweet. So each time we experience it again we recognize it, and we think we know what sweet is. We've left the apple itself in the background. Do we know about the apple? Do we know about the apple tree? Just getting to the sweetness, we cannot even connect to the apple, let alone to the tree. So how are you going to know about what a tree is? Is there knowledge other than the ideas you have had about the tree, the names you have given to it, the memories you have about it, that bring a recognition? When you see it you say, "That's an apple tree; I recognize it because I've seen it before so I know it." You have certain names associated with certain pictures, certain impressions. But when you look to see whether you really know it, instead of knowing *about* it, you have to get a little closer, look more intimately, to something like the apple. Then you have to leave even the apple, to get to something like sweetness, to experience a little more directly. We are moving from one level of perception to another, not only between the categories of the mind. The categories of perception little by little are getting closer to our own personal direct experience.

Now you are tasting a sweet apple. If you do not think of it as an apple, if you do not use the word, "apple," then you leave behind your mind's experience of the past, and go about it wanting to know it in a fresh way. You really want to know the apple not according to what you have experienced in the past, not according to what you have heard, or known, in the past. You want to know about the apple in a direct, fresh way. If you do not use the word, "apple," which means not to have the associations with the word "apple" from the past, what are you experiencing? Is this still an apple?

Let's take this exploration closer to ourselves now, to our immediate experience. Take a moment to sense yourself, to experience something in yourself. Be aware of your inner atmosphere, your inner environment. You might find sensations, emotions, feelings, tensions. You might say you are feeling sad, angry, pain, tension. Well, what do you mean by these words? You have the words: sadness, anger, pain. These are words you have learned to apply to certain categories of experience, and all of this is your mind.

How do you experience yourself if you do not use the words? The words are not the experience. If you do not use the words what are you experiencing? What is really there? Just be aware, whatever is there. Whatever experience you have, if you dissociate from the word in your mind, what do you experience? You say, "I know sadness," or "I know pain," or "I know tension." If you eliminate the words with all their connotations, what is it you really know right now? I am advising you to do this exploration right now. When you say you experience a nerve pain, ask yourself, what is a nerve? Do you know what a nerve is? Have you ever been a nerve? A nerve is a word. You have probably seen a drawing of it in some book.

You notice furthermore that your inner environment has different kinds of feelings; maybe there is some tension;

you might be aware of some emotions, some temperature variation. How about if you do not use the labels "tension," "emotions," "temperature"? All these words which connect with knowledge that comes from the past make you believe you know what you are experiencing.

If you do not use this past knowledge or the labels—if you want to know directly, right now—your experience will be fresh. What is it you are experiencing? You might be aware that there is pain here, and there is emptiness there, but if you realize that these labels are just words, you might notice that what those words do is differentiate one form of experience from another. Saying "tension" differentiates something from something else that is not tension. If we think there is a hurt here, there is a differentiation between pain and something that is not pain.

So words create demarcations. Now if we do not use the words, what happens to that demarcation? Is it as definite? What happens? The mind is creating that demarcation between pain and not-pain; your experience, your conceptualizing and labeling, and your concern about it, go together. The moment you stop conceptualizing it, stop using the words, the demarcation begins to lose its definiteness. Check in with yourself now. Do not think about what I am saying—sense your experience directly. What you know consists of words connected to slight variations in your sensations. Ultimately, when you sense yourself, if you do not say that there is anger or sadness, hurt, pain, heat, or cold—if you do not use these words that are pregnant with all kinds of meaning from the past—if you look at it in a fresh way, isn't it all just sensations? Is it anything other than sensations that you have names for? This collection of sensations might have a slight flavor you call pain, and another collection of sensations might have a slightly different flavor that you call tension. A third collection of sensations with a slightly different flavor you might call pleasure. But they are all sensations. Are they anything more than that?

What we call knowing our inner experience is nothing but superimposing concepts on our sensations. And as you focus on your experience through the filter of the concept, the sensation will tend to continue in the same way, and become more solid. When the sensation is pain, it tends to persist as we identify it as pain. If it is felt as tension, it continues to be tension, because the mind fixes it as soon as it sees that that is what it is.

What would happen to your experience if you changed the names of everything inside you? Could you call those new labels knowledge? What we call inner experience is nothing but the mind, words in the mind that you have learned from others, or out of the dictionary. We've been told many times, "What you call this is tension." After a while, there really is tension. Before you had the word "tension," there was no tension. God knows what was there. Before you had the word "pain," who knows what it was— some sort of intense sensation.

As you sense yourself, you experience all these sensations inside you now, and the less you use words to describe them the less the demarcation will be there. The form is not as solid, not as definite. This means that the solidity of your knowledge is decreasing, becoming thinner, as you separate your concepts from the experience, because we want to know what the experience is without your ideas about it. You believe you know this world; I am saying, let's find out. What do you really know about it if you do not use your words? What do you know directly? What is the direct, fresh experience without the past? To say that you know that what you are experiencing now feels like tension, means you are using past knowledge. Your mind is in the past. You are not completely here now; your experience is not completely direct. You are looking at experience through the filter of a concept you learned in the past. What do you really know right now?

If you are experiencing yourself without labeling your experience, you might become concerned about communicating your experience to me. How could you do that without words? But maybe you do not have to use words to tell me that knowledge. Maybe I'll know what you know regardless of what words you use. We want to know. To know implies using words, right? Then what is it you know right now? Is all you know just words? If all you know is just words, why do you say that you know the world? Why do you believe you know yourself? Why do you assume that you know your car? Why do you say you know the table if what you know is just words? We are trying to see experientially that you do not know what you believe you know. What you know is mainly words; what you know is so veiled by all these words that you haven't the vaguest idea what it is you are actually perceiving. When someone asks you whether you know something, and you know the name of that something, you conclude that you do know that something. But what is the direct perception without the words?

If you see the world directly, what do you see? What do you experience? If you look at your inner experience without the words and concepts, what do you experience? What do you perceive? Maybe you can tell me what happens in terms of changes. Is there a change that happens? What is the tendency? You might not be able to say completely, exactly, what you experience; trying to put it into words is a stretch.

Little dots flashing on and off—that's basically what sensations are, right? If you really look inside yourself without using words, without using the mind—which means you aren't using the past, which is not here any more—what remains is little dots. First it is just sensations, a swarm of sensations that collect in various constellations, just as the universe has different constellations of dots, which we call stars, or planets or galaxies or clouds. But what are they? Do we know them? We call this collection of dots a table; that collection we call a rug. The concept puts certain constellations together, and then we think we know what is there. We believe we know the world. But when we know the world through concepts, the world is dead, because what we know are words—dead, empty words from the past. You do not know the thing directly then. If you do not use those familiar discriminations to recognize your experience, if you look at your inner experience directly, without the mind, what do you experience? What do you see? What is there?

Experience is always changing; there is always movement. So you end up with a collection of sensations that are in constant flow and change. If you stay with it, if you do not use the word "sensations," what do you experience? What do you perceive?

Student: It is more a negative experience, and I do not know any more what is me, what is something else.

AHA: Right.

S: Loss of differentiations. I do not really know what is one thing . . .

AHA: Right. You start losing your sense of *me* and *other*, *inside* and *outside*. Right? Because *inside* and *outside* are words. *Me* and *other* are words. So what is the experience without the words? What is the perception without the words? What we are seeing so far is mostly our words applied to our perception. The world is drab, old, and ordinary because our words are old. You see a tree, it is a tree. I've seen a tree a thousand times before. Nothing new in it. If you do not call it a tree, what do you see? Is it old? Can it be old? The tree cannot be old because the tree you see here is not the tree from yesterday. So what is the experience without the words, if you do not say it is sensation? What is the perception?

S: It seems that there is response. I do not know where that comes from. There is no . . . It is like there is immediacy. The shadow comes, the color comes, it responds, it goes out. And it is constantly changing. Constantly, within . . . as one perceives these dots and colors and patterns moving.

AHA: So you see colors and patterns and dots, right? And the colors, you recognize them?

S: Rather than recognize them, it is like a response to warmth, coolness, dark, light.

AHA: Right. But these are words too.

S: That's right.

AHA: Warmth, coolness, right? Red, green, dark, light. You are still in the mind, you see? And you think you know. You say, "I know what I'm experiencing. It is green, it is black, it is dark, it is light. Words from the dictionary. But if you do not respond, if the mind does not respond for a minute, for a second, the mind does not bring in a label, what is the perception?

S: Constant changing.

AHA: Constant changing, right. Now, the *changing*, isn't that a word?

S: Yes, and I was going to say movement first, but that's still a word.

AHA: It is still a word. You see how there is always a trap if you go from one word to another word, the word just becomes more general, more diffused. But they're still words. You see? They are just as good as other words. They're all words, they fall in the same category. They're concepts.

S: Is the word coming through in order to respond to your question?

AHA: Might be. It might be coming to respond to my question, that's possible. But, you know, the idea here is not to respond to my question. The point here is to see what is the perception. What is the pure perception? Forget about answering my question.

S: *Perception* is a word too.

AHA: *Perception*'s a word too. This is not a quiz, you see. It is a guided meditation.

S: There is a perception of some differentiation, a perception of structure, that things . . . It is as if, seeing the tree is sort of like seeing, feeling it coming out of the archetype of tree, but now . . . I mean that's just a way to describe it, sort of, but it is like now it is only coming out right now as a form, as structured reality. In other words, it is not that there is not any differentiation of structure, but that . . . it is as if there is such a thing as a purified word, sort of, or a . . . there are categories . . .

AHA: That's true.

S: But they're not solid, exactly, and they're not about things. They're about . . . I do not know how to describe it, but there is differentiation. It is not all just dots and . . .

AHA: There is differentiation, I know, but if you suspend the word what happens to the differentiation?

S: What I see is like electrical energy. The dots are energetic.

AHA: Yeah. So it feels like electrical energy and that's a good way of describing it. But you see, you resorted to words. And that makes sense to you now, right? Like electrical energy. But the moment you do that, you make it an old thing. It is not completely fresh.

S: But you cannot really communicate without using words.

AHA: That is true. At some point the communication will break down, but I do not know whether we have reached that point.

S: Well, we have to go back awfully far because according to the tradition, the first thing Adam was charged with was naming everything.

AHA: Yeah, that's what we're doing here. Going beyond Adam.

S: That is a long way.

AHA: Before Adam came. *Adam*'s a word too, right?

S: *Adam*'s a word.

AHA: A *word* is a word. First there was a word. *Word* is a word.

S: When I try to suspend the words, I experience myself as a magnetization of those concepts. Any perception. The concepts, first they're vague, then they get more specific. Things come rushing in.

AHA: So the concepts become like magnets. They bring things together somehow, you see? We want to see, do we really know the world?

S: We experience it but I do not think we really know it.

AHA: What is it you experience?

S: Well . . .

AHA: Do you know the experience without words?

S: No.

AHA: Well, that's what we want to see. Maybe that's what needs to happen. Before we say that something is an old thing, we need to see is it really an old thing? What is it that's old? Is it this world that we see or is it our words? Is it the environment that is old or is it our mind? We blame it on the world, and say it is old and drab. We say, "I want to go somewhere where it is more pure, more spiritual." But what is old and drab is your mind, your words. It is not the trees, it is not the rocks, it is not the room, it is not these people. It is not what we perceive that's old, it is the labels we put on them. Let's find out what it is like if we do not put the labels on them. Do they seem old then?

S: Without the labels I definitely get out of my head. It is more like my organism has a response, a whole response to whatever is the object.

AHA: That is true, your organism has a response. But there is still a trap. There is a trap of response, and before that, the trap of organism. Both are words, concepts, still. See how tricky the mind is? It moves from one word to another. See how the mind is trying to explain it? It cannot be explained.

There is nothing you can ultimately say, but you have to exhaust all the words. You cannot say, "Oh you can't say it . . ." while you are still believing your mind. When you say you can't say it, you are using words: *you can't say it*. And each one of them means something to you. And as long as you can say that, it means something to you; you are still explaining it. You have to say you cannot explain it without knowing what you are saying. Otherwise you are still trapped in the words.

S: You could work yourself to a non-verbal . . . something like "bleah!" (Laughter)

AHA: The way the Zen master used to do this is to tell you a story. One Zen master asked his students if they knew what the Zen truth is. And one student came up and the teacher, said "Okay, what is the Zen truth?" The student slaps the teacher in the face. And everybody thought, "Uh-oh." And unthinkingly, the master slapped the student back. The student goes and sits down. They both look happy. And everybody's wondering, "What is the meaning of this? Is it slapping each other? That's the meaning of Zen?"

We kill the world, we kill our lives, we kill our perception by believing that we know. I'm just analyzing it to help you see that we do not really know, not directly, not in an immediate way. What we know is through words and concepts that we acquired from the past. The meanings and connotations of words has a lot to do with what your mother and father believed. The world you see, you are seeing through your mother's and father's eyes. You are not really seeing through fresh eyes. You are seeing through your mother's eyes, and the eyes of the mother of your mother, and the mother of that mother. It goes back to the beginning. But if we can look innocently, purely, directly, then we might see whether we know or not. And the moment we say we know it, the moment we say, "I know who I am," or we say, "I know what life is, I know what death is, I know what a table is, I know what this world is about," we put a big barrier on our perception. The barrier is your words, your knowledge, your mind, your past, your experience, and what you know is no longer the world.

S: I've had the experience of listening to music that was so beautiful that I *was* the music. As soon as my mind came in and said, "Wow, this is so beautiful," it wasn't that beautiful anymore. Is that relevant to what we're talking about?

AHA: Right. What we see around us we do not really know directly, right now, in terms of immediacy. We need to see that fact in a very deep and fundamental way. You need to see that when you look at the table you do not know what you are looking at. What you know is a word, the concept of a table. You do not know what you are looking at. And the moment you really see through the word, you see that the reality that you are seeing around you is a mystery; that we live in complete, pure mystery; that the world around us that is old, drab, and normal is actually a wonder, a mystery. It is a mystery that defies our minds, that defies our best efforts.

But we kill that mystery, we separate ourselves from it by putting up a barrier of words and concepts. Then the best thing we can do is know it through words and concepts, through the old. But if you confront your assumptions, you see that in reality, you do not really know. When you say, "I know this table is made out of wood," what are you saying? What is wood to you? What do you know? Do you really know wood the way wood knows itself? It is something you have seen, you have touched, you have read things about, you have used. But you still do not know what wood is. *Wood*, ultimately, is a word, and there is a mystery underlying that word, but the mystery is eluding you through the word *wood*. But you see the words, our mind, is actually what we perceive. We not only perceive *through* the mind, we perceive *only* our mind. When I look around, I see the table, I see people, but what I'm seeing is my mind. The table is not separate from my mind, from the word *table* in my mind. The person is not separate from the concept of person in my mind. It is the same thing. It is my mind that I see around me. And if I want to penetrate beyond my mind and see what is there, it is a mystery. It is unknowable, completely, one hundred percent unknowable.

It is so unknowable that the moment you begin to get a glimpse of it, your mind is blown to smithereens. You realize that your mind lays a kind of curtain over things, a veil, a colored sheet with drawings on it that overlays our reality and says, "That is reality." But the reality is beyond that: you open that curtain, open the window and it is unknowable. If you truly look, you do not even know you are looking, and you disappear. Your mind is there, but nobody's looking. The reality is there and you do not say there is mind or there is reality. And then, what you perceive, although it is mysterious, it is unknowable, we give it a name. We call it *truth*, we call it *God*, we call it *reality*. These are just words, words to refer to the unknowable, to the unknown, to the mystery. We can say these words knowing that they do not describe something, but are pointers to what is ultimately mysterious. It is not somewhere else—it is not inside, it is not outside, it is not in heaven. It is nowhere. It is all that exists without even saying "all" or saying "that exists." You see? You cannot say anything after a while.

But in this process you have to go all the way with the word, all the way, exhaust your words, your mind. You do not stop and say, "I read in one of those Zen books that you cannot know reality. Reality is beyond words . . . okay, that's it." Bullshit! That does not work because what you are doing there is using your mind and believing your mind, and maybe believing that you are going beyond the mind.

You are not seeing the truth, the mystery. The mystery appears when you use the words all the way, looking honestly, genuinely, truthfully at your own experience, and realize that what you are seeing is your mind and nothing else. You cannot see this by using some belief, or remembering a story you heard from someone. You actually perceive, "This table is my mind. It does not matter that I feel that I am touching it." It is like in your dreams—you could touch a table in your dream. Isn't it your mind you are touching? You do not believe that you are really touching a table in your dream. Why do you think you are touching a table now? It is the same thing. It is your mind, and you can actually perceive it is your mind if you can just stop for a minute believing that you know. If, for a second, you stop believing that you know what reality is, if you stop being arrogant for one second, then you might see that it is your mind and all its concepts that you are seeing when you believe you see the world.

The real world is nothing but the beauty that expresses the truth, the reality, the mystery that, in itself, is completely unknowable and inexpressible. Seeing this, we see that God is not somewhere else, that spirit is not something else, it is nothing specific, nothing in particular, nothing in the past or the present or the future, here or there, and has nothing to do with these. All these things are words anyway. *God* is a word. *Truth* is a word. If we are simply knowing a word, what is the mystery then? The mystery is not somewhere else, the mystery is nothing but our world, reality itself when we truly perceive it. There is nothing else, nowhere else; there is no heaven somewhere where God lives, running the show. This is God and he's not running the show, he's just living.

To see this we first need to dare not to know. We need to acknowledge our humility, which is not just being good and spiritual. Humility means to objectively see that you do not know, not to think that something is wrong with you because you cannot know. Nobody can know. You cannot know the mystery. The only thing you can know about the mystery is that it is unknowable and untouchable. You see it, you perceive it, but you do not know what it is. The moment you try to penetrate it, you forget you are trying to penetrate it.

When we're doing the Work, we're not trying to reach a reality inside us, to have some little experience, some little sensation. We're trying to experience what is the actual state of affairs. What is the truth? What is the reality? What is really happening? What is here? We're not trying to climb some divine ladder until we get all this light and talk to God over there, "We pray to you, O God." Who is praying? Who is there? *God* is a word. *Prayer* is a word. *You praying* is all words. What is it beyond those words? The word *prayer*, with all the feelings you have about it, has a lot of your mother and father in it, and the church you went to. It is all stale. Can you truly pray while you forget everything that has ever happened to you from this moment backward? What would prayer mean then? What does God mean if you forget all that? If you believe God truly exists, that he's really there, you do not need to remember anything from the past. You do not need to remember what Christ said, or what your mother said, or what your church said. If you believe, truly, that God exists, you will be willing, right now, to just drop all your belief in your ideas and apprehend it. Let it happen. Do not tell me, "No, no, I really believe in God. I have to pray to God." Bullshit! These are all stories you tell yourself because you still do not believe in God. If you actually did believe in God you would drop it; your belief would become knowledge. Then you would feel, "Why should I believe? I know. Why should I take what someone said in the past and apply it to God? If God is there he'll show up."

Conceptualizing is nothing but putting a boundary around part of reality and imagining that boundary actually creates something. It is the same thing with feelings and emotions. We put boundaries around them, and then we make those boundaries define things we take to be real. Then there is anger and grief and pain and all that. These things are nothing but boundaries. If we go beyond the name there is just an awareness of something. There will be a sensation, and sensations take forms, and we give these forms names. If you go beyond the names and differentiations, there is an awareness of presence, of something. That's what we call consciousness. Ultimately, all sensations are nothing but consciousness. There is consciousness of consciousness, right? Pure consciousness, then, without any differentiation.

Consciousness is the last concept, the last form. And it is hard to say it is a concept, because it is just the fact of consciousness. Beyond that, there is no consciousness. If you go beyond consciousness, it is a blackout. If you continue investigating, seeing the concepts, seeing the forms, at some point you forget you are seeing concepts. And then you wake up again. That is a resurrection. The world is back, but fresh.

S: Well, in one sense it seems like if you get a fresh perception, in the way you have been talking, there is nothing there. You do not perceive anything. If you really have a fresh perception, take away all the concepts, then there is nothing there, because there is no differentiation. The closest I come to what I feel is a fresh perception, I still have differentiation. I do perceive things even without names . . . and I cannot tell whether I'm still . . .

AHA: A fresh perception does not mean there is no differentiation.

S: Well, how . . .

AHA: While you were talking I was looking at you. I'm seeing you without the conceptualization about who you are.

S: But how do you see me if you do not have a concept . . .

AHA: I see phenomenon occurring there.

S: But how do you differentiate this phenomena from everything else in the room?

AHA: I'm seeing it as part of everything, not separated. Like part of a tapestry, or a rug. There are differentiations, but all of it is one rug.

S: What causes any differentiation at all, then?

AHA: It is possible to go beyond identifiable differentiations, if you go beyond the mind. But as long as you are looking with the mind you see knowable differentiations. It is possible to go beyond the past and still see differentiation, but the differentiation then does not have the labeling, does not have the past put in it. It just looks like a picture. There is differentiation without separation, without knowing.

S: Okay, well . . . there were very distinct outlines.

AHA: There could be distinct outlines. That's what I mean by the resurrection, you see. First you have to go through the usual perception of the world, right? Go through your concepts. When these are blown away, and all the conceptual goes away, all the differentiation goes away, nothing is left. Then you disappear, and when you come back again the world comes back, but it is a different world.

S: But then, is it concepts that create those distinctions?

AHA: No. I mean, you might be looking without thinking "This is a table." But you are seeing something there. You are seeing the table without saying it is a table. Your mind is empty, not thinking. It is not recognizing. You could see without recognizing.

S: Now I'm confused. Let's say I'm looking at something and I just notice a line between dark and light. Is that fresh or is that . . . I'm getting confused. That's a concept . . .

AHA: You are confused between two levels. There is one level, the usual level, where you can see everything as real.

You see the concept as real. When you see beyond concept, you could still see differentiation, but you see them as concepts. You see? I mean, I'm looking at you and I see you. It is Jessica there, and Lance nodding to sleep. There is Tinka writing in her notebook. All these things exist, right? But I see you as pictures in a movie. I do not take you to be the solid reality that you usually assume you are.

S: Is what you are seeing there separate from the past? I'm confused between . . .

AHA: Yeah. You have to be separate from the past to see it.

S: To see it that way?

AHA: Yeah. You are in the present, you see. The more you see that way the more you directly apprehend the mystery, too. You could see the mystery sort of peering through the concepts. The concept is like a transparent film through which the mystery looks you right in eyes. And if you keep looking, the concept by itself thins away and disappears.

S: I actually felt sometimes that my seeing anything as a thing was dependent upon my seeing myself as a thing. That there . . . when, the minute I conceptualized this little bug walking across, there would have to be . . . I would be positing someone who was seeing it. And so that got more and more clear so that, the person who was talking about boundaries, it is like my self-boundaries became more and more rigid and solid and everything. And I finally felt for quite a long time that I was trapped in this terrible world of concepts, you know, like this huge weight that was violating me, or violating something, because it got more and more opaque. But it all had to do with having to postulate that there was a *me* who was seeing these things.

AHA: The moment you see one thing in the world, you have to be there with it, even if that one thing is God. If you postulate even God or the truth as something separate from you in the world, you have to be there in relation to it. There has to be an object relation. Then there is the separateness and the isolation, all of that. You cannot see concepts as real without having a concept of yourself.

S: That was the thing that was the most apparent to me, that the more I looked at it that way the more everything became solidified into all these separate things. But when I would spot something and see something, the concept wasn't there until Mary would say, "What is the concept?" And with inanimate objects it was always what it was used for, and with animate it was movement and phenomena and color. Especially if I looked at the back of a person's head. If I saw their face and recognized them, the experience began to change from phenomena then to a memory of who that was.

AHA: Recognition. That's basically what the concepts are for. They're for practical things. You need to have a concept of the table so that you can use it. But that does not mean we know what the reality is. The fact that we can use it, does not mean we know it.

S: Well, that's what I began to feel as I would watch that. I realized I had no judgments about it, but it was all seen as how it was going to be used. A lot of times in my art work I'll put objects in juxtaposition to each other, like a purse on a head. But as I watched this I realized it was still a purse. I still saw it as a purse on a head and that was funny but that's still what it was. It was an object being used for something other than what it was meant to be used for.

AHA: And the ultimate outcome of that perspective, that there are objects to be used, is materialism. If you keep going that direction and forgetting that there is reality beyond the usefulness of things, finally you arrive at a completely material universe of discrete objects. And these objects are completely disconnected from the spirit. Then we start looking for the spirit inside ourselves, or inside one of the objects, while it is everywhere. It is everything. So, what we want to see from today's experience is the fact that

Essence or Being or God or truth is not somewhere else, is not something else, it is not something otherworldly. It is quite worldly, in the sense that it is all that we experience any time, at any moment. That is it. There is nothing else. But that it is it. It is the truth only when we realize its mystery, its unknowableness. As long as we perceive it as something we know, we're not seeing the truth, we're seeing our minds. The world we live in, including us, is an unknowable mystery. We do not actually know it.

We have concepts about many things—the table, the rug, electricity, life, earth. We have all these concepts, all these words, and from these we construct stories, theories that explain the world, explain us to ourselves. We call that knowledge, and we rest then in the security that now we know. There is me, and there is you, and there is the world. I have this life, I'm going to die one of these days, I have kids, and I do not have this or that: this whole big story that you explain and use. But this story is made out of the building blocks of words and concepts, so all the world that you know is a story. You do not know what is really there, what is actually happening. This is not bad, though many people think they should know. They believe that if you do not know what is happening, or feel you do not know, you are deficient. But our perspective is that when you start feeling you do not know, you are beginning to be truthful and humble. You do not know, not because you are bad or deficient, but because you cannot know. You cannot know because the truth is not knowable in the way we think things can be known.

So today we learned something about knowing. What we call our knowledge is nothing but a recognition based on concepts taken from the past. It is labeling things. I mean not just rugs, but things like divine light, angels, love. All these things are concepts too. They are just as conceptual as a rug or a tree. They're not more spiritual. They are the same thing, ultimately. They are created by your mind in the sense that they are concepts too. We're not saying concepts are bad, we're simply saying they are concepts. We have to see what the knowledge of the mind is, what true perception is. One of the most powerful ways of waking up is to see that what we think we know, we do not really know. To acknowledge our profound ignorance, our deep, fundamental, unchangeable ignorance. And that ignorance really, that profound ignorance, is ultimately our salvation rather than our deficiency. That ignorance is the entry, the door to the wonder, and the mystery.

FOURTEEN

Concepts and Thinking

I have discussed before that there are two complementary approaches in our work, the psychodynamic and the phenomenological. Psychodynamic work deals with personal issues that are generally determined by conditioned patterns from early childhood. The phenomenological approach involves exploration of perception and cognition. This means confronting and seeing through limitations on our awareness that are not dependent on personal issues. The phenomenological barriers ultimately reduce to the barrier of making reality mental, taking concepts to be truth, to be reality. All phenomenological issues finally dissolve into a consideration of conceptual reality. Psychodynamic issues, the personal patterns, are based upon images, memories, and events (and constellations of these) but each image, memory, or event is based on words or concepts.

All psychodynamic issues are based on concepts; so if you have an issue of difficulty in separating from your mother, we can deal with that psychodynamically in terms of what actually happened between you and your mother. But that issue is not determined only by what happened between you and your mother; more fundamentally, it is based on the fact that in your mind there is such a category as separation. The concept of separation has to be there before there can be any issue about separation from mother. And the concept of separation implies the concept of mother and the concept of self. The whole issue of separation would not exist if there were no concepts. All psychodynamic issues ultimately are based on concepts, and so finally reduce to phenomenological considerations, which ultimately reduce to the question of the conceptual mind. So the ultimate or most direct method of work is phenomenologically working through concepts.

Most spiritual techniques are based on the need to go beyond concepts, and beyond the words that reflect them. To see reality as it is, to experience the truth as it actually stands, one must go beyond one's mind, beyond one's words, beyond one's ideas. This is why it has been very important for us here to understand concepts, to understand what a concept is. How do concepts affect our lives, our minds? How do we create our reality through concepts? It is simple but not easy to understand what a concept is. The moment you understand truly what a concept is, you go beyond concepts. You begin to perceive nonconceptually, to see without the overlay of your own mind, your past history and prejudices. In most spiritual traditions and teachings, the ultimate point of view is that you have to go beyond the mind to see and know reality directly, without veils.

We work with psychodynamic issues not because working through these issues will ultimately bring us to reality or complete freedom, but because we are cut off from reality by so many entrenched concepts. We believe in the ideas and memories that have conditioned us so completely that we have to focus on some of them and their associations to lighten them up, before we can even entertain the possibility of approaching them as concepts. With all the memories and feelings you have about your mother, it is very difficult to start seeing that *mother* is a concept. You see? We have to deal with all the psychodynamic issues to get a little space from them before you can come to a place where you can truly see that *mother* is a concept, and doesn't really exist in the manner you normally believe.

The other reason psychodynamic work is important is that many of the concepts, especially the main concepts that we believe in, are unconscious. We have unquestioned belief in concepts that we don't even know about. This is why we need to make the unconscious conscious. We have to be aware of the notions that control our experience before we can make them more transparent. But at some point we have to come to the question of concepts themselves. We need to see how we view ourselves and our reality conceptually. Otherwise, psychodynamic issues will persist forever. There are millions of them. We have to penetrate to a place beyond concepts to really penetrate into reality, because this penetration into nonconceptual reality will expose our conceptualizations.

To understand more about concepts, what they do and how they develop, I will read you a chapter from Tarthang Tulku's last book, *Knowledge of Freedom*, and discuss it and work with it. It's a chapter about concepts called "Limits on Meaning." It will give us a sense of what concepts do and this will bring more texture to our understanding of concepts.

We all live within an inner world of images, thoughts, and memories that shift continually, evoking a rich texture of feelings, emotions, and moods. Sometimes images arise vividly in our minds and spark a chain of thought; at other times we can sense our minds bringing an idea into focus. At first we may simply sense that we are seeing images or thinking thoughts, but soon thought becomes more substantial; we are aware of the actual words in our minds as we think or express them in speech or in writing.

The words expressing images and thoughts are concepts, linked together in strings that clarify their relationships. Concepts are the building blocks of our language, and their meanings are the substance of our knowledge. Many concepts we use today had their origin long ago. Throughout human history, one concept has grown out of another, branching and proliferating like vines in a jungle.

Concepts may be simple identifiers like 'tree' and 'house' or more abstract notions like 'freedom', 'love', or 'justice'. They are built up through a process of distinctions, following a logical pattern that contrasts 'this' and 'not-this'. 'Green' is distinguished from 'not-green'; 'tree' is distinguished from all that is 'not-tree'. These distinctions depend upon each other—'tall' takes its meaning in comparison with 'short', 'big' has meaning in comparison with 'small'.

Thus concepts don't have meaning on their own: There is no such thing as "tall" without "short"' So "tall" cannot stand on its own. It's relative.

One way of seeing how we create concepts is to consider, for instance, the concept of mountain. As the Zen saying goes, "First there is a mountain, then there is no mountain, then there is a mountain." We start studying by seeing there is a mountain. So we investigate, what is a mountain? Suppose you're driving on the plains and a mountain comes into view. Where does the mountain start? There's the plain, then a curve arises and the mountain comes up. Where does it start? The point where the curvature begins, do you call that the mountain? Suppose you say that a mountain is something that protrudes out of the earth. You've taken part of the earth, one part, and said, "It's bulging. It's different from flat." Right? So you call that a mountain, and this flat land. But it's all earth, right? So a mountain is a bulging out of flat lands. But that doesn't completely do it—how about a little hill two inches tall? It's the same thing: the bulging out of land. Is that a mountain? It's the same thing, except there's a difference in size. So we have to invent another concept for a molehill, another concept to differentiate size. But is there a molehill in reality? Is there a mountain in reality? It's all relative to us, the observers; the mountain is a mountain in relation to our size.

There is no mountain that exists on its own. We see distinctions in reality; one perception differs from another. We call one perception a "mountain" and another one something else, and then we believe that there is a mountain. After you use the word for years, a "mountain" has reality. You believe that it actually exists on its own, independent of your mind. It's not easy for us to see the import of this phenomenon, the significance of our conceptualization of a mountain. When you say that there is a mountain and there is flat land and they are different, your mind automatically, naturally, becomes crystallized around the concept of a mountain as reality and flat land as reality. This crystallization prevents you from seeing that they are one thing. You do not see the reality that is beyond the distinctions, because you are looking at the distinctions, at the differentiated concepts. Because you think that reality is composed of those differentiated concepts, you don't see the unity beyond the concepts. And if you don't see the unity beyond the concepts you don't see reality, you only see concepts.

As we continue to meet with new objects, we can label them by distinguishing them from what we know. An elephant seen for the first time is 'not-anything-I-have-seen-before', 'not-dog', 'not-cat', and so forth. Then we can adopt the name 'elephant'. These simple distinctions form the foundation for more complex concepts that draw upon the meanings of many other concepts. 'Freedom' has meaning because we can define what it means to be 'not-free'.

When you believe that there is such a thing as "freedom," you then want to search for "freedom." But freedom is a creation of your own mind.

We can form an idea of 'love' by contrasting all we associate with love with what is 'not-love'.

And then we spend our lives looking for love, something that our minds created by distinguishing it from other things.

At some point in our childhood, we found ourselves thinking and speaking, using and reacting to concepts.

Of course, we didn't know that's what we were doing. We were excited that we were learning about reality. We didn't know we were creating it.

From parents, friends, and the other influences in our complex social conditioning, we absorbed our basic conceptual framework. As infants, we were fascinated by moving forms and patterns of light and shadow; we learned to recognize our parents, as well as to distinguish objects. We were already making associations between what we saw, heard, smelled, tasted, and sensed through our bodies. We may have developed a sense that our associations had significance, but we had no words to express their meaning.

Listening to the spoken sounds around us, we learned to name the forms and qualities of our world. This process unfolded by trial and error; the words we first linked to the objects around us may not have always matched the words used by others. Two objects completely different in size and color were both named 'dog'; two others, nearly identical, were 'dog' and 'cat'.

For a kid, that's what the kid was presented with, it takes a while before he could tell what's a dog, you see.

Corrected and recorrected many times, we shaped our early impressions to fit adult concepts and began to associate forms and sounds 'correctly'.

So the reality we came to know is basically inherited from our parents. The concepts we formed were learned mostly from other people.

Eventually, we did not have to listen to the sound as sound—the sound touched our concepts immediately, and we 'heard meaning' directly. Concepts became a kind of shorthand, a convenient way to refer to familiar objects without having to describe precisely what we were seeing or exactly what we meant.

Simultaneously, we were taught how to react to these concepts: what we could and could not touch, what to value, what to desire, and what to reject; we even learned what to be happy and sad about.

We now call these reactions our "preferences."

According to the customs of our culture, we were taught the proper way to categorize, use, and think about everything in our experience.

Gradually, many associations began to accumulate around concepts. They could touch memories and evoke complex reactions. We could, by uttering the word 'home', evoke a wealth of feelings and associations that gave this concept a special meaning to us. Perhaps many words took on a deep private significance, just as certain sights, fragrances, sounds, and sensations sometimes seemed to resonate with rich, unexplainable meaning.

But whatever had significance to us personally had to be expressed within the concepts available in our language. We had to accept the meanings we were given, and leave unspoken the meanings and feelings we could not communicate. The concepts we learned reflected back to us, and we began to think with the words of our language. The words that now form so spontaneously in our minds are all concepts transmitted to us by others. These concepts now condition how we view ourselves and our world, how we think, and how we respond to what happens around us. They create our everyday reality, and we use them to interpret all our experience.

All our experience: The effect is universal and complete. It is within that world created by those concepts that we seek what we believe we need. We believe some things are valuable and we need to seek them, and that other things are not valuable and we need to avoid them.

Concepts begin as fluid and flexible, . . .

When first we learn about any concept, the concept is usually fluid and flexible.

. . . but become more fixed as we mature. When we are first learning a concept, such as 'space' or 'aware-ness', we are most receptive to nuances around it; we

may play with it for a while, question it, and explore its possibilities. Once we feel we 'know' it, we tend to lose interest.

It's filed away, basically forgotten.

Our willingness to reexamine, discard, or expand the scope of the concept decreases; the word is no longer alive, subject to modification in light of new knowledge, but frozen into an item of information that we possess. We rely on it automatically in our thinking, which becomes more a matter of recollection than a creative activity.

Thinking itself is not necessarily uncreative. But thinking is uncreative when it is a matter of recollecting concepts from the past, or a matter of logically stringing together concepts. This kind of mental activity is basically computer-like. A computer does not invent anything new. What it can create is already there in the concepts. When we live and know through our established concepts, we don't have anything new in our lives. True creativity disappears, and everything we might think we're creating is only new combinations of what we already know.

Thinking *can* be creative when we allow ourselves to be open to what is beyond concepts. Then even words, even thinking can express that reality, can creatively unfold like a fountain of insights coming from explosive perceptions of nonconceptual reality. Thinking can be spontaneous, original, and creative when it directly expresses the experience of the moment. This is true communication. But usually we use our words to relate things about the past, to relate old concepts and memories. So our expression, our thinking, is dead.

I'm saying this to emphasize that conceptualizing on its own is not necessarily bad. Thinking can be a creative process when we are in touch with the nowness of experience, and that nowness is the source of our thinking. However . . .

> *Relying exclusively on our conceptual patternings, we slowly constrict the natural openness of our minds. It becomes more difficult to perceive the subtle nuances of the changing moment. At the moment of perception, our minds grasp and interpret sensory information, and supply us with prepackaged concepts that have specific associations and emotional tones based on past experience.*

When you see something, the input goes into your eyes, into your brain. At the moment the sensory input reaches our awareness our mind grabs it and interprets it, so the experience of reality is not pure.

> *. . . our minds grasp and interpret sensory information and supply us with prepackaged concepts that have specific associations and emotional tones based on past experience.*

Our experience of what is happening is not of what is actually happening. Actually when you perceive, the impressions, sounds, sights, or sensations are new—they're one hundred percent new as they happen. But we don't see them in their newness, we see them through our concepts about the various kinds of impressions. Not only do we see them through those concepts, those concepts automatically evoke emotional associations and feeling tones. So our experience is not a pure perception, but the thoughts, feelings, and memories that our concepts bring in. We have an experience only in the present moment, but that experience is not really an experience of the moment. Your experience is already your own interpretation of the moment. This happens every second. We never, or rarely, allow ourselves simply to perceive.

These associations arise simultaneously with the concept, projecting a past situation onto the present and conditioning how we view an experience. We do not necessarily respond to the immediate experience, but to the experience as it is filtered through concepts, memories, images and associations.

Seeing a present situation as similar to a past one, we tend to react automatically, decreasing our ability to assess the present situation freshly. Bound to the past in this way, we cannot perceive the vast range of alternatives available in the present and so diminish our options for action.

Our emotional patterns are based on concepts already crystallized in our minds. Every perception involves our concepts, their associations, and the patterns of these associations. Your responses are prepackaged. Your personal mind, which you inherited from many people, responds to each fresh moment in a specific way, and we do not see other possibilities in the situation. So there is no freedom here: You are imprisoned by the fact that you're operating through concepts. Concepts are much more basic than patterns or past events.

This tendency obscures awareness; losing touch with the open dynamic of the living moment, we live in a deadened world.

We are concerned here with the most basic, fundamental conditioning—the automatism of the mind. This conditioning is beyond your personal patterns and issues. Reacting to reality through concepts underlies all your personal patterns and issues and history. Concepts are the building blocks of our reactions, our knowledge, and our cognition. But it happens so automatically that most of the time we think we're seeing reality. We aren't aware of that split second of interpretation. The input comes in and we perceive a word or an idea. Otherwise you couldn't say, "This is a chair, this is a person." Without these ideas pure perception is just colors and sounds.

When we perceive through concepts, it's hard to know how a thing might actually look when the perception is fresh. What is it like? Tarthang Tulku calls it the "open dynamic of the living moment." The openness of the living moment is dynamic and fresh. But we have lost that freshness because we don't experience the pure perception in the moment. It's not as if it's not available; it's happening all the time. Perception has to happen for us to have any experience. But our mind instantaneously responds and we instantaneously react. And this response and reaction is completely governed by inherited concepts.

To go beyond the mind means simply to perceive without conceptual or cognitive response. It means to put your mind "on hold," to put that automatic neuro-linguistic response "on hold." Then you can see what's actually there. Then what we see becomes a source of creativity so that even our words begin to express that creativity. When we perceive without concepts, our concepts can change. They become more alive; they are closer to the immediate experience, rather than thirty years old.

> *When concepts become this fixed in our consciousness, we can perceive nothing new. Unable to perceive the subtleties of each changing situation, we even repeat the same gestures and the same comments in situations that appear the same.*

That's the patterns.

> *When our minds become habituated to such automatic responses, they grow lazy and inattentive, especially in familiar surroundings. Our fixed views give us a sense of security.*

We feel we 'know' the objects in our world; we feel we 'know' people and other living beings. We count on things to stay the same and to fulfill our expectations of what they are supposed to be and do.

This statement brings out a psychodynamic issue related to concepts. We use our conviction that concepts are real to give us a sense of security. They function as supports for our sense of ourselves and the world. As we explore conceptual and nonconceptual reality, we will deal little by little with some fundamental, entrenched concepts and with the psychodynamic need for concepts. But first we're working to understand concepts. We need to contemplate this issue of concepts if we are to truly understand reality. And we need to come to appreciate that reality is beyond concepts.

The more we reinforce this passivity by relying on deadened concepts, the more our minds resist reexamining what we know. As we force our experience into rigid molds, our inner world can become smaller and more limited, rather than enriched by our daily experiences. Confined to concepts that limit our expressions of feeling and insight, we can only duplicate the patterns we have learned, like our parents, grandparents, and their parents before them. All the knowledge we gain from our formal education and from our experience may only be an increasingly complex association of concepts that have little meaning to a human life. Such concepts are too frozen, too particularized, too distant from the realm of living things to express our deeper levels of experience.

The more fixed and rigid a concept is, the farther away it is from the living experience. Rigid concepts limit our inner experience, make our inner world smaller and smaller. They make our world in general smaller and more restricted. We are controlled by prejudices that we feel we need to uphold and fight for.

> *Until we question, analyze, and reassess the concepts we use to express ourselves, we are restricted to only one set of interpretations for our experiences. Whether they accord with the reality of what is happening or bring us unnecessary pain, we leave ourselves no choice but to live in this limited realm.*

This means to keep living in a world that is a creation of our own mind.

> *Even if our mental world is lonely, and we gain little pleasure from our experiences, our thoughts are familiar and give us an illusion of security and control that binds us to them. We may see no alternative to this way of understanding ourselves and our world.*

. . . because we believe it's reality. How can we think of an alternative? Even if we think of and long for freedom, we think of freedom within that world.

> *But when even such thoughts as these depend upon concepts we have never deeply examined, how would we know there are no other possibilities? Can we even think about something for which we have no concept? If we had no concept of love, could we form expectations of what love is like, become disappointed when our experience did not match these expectations, or fantasize about people we love? If we had no notion of love, could we hate? What if we had no concept of 'I,' or of ourselves as somehow separate from others? Then what would be love or hate . . .*

. . . if there were no concept of a separate entity? What would it mean to love or hate somebody?

Could we become attached to people or things, experience insecurity, or fear rejection? If society could not present us with ideals that did not match the reality of our situation, would we feel guilty that we could not live up to them?

That's showing you here that if there are no concepts, there are no psychodynamic issues.

How might the quality of our lives be different if we had no 'should' or 'would' in our language?

If we look carefully at our experience, we can see that many things that seem substantial and real are actually notions formed by our minds. Thinking about them and using them daily, we tend to forget that they are mental formulations and relate to them as real. Thus happiness, for example, is not inherent in the objects we desire, but grows out of the way we interpret a certain kind of excitement. However much we value happiness, it too is only a concept, a name that we learn to apply to certain types of situations or feelings.

Without our idea of happiness and the many related notions concerning what makes us happy, would we know if we were happy? Could we be unhappy? Would we have the same feelings if we lacked a word to express them?

Would we ever feel happy if we didn't have a word for "happy"? Would we ever feel unhappy if we didn't have the concept of "happy"? We create the concept of happy, then we live our lives feeling unhappy and trying to be happy. See the trap?

How could we spend time thinking about whether we were happy, or feel deprived if we were not?

It is nearly impossible for us to imagine what life would be like without such familiar concepts. We have come to trust our present conceptual patterning as a reasonably reliable reflection of truth, and see no reason to question it. But does our conceptual patterning increase our options for being and acting in the world, or is it too limited to serve our needs? Are our present concepts able to accommodate all the knowledge possible for us to gain, or have they become too rigid to sustain a more comprehensive perspective on knowledge?

When we depend automatically upon concepts, whether in thoughts, speech, or writing, we can actually decrease our ability to communicate. We all live in our own mental realm; our individual experiences have conditioned the specific connotations of the concepts we use. Although our mental worlds overlap those of others, they are never completely identical. Depending on knowledge filtered through concepts, we cannot wholly communicate our intended meaning; instead, we are subtly isolated from one another. Although we all use the same words daily, there is a gap in our communication that cannot be fully closed. . . .

If we reflect on the nature of concepts and how uncritically we accept the reality they create, it may seem that we are caught in the midst of some elaborate computer program that is operating without our conscious decision. And yet we tend to feel that we are in charge of our thinking. Are we running the program or is the program running us? Can we separate ourselves from the program and allow our thoughts and actions to be informed by a more comprehensive and trustworthy knowing intrinsic to our own being?

In the light of greater understanding, could we retrain our minds into a more satisfying way of seeing? Is it possible to see through our conceptual patterning? Might there be a way we could open up our concepts and revitalize them with meanings that allow us to communicate our ideas more completely? Could we find concepts that are closer to the immediacy of our experience and more in tune with our insights and feelings?

There may be ways to glimpse a more subtle side of our consciousness that could allow us to examine the fixed patterns of our minds more clearly. When we relax the body, we can slow the flow of thoughts and images, and observe more directly the thought process itself.

Such relaxation need not involve any special technique. It is simply a matter of observing the thoughts that come, without comment or interpretations. When we try this way of observing the mind at work, what we see may not be quite what we expect—it may not appear to be very important. But over a period of time, we can begin to observe with an unforced, relaxed concentration that may be a new experience in itself. This way of looking inward might lead to important insights into the nature of thought, as well as a new awareness of the connections between thoughts and feelings.

Left to themselves, thoughts tend to carry on to a point where they pause, almost as if they have converged at a blank wall. We might have experienced such a pause when rigorously following a particular train of thought or when we found ourselves 'stuck' on a problem. At any time the mind may be silent for a moment. If this pause is noted, we usually consider that we have reached the end of a train of thought. If no new thoughts arise to continue it, we turn our attention to another subject.

But that seeming 'dead end' where thoughts melt into a single point could also be a gateway to new knowledge. Focusing on this point with a balanced concentration, we might see possibilities for a way of knowing that lies beyond our accustomed pattern of thinking.

*If we can remain relaxed and aware, we might sense
a feeling of brightness, as if light were shining through
the silence. Our usual flow of thoughts and our habit
of focusing attention on the content of thoughts give
us few opportunities to sense the presence of light in
our mental imagery. If we relax our hold on the content
of thought and are attentive to the thoughts themselves,
we might sense thoughts arising from within this
brightness just before they form into words.*

We will do now a certain meditational practice that this
refers to. In this meditation, what you do is observe your
thoughts. Now, to observe your thoughts does not mean
to try to find out what you are thinking about. You're not
concerned about the content of the thoughts; you're concerned with the thoughts themselves, with the thinking process. So the idea is not to get caught in the thought, to be
influenced and run by it so that after a while you're pursuing some idea. You want to be aware of the thought happening. You want to be aware of the thought: when it's there,
when it stops, the gap between the thoughts, as another
thought arises. It doesn't matter what the thought is, what
words are in it, what the sentences are. You want to just look
at the strings of thoughts. If you continue looking you
might see that there are gaps between the thoughts, and you
might experience what the quality of that gap between the
thoughts is.

So the important thing is that you're not interested in
looking at what the thought is about, you just want to see
it as thought, just the thinking itself. As it goes through you,
just become aware of it in a relaxed, balanced way. Relaxed,
balanced way means you're not trying hard, you're relaxed,
you're just looking, you're just aware. You're not trying to
do something to the thought. The moment you react to the
thought, you're involved in the thought, in the content of

it. If you react one way or another, you're involved in the content of what the thought is. You don't want to react to the thought. That doesn't mean you want to control your reaction because your reactions will be thoughts too. What else can they be? You just continue being aware of them.

So it doesn't matter what the thought is, whether it's original, whether it's a reaction, it's a commentary, or it's a thought about thoughts. They're all thoughts. It doesn't matter what the thought is, where it comes from, what it's a reaction to, what quality it has—wonderful, good, happy, unhappy, about you, about somebody—it doesn't matter. It's just a thought. So just be aware of the passage of thoughts.

So, I'll continue reading the chapter:

> *The process may occur so fast that we immediately identify thoughts with words or perhaps whole strings of words that begin an inner dialogue. As more interpretations follow, involving combinations of concepts that evoke strong emotional tones, we may become aware of feeling burdened by a sense of heaviness that appears to be dark and serious. What thoughts contribute to this heaviness? What has happened to the qualities of openness and light with which the process began?*
>
> *Perhaps as we ask these questions, the flow of thoughts again briefly pauses. But almost at once, a new flow of thoughts is in motion, lasting a long time or perhaps only a few moments before another sequence begins. Where are these strings of thoughts coming from? What happens when we take possession of the thoughts and consciously guide them in a specific direction?*
>
> *Perhaps there does not seem to be a pause in the flow of thought: We are caught up in one sequence that has a theme or 'story line', when suddenly the content shifts, and we find ourselves in the middle of another story. How did we get from one story to the other? Does each*

*one have a beginning and an end, or are they contin-
uous? Do they overlap, influencing each other?*

All these you could observe by doing this practice.

*Questioning thoughts in this way, we can relax our
fixed hold on the concept of thought and gain new
insights into our mental processes. Every thought is an
opportunity to observe and learn from our mind. With
experience, we can begin to see how thoughts can actually create confusion and prolong unpleasant states of
mind. Eventually it will become more obvious how one
thought generates another, and how the momentum of
thoughts tends to build on itself, cycling and recycling
impulses through the mind.*

*Just as a weaver creates a tapestry by establishing the
basic threads of a fabric and embellishing it with pattern after pattern, our minds seem to weave thoughts
and images in endless replications. When we catch the
beginning of a thought, we can observe how it begins
with a simple pattern that is open and spacious, growing more dense as images intertwine in ever more complex patterns.*

*Stimulating memories and associations that evoke
universes of feelings and emotions, thoughts lose their
openness as they proliferate and intermesh. Simultaneously, we can sense our critical faculties at work, labeling
our experience as happiness, depression, ecstasy, bore-
dom, or anger, as noble or blameworthy.*

He is discussing the whole process, from the beginning
of thought through its development.

*As each experience is sealed and witnessed by the
mind, our thoughts about it become more substantial
and 'real'; we then identify with the experience and
react to it according to our conditioning.*

When we're in the middle of a thought, the complexity of thought patterns becomes more substantial and feels more real. It feels real and substantial, as if it is solid reality.

> *Out of all the possibilities for viewing a particular experience, we may choose to call it 'pleasure'. Then we project the experience outside of ourselves, and decide that we want to have that experience.*

Which is another thought, right?

> *Reaching out for things we associate with pleasure, we encounter our own image of what pleasure 'should be'.*

Which is another thought, another concept.

> *Grasping for an object, expecting to experience pleasure, and wanting to prolong it, we feel pleasure for only a short time. Almost immediately, we feel it slipping away.*
>
> *Observing the ebb and flow of thoughts allows us to see how the mind attaches labels to perceptions, feelings and emotions, and how it then produces commentary after commentary on what we are experiencing. Seeing these patterns of thoughts being woven together before our eyes, we may ask whether they actually create a solid cloth. Perhaps it is possible to view ourselves—not just our personality, appearance, and activities, but the very root of our being—in a different way. Such a fresh and open view could relieve the mind of the tendencies that freeze experience and make us vulnerable to confusion. Once we know it is possible to loosen the hold of concepts that entangle us in emotional pain, we have taken the first steps toward a new understanding that could transform the quality of all our experience.*
>
> *With greater insight into who we are, what we are, why we perceive, feel, understand, and interpret in the*

manner we do, everything we know might be considered from an entirely new perspective. Then we could analyze our assumptions more deeply, deciding for ourselves what it is possible to change or not to change, which ways of thinking are healthy and valuable, and which involve us in needless suffering. As we continue to question, our thoughts may grow more vital and clear, opening up new possibilities for self-understanding and more control over the direction of our lives.

So we're not trying to eliminate thoughts, we're trying to understand what the thinking process is. What happens when there's a thought? What happens when we observe a thought? What happens when we're involved in a thought? What happens when there's a complex of thoughts? We want to understand how the thought process determines our reality, and to penetrate and see through that process. Then, as Tarthang Tulku says, even thoughts will change quality. When you penetrate through concepts, even thoughts become more alive.

Thoughts are always being created, in the sense they are spontaneously arising. But they usually arise as responses from the past. However, thoughts can arise as an unfoldment of the present moment—you might see that your thought is an insight, arising right in the freshness of the moment. The thought is in touch with the very moment. It's fresh, it's open. When an insight has form, when a direct perception has a form, it's a thought, but it's a creative, new kind of thought.

Insight requires concepts. So in some sense, it is not one-hundred-percent fresh. But it is closer, fresher. It's seeing something about reality that is closer to the immediate experience. If you get completely close to the immediate experience, of course, there will be no form then. The form disappears little by little.

Student: You could analyze your thought process and I'm not quite sure how that creates the whole opening of the thought that . . . being able to be more fresh.

AHA: Analysis is not the same thing as the practice of meditation itself. You do the meditation, you have some experiences and then, of course, you can analyze in the sense of understanding it. In time you understand what causes what, what actually happens. That's what he means. The insights about it help you to do the practice even more easily or deeper. Do the practice through the meditation. Analysis is not done through the meditation; it is something else you do, maybe, afterwards. Our concern here is not with the analysis. Our concern here is just with the experience, penetrating the thinking process.

At the beginning we see thoughts in our minds and at some point, there's a gap, maybe lightness, openness, or space. But there are still subliminal thoughts, in some sense, happening there, determining our experience. I realize I'm in a thought, and I'm watching it, and suddenly I realize *you* arise as a thought. In time this process might go as far as seeing that everything arises as a thought, even your external perceptions. That's what I mean by creativity. What arises is absolutely brand new. It will happen only if there's a freshness in the moment, if the mind is being touched by the *now*. But if it's just putting two old things together, you don't really get anything new, just a combination of the old. So for there to be insight, there has to be in-touchness with the beingness itself, with the energy that's there in the moment. That combines the concepts in a fresh way. So you get a new insight that is not just a logical combination.

It is the difference between a recollection and an insight. Recollection is remembering something that happened; you can think about it and make connections. But that's not exactly an insight. Insight is an explosion. It will produce thoughts but it is truly creative. Something actually new arises, not merely a combination of old things.

This process can go deeper and deeper. I'm just describing some examples of what we mean by creativity—in this case, how involvement in the moment and penetrating thought can lead to thinking as a creative process.

FIFTEEN

Physical Reality and Nonconceptual Reality

N onconceptual reality is a term I use to refer to what actually exists. That reality can be perceived and apprehended not by going beyond concepts, but by going through concepts—seeing and recognizing concepts, a process which can make them transparent.

We generally live from an incomplete perception, taking a small dimension of reality to be all that there is. Then we try to live our lives according to that partial view. We try to solve our problems from that incomplete perspective, which doesn't work. Unless we actually realize what the whole truth is, what is actually there, what reality is in its totality, we will be misguided and inefficient in dealing with the situations in our lives.

We generally can't even imagine what actual reality is like, because we have taken a dimension of what exists and focused on it to the exclusion of the rest of reality. To actually comprehend the greater reality not only helps us to deal with our lives, but also shows us that reality is something more beautiful, real, and majestic than we have imagined. It is ultimately a beautiful mystery—the way things are, what actually exists, and how things function. Reality is so mysterious, so amazing, so magical, that seeing it is bound to change us and change our lives. Knowing what is real, we can't continue to live in the same way.

One of the reasons I like science fiction is that it stretches the mind, and makes it less attached to the usual way of seeing things. It opens new possibilities of experience and perception. This newness can happen, however, simply by opening our perception to what is actually here now. I always wonder why people don't write science fiction stories that simply describe how reality actually is. It's much more fantastic than the best science fiction.

To see things as they are is to see them without filters, without veils. To see what *is* means to perceive objectively. Objective perception requires that we apprehend or perceive without the usual filters, without the projections of the past onto the present. What is, obviously must be in the moment—now, because only now exists. Only this very moment exists. You can see that logically for yourself. I am not saying anything esoteric here; what exists is now. The past reality is not here. The future hasn't come yet.

To see what is means to see the *now*, as it is. But to see the *now* as it is means to see without the influence of the past. In the various aspects of the work we've done, we have seen that many of our problems and illusions come from past experience. We have seen how we project our patterns on our interpersonal relationships, how we project our relationships with our parents and others in our early childhood onto our present life, how we react in ways that have nothing to do with the present. This is one way of seeing some of the more obvious psychological and emotional filters. We don't see people the way they are; we see them according to our past experience. We are always projecting images and patterns of relationship that do not actually exist now.

The most fundamental and subtlest of these projections is the projection of concepts. Concepts actually constitute the material of our experience. They constitute the content of our minds. We have seen how the mind is inseparable from the world we live in—that the world we believe we live in and our minds are not two things. We can come to a direct perception of this fact—it is not an idea. You can discover that the world you live in is determined by what you believe the world to be.

In the last few meetings, we have explored the subject of nonconceptual reality. We have approached the nonconceptual by discussing what concepts are and how they influence perception. Basically, we have tried to get a feeling for what we mean when we speak of experience with concepts and without concepts. Some of us have some inkling of what I mean by concepts, and what I mean by experiencing things without concepts. To experience things without concepts means to experience things without the past, with absolutely no mind, because mind is the filter we put on reality. When we speak here of experience without mind, we mean without discursive or discriminating mind, not without awareness. The nonconceptual is what is, without the overlay of our past experience, our past prejudices, and our minds. This is what is referred to when some traditions, such as Zen, talk about "no mind."

Today we will explore the various barriers and issues that prevent us from penetrating to the nonconceptual. For each of the next few meetings we will explore one specific barrier that manifests as a particular way of looking at things, or as an attachment to a certain way of perceiving.

Today I would like to discuss what has been called in the literature of the traditional teachings, "freedom from the senses." What does this mean? Spiritual literature contains a lot of discussion of how we are imprisoned by our physical senses. An important part of spiritual training is to learn to be free from the influence of our senses. So we want to see what this means. Of course, this does not mean that you don't see and don't hear. Our senses are part of our lives; we can't do without them. But it is possible to live in relative freedom from our senses.

The attachment to the channels of our senses is a major barrier against the experience of the nonconceptual. Understanding how the senses work will help to clarify the difficulty. This understanding is not available to someone who has not experienced anything beyond the senses, or who might not even think about such a possibility. But when you experience things without using your physical senses, you begin to see how your physical senses tend to prejudice you in a certain direction.

To be imprisoned by our physical senses means to have the conviction that the information about the world that comes from our physical senses is actually what exists, and to take the information that comes through the channels of the senses as complete information about reality. In other words, it is believing that what we see is what we get. Obviously, all of us are to some extent imprisoned in this way. But we don't believe that we are imprisoned. What we believe is that the world that we apprehend through the physical senses is the world as it is. We believe that what exists is what we see, hear, smell, taste, and touch.

Let us explore what this means. If we take reality to be only what comes through those channels, then we are convinced that reality is nothing but the physical world, that nothing but the physical world exists. True reality, we believe, is what the physical senses tell us. If you touch it, it's there. If you see it, it's there. If you don't touch it, if you don't see it, it isn't there.

You might say, "I've had experiences that are not seen by the physical eye, and I know they are there." Yes, but do you act according to them? You don't, because those experiences are like a dream for you, like a little scratch on the surface of your brain. You are still convinced that what your physical senses tell you is what is real. You believe that only physical perception is objective perception. That is the rock of reality, and that's what you have to pay attention to and take care of. Other things, perhaps more subtle experiences, are nice; they come and go, and maybe they are real, maybe they are not. They are goodies, extras—not really as important as physical reality. So your focus, your valuing, and your conviction are based more—a million times more—on what comes through your physical senses than on what comes through any other channel.

Our belief in the perspective of the physical senses influences our consciousness in a powerful, dramatic way. We cannot know how powerful this influence is until we perceive the nonconceptual. So freedom from the senses does not mean not using them. It means not believing that the information that comes through them is the whole story. For example, when you have done some meditation practice or had an insight or some energetic opening, you have undoubtedly seen in many such experiences that your perception becomes very different—you experience yourself in a less opaque way, but also the perception through your senses is much more vivid. The world you perceive often will look more vivid or bright, or more precisely itself, clearer. Your sight has been cleansed; you hear sounds you were not hearing before—the sound of birds outside is clearer, more present, more beautiful. Smells and tastes are more clear and full. You are living in a different world. So clearer information is coming through the senses; you are experiencing the physical world with less filtering through concepts.

In such experiences it is not only that the physical world becomes more vivid; at the same time you become more open to your own presence and awareness, more available to the living, direct perception of what is manifesting in your body, your feelings, and your essential presence. However, even though you might have hundreds of such experiences, it is not easy to actually shift your orientation away from the completely materialistic perspective of the ego. We usually remain utterly convinced of this perspective. To say that you are materialistic does not mean necessarily that you like physical objects, that you think that something like having a car is more important than love. The fundamental attitude is more basic: It is believing that the material is ultimate reality, that it is what's really important, what's really there. You believe, for instance, that you are fundamentally your body, and that the body is the most important thing about you, even the most real thing. As we have been seeing in our exploration of nonconceptual reality, you have built up solid, opaque concepts of the world and even of yourself that cause you to experience yourself as a solid, physical, separate entity in a world of solid, separate objects. If you believe that perspective completely, you become complete, pure ego, and you become truly materialistic.

So materialism is not only a matter of having materialistic values. Materialism is the conviction that the physical universe is the only universe, and that what we perceive through the senses is all of reality. If you believe only in natural science, you become a materialist.

Some forms of spiritual training attempt to detach the consciousness and the perception from the physical channels. They involve developing the ability to perceive without being restricted to those channels alone. It does not mean not valuing or disbelieving physical perception. Spiritual perception, perception of what is real, puts sensory perception in its place as part of the information that is possible for us.

To be imprisoned by the senses means to be solidly convinced that physical reality, or reality as we see it through our senses is absolute reality. The prison is the belief that this reality is the most fundamental, everlasting, solid reality—the most real. If you consider the way you conduct yourself, the way you think, feel, and behave, you will see that you have this underlying conviction. The way you think of yourself and the way you live your life are very much influenced by this conviction. It is the strongest conviction in your mind. Even our spiritual experiences, perceptions of the transcendent or essential, which are clearly not physical, do not shake this conviction. Our belief in the fundamentalness of physical reality remains solidly entrenched in our souls. In any authentic spiritual work, this conviction must eventually be confronted, shaken, and dismantled. It must be shattered before we can perceive totally, completely, what is actually there.

In general, deeper or more subtle perceptions do not affect the belief in the physical world. You still believe that you are your body. You believe that your body is the most important part of you, that it is what defines you. It is who you are. And you believe that the needs and desires of your body, and the attractions and repulsions of the body are *your* needs, *your* repulsions, *your* reality, regardless of experiences that challenge that belief. You might even have had experiences in which you realized very clearly that what you are is not the body, that the body's physical experiences are restricted to a certain realm. You can spend years having all kinds of spiritual experiences and psychological experiences, but the tendency is very strong to think, feel, and behave as if the physical reality of who you are is the most important part of you, the most basic.

Spirituality does not just involve seeing that there is spirit in addition to the physical. It involves seeing reality as it is—what actually is there, physical or non-physical. To make that possible, we need to be free from the conviction that makes us focus on the dimension of reality that comes through our physical senses. This conviction is so deep, so solid, and so entrenched, and it pervades our consciousness so completely, so universally, that we take it to be reality. We don't think of it as a conviction, we think of it as unquestionable reality. Most people never question it.

So everyone tries to live their lives from this limited perspective. You take the input of your senses as all of reality and then try to deal with your life from that perspective. Then you get in trouble because that's not all of reality. So your beliefs are bound to be inaccurate, and your actions are bound to be ineffective. The simplest, most common example of this is that from the materialist perspective you tend to believe that if you have material success, you will be happy, or if your body looks a certain way, you will be satisfied with yourself. But in holding this perspective, you are actually bound to be unhappy, because the perspective of the physical dimension is not the whole truth about you.

This is a vast subject, a very deep subject to explore. In one sense, it is obvious. But it is also subtle. As we have discussed, the universe we see is not separate from the concepts in our minds. But the universe we see is mostly the physical universe. The mind develops by focusing on the physical universe. This is true for every human being. The restriction of consciousness to the physical and the development of the mind constitute the same process. It's not that you grow up and then you believe this perspective. As you come to know yourself growing up, the materialist perspective is developing. The perception of physical reality as fundamental becomes more and more entrenched; it becomes part and parcel of your mind, the way you think, feel, and perceive. This is why it is so difficult to see through or beyond it. We can't imagine how we could perceive or act without this perspective.

We have discussed how the developing child forms concepts of himself and the world. From the beginning, what does the child know? Daddy, Mommy. What is that? A body that moves around. The first words that kids learn usually denote some physical reality. The child learns "table." Mommy says, "Elbow. Finger. You." And the child says, "finger" a thousand times. How are the parents training the child? They are training the consciousness to focus on the physical. The parents already focus mostly on the physical. That's the world they live in. They do not point to the essence of the child and say, "Essence." They just say, "Nose," and the child says, "Nose." So after a while, what are you? I am nose, eyes, cheeks, and cute. Why am I cute? Because I have a dimple. You are not cute because your heart is pink and fluffy, is full of sweet love. Everyone is trained within the context of these physical concepts.

The building blocks of the mind are concepts of physical reality, or concepts based on physical reality. For example, the concept of relationship is the relation between two physical objects, for people are seen as physical objects. The most basic objects, the ones the child can most easily perceive, are physical things. The child does not perceive something like freedom, for instance. In the beginning you cannot tell a child what freedom is. A fourteen-month-old child will not understand freedom. There is nothing in his sensory experience that he can see as freedom. But he knows his nose because the senses are there. He can see it, touch it. The physical realm is the most obvious for the consciousness to see. Also, the child does need to focus on the physical to learn to function and survive. At first the child doesn't have a notion even of solid objects. In order to learn to function, he needs to learn that his body and the table cannot occupy the same space at the same time. In the course of this learning he develops a concept of "me" as a solid physical object, and of "table" as a different solid physical object. This is a necessary learning, but the process of reification—of coming to see these concepts of the physical body and the physical world as fundamental reality— eventually cuts off other modes of perception.

There is a connection between early physical experience and learning, and later forms of learning. Learning about eating, defecating, cleaning, sleep, and so on, all have to do with the physical body. Later, a child learns about love, gentleness, and other more subtle phenomena. But most of us cannot know what love is if we have not been touched. You will not believe that your mother loves you if she doesn't touch you, or if she doesn't take care of you physically. The orientation of the development is physical. It takes a lot of maturity to realize that someone could be loving in attitude. How many of you can really believe that someone loves you if they don't want to sleep with you? Is it easy to believe that someone loves you if they don't feel you're attractive enough to sleep with? The physical thing is important. It's what makes sex such a huge force in our relationships.

In the beginning it does appear that the infant's perception is not limited to the physical senses. There seems to be more of a total, holistic apprehension that includes the physical. But the developmental task of focusing on the physical causes that more total apprehension to change, to become restricted to what is known through the physical senses.

For instance, by talking about noses, tables, blankets, food, and things like that, we tend not only to point to the physical, but to point to particular components of it. We say "table," distinguishing it from the rest. We say "food," distinguishing it from the plate, from the hand, from the stomach, from the mouth. Making those distinctions, just saying there is a *table* or there is *food*, begins the process of

reification in which the table and the food end up as separate, completely independent entities. Again, this process
tends to shut off the other capacities of perception, leaving
the physical senses as the channel for information about
the world and ourselves.

If we look only through the physical senses, we tend to
look at reality from the perspective of physical things. If I use
only my physical senses, only my eyes, ears, nose, touching,
and my tongue, I will tend to see things in terms of physical
objects in space because that's how the senses function.

We have been seeing how physical reality and reified
concepts are actually the same thing in our experience. The
world of entities, discrete entities like tables and people and
trees, is what we call the physical world. But that physical
world is made up of what I am calling concepts. The conviction that physical reality is the ultimate reality is the
same as the conviction that concepts are ultimate reality.
This is a radical notion which seems to be the opposite of
common sense. Conventional understanding has it that the
physical world is independent of the mind, and that what
we see, smell, feel, and hear is objective reality.

Taking the physical world to be ultimate reality means
taking the table as an ultimate reality, as something independent. It seems to exist without you, without people,
without consciousness, so it must be ultimate reality. But
a table is a concept. Before the child learns this concept, the
child doesn't necessarily know that there is a table separate
from the floor. When you see through your concept of
"table," when it becomes transparent rather than opaque,
you realize that the table and the floor are not separate. That
nonseparateness is not on the physical level; it exists on
another level, which we cannot see through our physical
senses. The unity which makes concepts transparent is
apprehended through a capacity to perceive which has
nothing to do with the physical senses. The basis of unity

is not in the physical world. It is a little bit confusing for me to say it that way, because I don't see the physical world the way we generally think of it. There is a physical world only from the perspective of the physical senses. If more of you is operating, the world you inhabit is not just the physical world, and in this world there are no objects that are separate and absolutely independent of each other. In perceiving the nonseparateness, or unity, you do not lose your capacity to discriminate in the physical world; you just do not see differentiated objects as actually separate.

As we have been discussing, the process of discriminating and conceptualizing objects leads to reifying them as discrete and separate entities. This process in turn tends to restrict our perception to the physical senses, because it eliminates our experience of the unified awareness that underlies the concepts; it excludes the perception of the unity of reality.

In reality differentiation does not mean separation. My lungs and my heart are different, but not completely separate. The cells of the body are finely differentiated, but the cells are not separate from each other. They constitute one body. It is more fundamental that they constitute one thing, the whole body, than that they can be seen as separate. And the unity of reality is more fundamental than the separate existence of tables and chairs on their own. In other words, the dimension of unity is more fundamental, it is a more inclusive reality, than the dimension of the physical.

Reified concepts are the main barrier to penetrating to what is, and the basic concepts that form our experience are physical. You are more convinced, for instance, in the existence of your body than in the existence of inner freedom, because while your body is a physical thing, freedom is not a physical thing. It is particularly these physical concepts that we have to penetrate in order to perceive what is. The ground of the personal mind is constituted by physical concepts.

Our perception of relationships between things are based on that ground of personal mind. We perceive that this object is round and this one is square; this object is distant from that one, and this object is near that one. This object is free from that one, this object likes that one and doesn't like this other one. These relationships develop as a super-structure on a fundamental ground which consists of physical concepts, the concepts of what we call physical objects.

Because we believe the physical universe is the most fundamental reality, we are afraid of death. Why is death a big deal? Because you believe that you are fundamentally your body. More than anything else, your body defines who you are. And because you believe your body defines who you are, there is such a thing as death. What we mean by death is death of the body. And because we think it is who we are, the idea of death of the body is deeply frightening for us.

We are continuously concerned about what happens to the body—about whether the body is comfortable or not, whether the body is getting what it wants or not. Is the body getting comfort and pleasure, or is it in pain? Is it secure from threat? Is this body liked or not liked? Is it thin or fat? Tall or short? All these are big concerns in our minds. Our deepest issues are based on physical concerns, rather than on concerns about whether we are loving, compassionate, or free. Even though we might have these latter concerns, they are not as fundamental as our involvement with our physical body and our physical world.

The perspective which assumes the ultimate reality and value of the physical universe, to the exclusion of other dimensions of reality, is the source of the difficulties of the egoic mind. This perspective creates most of our suffering—the way we approach death, sickness and disease, pleasure and pain, issues of acceptance and rejection. In the course of our process of spiritual work, of discovering the true presence that we are, the basic identification with the physical body and the conviction in the physical world persists as an ongoing phenomenon, concern, and barrier.

For example, suppose someone begins to experience space. At first, you experience a kind of absence. As you know, the arising of each essential aspect usually manifests first as its absence, as a hole. In the case of the arising of space, the hole first manifests as an emptiness in the pelvis, the sensation of a hole. How do people see it? Do they experience, "Oh, I feel emptiness there. I am seeing the dimension of emptiness." No, most people react, "Uh oh. I lost my genitals. I have no genitals." That's how people react to it. Why? Because you approach the experience from the physical perspective. If you perceive an emptiness there, it means to you that there are no genitals. You don't think, "I'm just perceiving a different dimension. There is physical reality, but other dimensions of reality also exist." If you saw that, there would be no fear, no issue. You have not lost anything. You are just seeing another dimension of yourself. But because you assume that the physical universe is the most fundamental reality, when an emptiness arises, you tend to think, "Uh oh. I lost my penis."

If an emptiness arises in the head, you feel, "Oh, I lost my head. That means I'm dumb, I'm stupid." What does your physical head have to do with being dumb? Yet when people feel emptiness in the head, the most common reaction is that they decide that they are stupid. Why? Because we are looking at things physically. We think the intelligence is somehow inside the physical head. We believe the physical universe is what determines who we are.

When you see how fundamental, how pervasive, how deep and entrenched your physical orientation is, you will notice that you don't look at even your deep experiences from a total perspective. You look at them from the perspective of the body, from the physical perspective. Most of your issues arise from that perspective. When you feel that you are disappearing, what is it that is disappearing? Usually, it's the image of your body. You are terrified because you believe your physical body is the most important, fundamental, lasting, real, fundamental, solid *you*. If that goes, you go. You don't think, "I'm just seeing myself from a different place. My perception is detaching from the physical senses, and as a result, I am seeing something deeper than the physical." If you do see it that way, you won't feel that you are disappearing. You will be aware that you are not just seeing through your physical senses. Then there will be no fear, and no reason for the terror. So the source of the terror is our belief that the physical body is who we are—fundamentally and ultimately.

Our whole society focuses on the physical world as the most fundamental reality. We believe that human beings are discrete objects in physical reality, and therefore, physical death is the end or disappearance of what a person is. However, reality does not exist in discrete objects except in the physical universe. When you penetrate the physical universe and you see what underlies it, you realize that there are no discrete objects. Reality is a oneness, a unity. When we are convinced of the oneness, the unity, we are not afraid of death.

There is no physical reality that exists on its own, somehow separated from another world underneath or above it. The exclusively physical, materialist perspective is a partial perspective created by eliminating the other perspectives. In reality, it is one world. If you see the creation in its totality, it is a unity. If you see only its surface, you see the world of objects. So eliminating the subtle perceptions eliminates the oneness, the unity that is an intrinsic aspect of the nature of all that exists.

We are seeing, then, in some detail, what is meant when spiritual teachings say that we are prisoners of our senses. We are seeing why the spiritual traditions admonish us to

"Be free from your senses." In many traditions and religions, this injunction has taken on a puritanical meaning. The orientation is that sex is not good, pleasure is not good. You are told, "Don't focus on the sensual world, and don't act as if it is important." Unless you understand the way in which the senses are a prison, you might take the devaluing of the physical world literally. The message then is: Don't look, don't feel, don't desire. However, in our work we engage in the process with all our being, including the physical. It does not work to try to eliminate physical experience when you are working on the whole being. It is true you might have experiences of not identifying with the body, being aware of yourself as pure awareness, for example, but if this experience is used to move away from the experience of the senses, you will maintain and strengthen the duality between the physical world and other dimensions. The physical world, and thus the conceptual world, will never become transparent in your experience.

To know that the physical perspective is only partial is not to devalue the physical, but to allow the possibility that there are other perspectives. We actually need to include other perspectives or dimensions to enable our physical senses to function clearly. This is called the cleansing of the physical senses—becoming free of the physical senses means cleansing and clarifying them. Cleansing or purifying the senses happens when they function in a deeper mode of perception—perceiving through our being, through our essence, and through our hearts, instead of through reified concepts.

The current revival in the West of holistic medicine and alternative medicine is an attempt to acknowledge that there are things beyond the strictly physical senses. Orthodox western medicine basically looks at the body through the physical senses. That's all there is, so you deal with it. Other perspectives, such as acupuncture, work from the perception that something else is operating. When the energies you are working with are not only physical, it's called alternative medicine. To sense these energies is to penetrate the physical to other dimensions.

Let us summarize. First, we have seen how we are imprisoned by our senses, how, if the physical senses perceive through reified concepts, we tend to perceive only the physical world and are convinced that is all of reality. As part of that perspective, we tend to see reality as composed of discrete objects. We take ourselves to be discrete objects, fundamentally the body, in relationship to other discrete objects. In this perception, we are a body that lives in a physical universe with other discrete objects, some of which are alive. We call some of the alive objects "people" and "animals," and we interact with them. Other objects which are not alive, we call "inanimate." This perspective results from the development of the conceptual mind, and the training we receive in childhood. This conditioning makes it difficult to see through or beyond this perspective; we have taken it to be reality.

The materialist perspective determines the reality which underlies all our personal, emotional, and psychodynamic issues. The physical world and the world of concepts of discrete objects become the same thing. The conviction that the physical dimension is the most fundamental reality is one of the main barriers against seeing the truly fundamental reality, which is what is—nonconceptual truth, nonconceptual reality.

Student: I see the grid that we're all locked into, and at the same time, I also see that my perceiving myself as being incredibly locked-in is also a concept. And beyond that there is a force that I can't get rid of no matter what I do. There is something else operating that is available.

AHA: Exactly. The more you see yourself as imprisoned, the more you are imprisoned. But it is possible for the concepts to become more porous, without such definite separations. Nonconceptual reality is not the absence of the physical world; it is the perception that the physical dimension does not exist independently, that it is part of a larger reality just as the surface of the body is part of the whole of the body. If you see the skin as one layer of the whole, the rest of the body, the depth of it can be perceived at the same time. It is the same with physical reality—physical reality as a whole is a surface. Seeing the dimension deeper than physical reality allows the porousness, the permeability of the concepts.

Seeing nonconceptual reality, what is, does not eliminate the usual world that we perceive. It is as it is, except that it appears more porous. Things are not as discrete from each other as they usually appear to be. We see that they are made out of the same thing—the space, the earth, the table, the rug, me, you. We're all made out of the same thing. It's a homogeneous existence. This homogeneous existence is nonconceptual in the sense that there's nothing you can say about it. When you say something about it, you tend to close it off. The less you say about nonconceptual reality, the more it will open up and appear as it actually is.

When I talk about seeing the reality of what is, I don't mean that you are suddenly going to see all kinds of strange things in front of you. The physical reality is part of what's there: it's just not the only thing that's there. When you see the totality, physical reality will appear differently, as if you are seeing it in a different light. It will have more color, more harmony, and more refinement. You will see more the sense of beauty, the sense of grace in physical reality. But that sense of beauty arises through seeing the porousness and the consciousness that constitute the physical world. This basic, fundamental, pure consciousness and existence is independent of the various forms. It is specifically what I call nonconceptual. So a table is a table, but at the nonconceptual level it is not a table. The concept exists, but it does not exist on its own. The concept is simply a surface phenomenon of something more fundamental.

S: I've noticed two extremes. One is when I've been in touch with something beyond ordinary appearances. There is that kind of oneness and a kind of ordinariness, just a simplicity. But when I'm not in touch with that, and I look towards something beyond just the senses, I get this feeling that the physical senses and my whole relationship to them, the concepts, are a barrier or wall that's holding back nonconceptual reality. I want it to come through, and I'm also scared that if it comes through, it's going to create chaos at the physical level. I feel myself operating as this separate entity. I have this great desire to be operating connected with things, to have some greater power moving me than just my mind, my own ego. But I'm also tremendously frightened of that, afraid it's going to blow things apart, the joy's going to be too big, all those kinds of feelings come up, yet I have this real desire for that. I can see that it's so connected with this feeling that if it comes through, it's going to somehow have a physical expression. It's going to be upsetting.

AHA: That is one of the biggest fears. When we explore the insight that the physical universe is not ultimate, we are afraid we'll lose it, that there will be a loss of the physical component of our existence. If we go beyond the body, we will lose the body. This fear makes us feel that we have to hold on to it, we have to keep it solidly there, or it will fall apart. That is because we are holding the sense of the body together with our minds. We are not holding together the real world; we are holding together our idea of the world. So the mind can't let go of it. It says, "If I let it go, it will fall apart." If you just allow it to fall apart, you begin to see the real world. What will fall apart is the world you usually see. But we believe that is the real world that will fall apart, and this is why we're afraid. We believe that's it! We will be completely annihilated. You fear that you will lose physical reality, or you will lose your mind, you won't be able to think straight.

S: They'll give you medication!

AHA: Nonconceptual perception can sound like psychosis, but it is not the same kind of experience. It is a very different kind of experience: There is a sense of oneness, unity, integration, and harmony. Psychosis is a lack of integration. In psychosis, the physical world is disintegrated or fragmented. But that's not true in the nonconceptual dimension. The sense of disjointedness, fragmentation, and things falling apart might arise on the way to the nonconceptual. The disintegration of the structures of the usual mind seems similar to psychosis. But that's not what we mean when we say nonconceptual. The nonconceptual perception arises when you let go of those structures. They are gone completely, disintegrated to nothing. Then you can see things as they are instead of seeing them through the filter of your mind. A psychotic person sees the world through a fragmented mind. He is not looking at the world with "no mind."

S: One thing I've observed from working with you is my tendency to have opinions in reaction to this information. Do I like this or do I not like this? That whole contraction itself is a resistance to it. And I find it seems that one of the ways to penetrate that conceptual stuff is to just have a kind of direct practice of hanging out with your experience of the physical world, and at the same time, seeing what the mind is doing in terms of making up the context all the time. In other words, I'm still thinking I'm sitting there doing this, and that I'm in control when it is the opposite. So all I can do is just sit there with it. I can't try to penetrate. All I can do is see the content.

AHA: Then what's happening is understanding. The more you understand, the more you will tend to let go of the concepts. You don't try to stop. You can't do that. Today we're discussing something that might bring us some understanding. With the understanding, the mind will relax, since the mind holds on to mental reality only because it believes it is reality.

S: But what I'm saying is that in this case the relaxation is the understanding. It's like that's the only way you can do it. So understanding isn't a conceptual understanding.

AHA: That's true. One important point here is that we are discussing the nonconceptual experience in our work as an advanced state, an advanced perception that happens at a very deep level of understanding and realization. However, there are traditions that only work in this way. The Zen tradition, for instance. Their central method of penetrating reality is to see through the concepts. So working on the concepts, letting go of the concepts and the support for those concepts, such as physical reality, will allow the mind to relax and let go. This will free the unfolding of the essential aspects. The aspects are usually blocked partly because they are not physical, so they are being eliminated by the mental identifications. But as we see the limitations of our conceptual world, the general effect is more capacity to allow the perception of deeper realities. Of course, this openness allows the arising of Essence in its various manifestations.

Work on the nonconceptual is a way to activate Essence. That is how some traditions do it. We've done it the opposite way. We work with Essence, and then we get to the nonconceptual.

I would like us to leave today with an appreciation of our entrenched conviction that the world is a physical world. Just stay with that as a practice. Keep reminding yourself of how you are taking reality to be what you see with your eyes, what you hear with your ears, and how that restricts what you are and what your world is.

SIXTEEN

The Universal Mind

Today I would like to present a context in which to situate our exploration. We've been focusing on what I call "nonconceptual reality," the realm beyond the mind as well as beyond the specific qualities or aspects of Essence. Today we will discuss how the realm of the nonconceptual and the realm of Essence are connected. To do that, we need to look at the total picture that our Work involves. The realms of experience and dimensions of Being we will be exploring are of course not unique to our Work; they are described in various formulations throughout many spiritual traditions.

When we do these explorations, most of you try to follow me experientially. Today, don't try to do that. If it happens, that is fine. But it will probably be difficult to follow me experientially, so it's all right if you just mentally understand. You want to just get the overall picture. You might have a feeling for some elements of what we are discussing, or you might have experienced these realms. Also, some aspects of what we are discussing may arise in you as we explore. Today we will be exploring a wide territory, including the most fundamental dimensions of Being.

Whatever way you understand today's discussion is fine, even if it is mental or intellectual. Any understanding will be useful, because it will give you an overview, an understanding of how certain things interrelate. You'll get dizzy if you try to follow it experientially. Even if you follow intellectually, it might make you dizzy! We have been discussing in our exploration of the nonconceptual realm the possibility of awareness and even functioning beyond personal mind. For the ego self this can be a confusing or even alarming possibility. In the absence of the understanding of the dimension we will introduce today, some have the assumption that without the structuring of the world by personal mind, there will be chaos, a lack of order in experience. This is understandable from the point of view of experience that has never been outside the realm of the conceptual mind. However, what we will explore today will illuminate the true source of order.

We usually begin our work by exploring the dimension we call personality—the socially determined dimension of reality, of experience, of thoughts, emotions, and images. So in the beginning, it's important to be aware of our bodies, our thoughts and feelings, and to understand them. As we do that, we gradually approach another dimension of experience that we call the Essential, in which you begin to experience Essence in its various aspects. You might experience Compassion, Space, Joy, Value, or Truth. These qualities are in a different realm of experience than the one we started with. To experience essential Value, for example, is a very different experience from experiencing self-esteem in the realm of the personality.

In the realm of Essence, in addition to the many essential aspects which manifest in the soul, there are also many levels or dimensions. We call these the Diamond Dimensions. Essence manifests in many dimensions. Reality becomes deeper and more refined as you penetrate further into it. At the beginning, and for some time in our process, as we experience Essence and its various aspects and dimensions, our experience remains an inner experience, meaning that it is experienced inside the body. You feel Joy in your heart, or Will in your belly, or Clarity in your head. Your experience remains within the usual framework of the body; it seems to happen to an individual person who is having a spiritual experience.

At some point we reach a dimension in which our experience is not limited by the boundary of the body. We experience Essence as continuous, inside and outside. This is the dimension that's usually called "unity." In unity, we are one. There is no separation between people and things. We are experiencing Essence or Being, not as an inner experience, but as a total experience, a universal, cosmic reality. This level also has various dimensions and refinements. The general gradation from inner to unified boundless experience is a typical pattern in those who pursue effective long-term spiritual work.

To deepen our understanding, I'll explore the gradation from the last, most fundamental state first—starting from the top down. We have been discussing it from the bottom up, from the level of personality through essential aspects to boundless dimensions. Today we will start from the top down, which is the traditional way this gradation is presented.

The deepest, most objective state one can experience, in the sense that there is nothing that you can experience beyond it, is what we call the Absolute. The Absolute is absolutely unchangeable, absolutely itself, absolute in the sense that it's ultimate. You cannot experience anything beyond it. It does not make sense that there could be anything beyond it. Some traditions call it the "mystery," or the "unknowable."

The dimension of the Absolute is the peak, but it is not a peak in the sense of the peak of a mountain. It is fundamental. If you consider physical matter, for instance, and go deeper and deeper, until you get to the most elementary element, what is the furthest you can go, where you can't go any further? Without limitations on what levels can be perceived, what will you finally reach? The Absolute.

The experience of the Absolute here is actually the Absolute experiencing the Absolute in itself; we could say experiencing itself *as* the Absolute, but it is not really *as*, since there is no separation or mediation in the experience. This is the only way it is possible to experience the Absolute completely, as the Absolute experiencing the Absolute. If the Absolute is experiencing the Absolute, the experience is that there is no experience. Absolutely. That's why it's called the Absolute! It's absolutely empty of anything you can call experience.

If I experience myself as Absolute, then the experience is "I don't know." I don't know anything. And I don't know that I don't know. "I don't know" means that I am not conscious. I am not conscious of anything, and I am not conscious that I am not conscious of anything. It is similar to deep sleep. When you are in deep sleep, you don't know you are in deep sleep. It's as if there is nothing there. You are gone, absolutely gone. You're out of it. So the Absolute is like that. It is the ultimate, deepest nature of everything.

It is the level of existence, of beingness, where there is not even the perception of beingness. You *are* beingness. You are so deep, you don't know you are there. Being in the Absolute completely happens only in a state of profound meditation or in a state of deep sleep. It does not happen any other way. In this state you are not aware of seeing anything. You cannot be driving your car and be completely in the Absolute, because in the Absolute you do not see any car.

The ultimate nature of things is sometimes called the Absolute, sometimes called the Void. Some theistic traditions call it the Godhead; in Sufism it is called the Divine Essence. The ultimate essence of everything, including the human being, is a complete absence of all that can be experienced and the absence of knowing that there is nothing to experience. It is a complete lack of self-consciousness, and an absence of consciousness of anything. That is the ultimate source—the Origin.

This does not mean that there is nothing there. You are, you exist, but you are aware of it only when you come out of it, when there is some consciousness. The quality of the Absolute is that it is not conscious of Itself. In the Absolute, consciousness does not exist yet; it is not yet manifest. The Absolute is sometimes called the "unmanifest." Consciousness, awareness, is a development or manifestation out of the Absolute. The first level that arises from the Absolute is the capacity to be conscious or aware. Ontologically prior to this arising, this capacity does not exist. There is existence without awareness of that existence. The Absolute is what most fundamentally exists. But it does not exist in the usual sense, in the sense that we can experience it, or touch or feel or see it. It exists without any quality; it is "qualityless."

Awareness or consciousness is the first quality that arises. The Absolute transforms and becomes, or within its dark vastness arises, pure consciousness or awareness. This awareness has the capacity to perceive, but it does not perceive concepts or entities. It is ontologically prior to concept, just as the Absolute is ontologically prior to consciousness. The realm of experience and perception at this level is what I call the "nonconceptual realm."

The Absolute is nonconceptual because there are no concepts there; but it is deeper than simply nonconceptual. In the Absolute there is not even any consciousness. The nonconceptual is the same as the Absolute, except that there is consciousness. As the nonconceptual, which I call the Nameless because there is no name for it, I know, and I know that I know. But I don't know *what* I know. This level of knowing does not involve recognition of things. In the Absolute I don't know, and I don't know that I don't know. The Nameless is "I know." I know that I know, but I don't know what I know, because there is nothing there to know. It is just consciousness knowing itself. It is just the bare minimum of awareness of existence, which is pure consciousness. We call it nonconceptual because there are no concepts there. The moment there are concepts, you know *something*. The moment you say, "I know this," you have created a concept or become aware of a concept. You have put something in a category, delineated it as something. But the nonconceptual is not a something.

In the nonconceptual, there is no sense of space and time. When the nonconceptual is experiencing the nonconceptual, it doesn't have form, shape, color, location, or size. It is prior to time and space. To have shape and size and color you need the concept of space. The only thing left is quality, and the quality is simply consciousness. You almost cannot even call it quality; it's not exactly that. It's as if you're aware, and you know you're aware, but you're not aware of anything in particular. You are simply aware of the awareness itself, conscious of the consciousness itself. You don't know whether it's inside or outside. There is no concept of inside or outside. There is no concept of someone being there, being aware.

Consciousness is the first thing that is needed for any experience. You cannot recognize a table without the capacity to be aware of a table. You cannot have any conceptual experience, such as, "I have a body" unless you have the consciousness that allows you to be aware of a body. Then in addition to the consciousness you need the concept of body before you can experience "I have a body." Before that you might be experiencing a body but not recognizing it as a body. The nonconceptual does not have categories. It is just the bare awareness. It is purity itself. It is complete innocence.

The nonconceptual does not have a sense of time. Here, the closest thing to time is like a sense of eternity. But by eternity we do not mean something that goes on forever. The sense of eternity indicates a realm that has nothing to do with time. Time is a concept.

From the perspective of the nonconceptual, you cannot say whether something exists or doesn't, because existence and non-existence are concepts. When your awareness of yourself is nonconceptual, there's no one there saying, "I exist" or "I don't exist." When you are contemplating existence or nonexistence, you have already distinguished two things, and are thus in the realm of the conceptual. So this realm is beyond existence or nonexistence. And even though there is consciousness, there isn't an idea of consciousness. Consciousness is not saying "I am consciousness." There is consciousness because there is consciousness, not because it is saying, "I am consciousness." It's very subtle. Then, when you go to the Absolute, even that is gone. There is complete darkness.

The Absolute and the Nameless are both nonconceptual. With the Nameless there is consciousness, and the Absolute is beyond consciousness. It's the difference between the night and day. The night is Absolute, and the day is the Nameless or the nonconceptual. There is light. This light doesn't bring any particular knowledge; it's just pure light.

The next thing that arises is that the nonconceptual, or pure awareness, manifests as existence or presence. We become aware of ourselves as existing. That is what I call the dimension of Pure Being, or the Supreme. Being then exists, and there is awareness that there is existence. The consciousness becomes aware of itself as existing. This is the beginning of the conceptual. The first concept that arises is Existence, Beingness, Presence.

Here there is a concept, but there is still no differentiation. It's not that someone exists. It's not that I exist and you exist. There is one pure something, and that is Pure Beingness, Pure Existence. That is the first concept. If you go beyond that into the nonconceptual, you can't talk about existence or nonexistence.

The Pure Beingness is experienced as unity—there's just one thing. There is just one thing that doesn't have parts. The perception of unity is like the perception that the whole body is made out of one thing. If it were only made of water, for instance, that would be unity. It is also possible to experience the whole as oneness. In this case, there is differentiation and discrimination; you can be aware of the parts, but still this differentiation does not mean separation. In oneness the perception is like you are aware of the elements the body is made of—for instance, that there is water, and there are carbon-based molecules, organs, and so on—and you cannot separate these elements.

So, in oneness there is differentiation: You are discriminating things; you can perceive colors, and the colors are different from one another. They constitute one thing, like one fabric. Here we see that differentiation does not mean separation. We see one shirt with different colors in it. We are aware of one body with different elements. We see one house that has many parts. You can discern things, but also perceive that they are not separate. In oneness, there is time-space. With pure Being, there's still no time-space, but there is existence. For there to be differentiation, as in oneness, there must be space.

In this dimension, concepts exist. What we mean here by "concepts" is recognizable differentiations. There are recognizable differentiations in phenomena, which from a certain perspective appear as concepts or ideas, but which we call here "noetic forms." They are the forms in which manifestation is differentiated. These concepts or noetic forms are not mental phenomena in the sense that thought is mental. We associate concepts with mental images. But a mental concept of something is not the same as a form actually existing. Here, we are talking about forms which exist. In this sense, a house is a concept. A house is not the same thing as the hill it sits on, right? So they can be differentiated and discriminated. However, the house and the hill are not separate; they are elements of one reality. So the hill is a concept, and the house is a concept. Differentiation and discrimination happen through concepts. In the realm of concepts, you can recognize differences in what exists in reality.

Our usual notion of a concept of chair, for example, is the idea of a chair. But an image of the chair is not the same thing as the chair. In this dimension, when I say, "This is a concept," I mean the chair itself is a concept. The pattern exists in reality; I'm not creating it in my mind. This is the realm of what we call "universal concepts" or "noetic forms." A universal concept is not my concept, not a mental concept. Mental concepts are personal, and their content depends upon the person. The fact that there is a chair here, however, does not depend upon the person. Any person who comes here can see this form, although it might not be recognized as a chair.

So what we call a noetic form is what we call a discriminated something that truly exists, that truly appears to perception. Physical reality is discriminated in universal concepts—a rock, or the hill over there, are universal concepts. It's not just that I personally see it as a hill. Someone else cannot validly say, "That's not a hill; that's an ocean."

The discrimination doesn't depend upon my personal experience. It is actually what truly exists, what exists as a differentiated existence. This is a noetic form. We also call this kind of discriminated form a universal concept, in that it can be universally perceived. We call these forms concepts because from the perspective of the nonconceptual, the forms in which Being manifests actually appear as ideas. This is the perception that some traditions call the "Divine Mind." Those aware of this perception might be heard to say such things as "We are all just ideas in God's mind." When you are perceiving the existence or manifestation of noetic forms from beyond these forms, they appear as a kind of ideas.

Physical reality as it actually exists is the existence of noetic form. A door is a noetic form, a bird is a noetic form, and a human being is a noetic form, in the sense that they truly exist. These forms are not determined by what we call them or how we perceive them; they actually exist, independent of our beliefs. On the level of oneness, they do not exist separate from everything else, but are part of everything else. A noetic form can be differentiated because it has its own intrinsic pattern that is discriminatable, not because my own personal mind defines the difference between one form and another. I cannot change the differentiations; I can only recognize them. Definitions might change, in that we might call a hill a hill only if it is a certain size. Another culture might call what we call a hill, a mountain.

Here we are talking about perception, not naming. So a noetic form has to do with an objective perception in the differentiated realm. This table has a glass of water and a notebook on it. Someone could look at the whole thing and call it a table, and someone else could say, "There's a table, and there's a notebook." But they're perceiving the same thing. The first person is seeing the notebook as part of the table, but they can see that this is black, and this is brown. This discrimination has to do with actual perception, not labels.

Student: I'm wondering about oceans because it seems that water would be a universal concept, but ocean is an abstraction. A bay is one thing. An ocean is water in a certain configuration.

AHA: So "ocean" is a large body of water, right? We have a concept for that. Another culture might not have that concept, but they will definitely see a large body of water.

S: Water is the universal concept. Ocean seems to be a very particular way of looking at water.

AHA: Water is a universal concept, a noetic form. But when I'm talking about noetic form here, I mean anything that exists on its own, any perception that exists without your subjective mind distorting it.

There is a discernible perception, right? Now where you put the boundaries does not make a difference. You could put a line at the rug. You could put the line at the table. You could make it smaller. But the perception is the same. You don't have to put the boundary on the rug; you could put it on the outside of the house. But the fact is that there is a perception of different colors and forms. You can differentiate the color of the table from the color of the rug. You can tell there is a difference. You might not think of them as two different things.

Here I am referring to the level of discriminated perception before you give things a name. It is difficult to understand this realm, because we are not used to discriminating the forms of things separately from naming them. And only when there is some capacity to see the forms from the dimension beyond forms is it possible to perceive forms or "divine ideas" which are not influenced or determined by personal mind. When you look at what exists from the level of the nonconceptual, you do not give things names, you do not separate one thing from another. There is just one existence. You do see variations; you just do not recognize or mentally conceptualize what the variation is. If you look at things from the perspective of noetic forms, then it is possible to articulate the differentiation. The idea here is that the existence of the table is different from the idea of a table.

S: You're talking about objective, electromechanical reality.

AHA: The most obvious noetic forms are those in the physical world. We might call things different names, or establish boundaries at different points, but we are seeing something that definitely exists. Someone could look at a tree and not differentiate the flowers on it as flowers. The whole thing is a tree. Someone else could say, "These are flowers, and these are leaves." And someone else could say, "Really? There's no such thing as flowers and leaves. There's just a tree." They simply are not discriminating them. Someone might have the concept of a tree, but not of leaves. You see a tree with leaves, and they don't. But if you pointed to the leaves and said, "These are leaves," then they might say, "Oh, that's what you call leaves." They will not say, "No, there are no leaves." They will understand you. "So that is what you call leaves. I get that. I've seen them before. I just didn't give them a name."

So noetic forms are independent of our personal orientation, independent of our history of learning to name and discriminate things. As we have discussed, the process of conceptualizing the elements of our experience and reifying the concepts in our minds creates a world made up of opaque and separate entities. This reification constitutes a powerful barrier to our capacity to experience reality with no concepts, to experience the dimension of the nonconceptual. It also prevents us from seeing the level of oneness. Two elements of perception must shift to make a transition from living in the world of mental objects to perceiving the world of actual noetic forms: First, the perception of forms as separated, discrete objects must shift, so that there is a perception of oneness where there are discriminated perceptions but without separating boundaries. In this level of perception, forms and concepts are seen as transparent. Second, the capacity to be conscious and aware of reality without any conceptualization at all is needed. This is perception in the nonconceptual realm—what some call the "ground of awareness." These capacities do not necessarily develop in a particular order; they each have many issues and barriers associated with them, which we have begun to address in the past few meetings.

Besides the barrier of reified, opaque concepts determining our experience of the world, there are more specific barriers in the personal mind for each person to work through in the process of realizing these dimensions. As we have discussed, all the concepts of the self and others and of the world are developed in the mind of a child influenced by instinctual and emotional needs. That process is governed by seeking pleasure and security and love, and avoiding pain and insecurity. The development of the concepts of self and world are always colored then by reactivity, and by psychodynamic issues. The psychodynamic issues have to do with the history of the relationships with the parents, for example, as well as other factors.

Experiences of physical and emotional pleasure and pain greatly influence the formation of the concepts of self and world, and either attachment to or avoidance of certain concepts renders our mental world rigid and closed. An example of this is the concept of sex or gender: We learn in the course of growing up that we "are" a girl or a boy. The notion that one is a girl or a boy is always fraught with various value judgments, ideas of what male and female or masculine and feminine mean, and related beliefs about oneself and others, which may be very far from objective. So even though there are objective differences in the noetic form of female and the noetic form of male, the concept of male or female will for any given person be deeply subjective; it will be a personal concept, involving all kinds of judgments, reactions, opinions, prejudices, and associations. These reactions and associations then limit our capacity to see clearly even what we are personally believing at any given moment about reality, and tend to make the rigidness of our reified concepts even greater. In turn, as we have seen, this rigidness and opacity about ourselves and the world separates us further from the truth of who we are, and thus is the source of our suffering and alienation.

In our work here one way we address this vicious circle of reification and reactivity is to work on the qualities of the soul, the essential aspects. So far we have talked about the noetic forms of manifestation on the level of physical reality. Another realm of discriminated manifestation which exists independent of personal concepts is the realm of noetic forms which we call essential aspects. The aspects are universal concepts in that their form of manifestation is independent of the personal mind of the person who experiences them. For example, when you experience essential Compassion, and I experience essential Compassion, we experience the same thing. To say that the form is the same is not to say that you and I might not call it something different. But the quality itself is the same thing. It is not dependent on what I know from the past. It is not dependent on my personal mind. Compassion truly, objectively exists, independent of my personal historical mind. That is what Essence is.

When we experience Essence as Value, someone who does not know about the realm of Essence might say, "But that's your subjective experience." However, Essence is not simply a subjective experience; it is an actual, specific, discriminated presence in the soul. It exists on a level more fundamental than, for example, my idea of myself as a little kid who is hurt. This self-image affects how I see myself, how I feel emotionally and how I react, but it does not exist on the level of presence. It is not an experience of my actual state at the present moment. It's an idea in my mind. But if I experience myself as Value right now, that means that right now I am actually valuable. And the presence of Value is as palpable, as substantial, as anything physical.

So far today we have seen that as manifestation goes from the nonconceptual level to the conceptual, what first arises is what is called the realm of noetic forms, or universal concepts—knowable differentiations in reality. We can have differentiated perceptions without naming them, without separating one thing from another. If I am the nonconceptual perceiving the differentiated world, I won't say, "This is a chair, this is an arm." I just see the variations in differences without separating things out. At the next level we discriminate things out so we can deal with them functionally, and also communicate about them.

Mental concepts can be more or less aligned with true noetic forms. As you know, the process of becoming objective in our perception of ourselves and the truth of reality is a long and arduous one. It involves an orientation toward truth and objectivity, in which we consistently question the content of the personal mind with its beliefs and reactions, and attempt to see what is actually true and real in our experience. This process involves not assuming that we know the truth, which supports our experience of space and openness. The process continues into the realm of nonceptual reality, in which the concepts of personal mind no longer determine what we perceive. Here we see the significance of our work on essential aspects: we are working with a knowledge of discriminated reality in realms independent of the personal mind. This work eventually brings us to the realm of the Universal Mind, or what the Greek philosophers called the Nous. At the level of the Nous concepts are more fundamental than ideas in the mind. Awareness of concepts at this level makes it possible for us to communicate and function without relying on the content of personal mind.

Objective discrimination in the essential realms is possible, just as it is in the physical universe. For example, a fingernail exists in the physical world, but someone might not think of it as something on its own. They might perceive only a finger, without separating the nail from the finger. But they can see that there is a difference from here to here. The finger is hard here and soft here. They just might not give it a separate name. In the essential realm, some people might not differentiate Compassion from Love, but they are distinguishable.

The realm of noetic forms is the realm of the manifestation of what is, independent of our definitions or our prejudices. Our learned definitions and our emotional prejudices determine which elements we pay attention to and recognize. These factors determine the content of personal concepts, of mental images of ourselves and others and of the world. Thus the content of our personal concepts can change.

We are traversing quite a territory today. So far we have elucidated the difference between the nonconceptual and the conceptual, the realms where there are no concepts, where there are concepts, and where concepts are possible. Here we are describing the realm of objective reality, things that actually exist. This realm has many levels, from pure Beingness to other levels of Essence, all the way to the physical levels. These are the gradations of reality. We can experience everything as beingness, but at the same time perceive that beingness as differentiated. The chair is beingness, the glass is beingness, the rug is beingness. They are all one beingness, differentiated.

What is this territory we are exploring? The totality of all that exists, with all this variation, is the Universal Mind, or Nous. The Nous includes everything that exists in reality, with all the differentiations. It includes everything that can be perceived or experienced, and anything that can be conceptualized. What we call in our Work the Diamond Guidance is the Nous on the level of Essence, the manifestation which allows the individual soul to be affected by the Nous. The Nameless or nonconceptual is beyond the Nous; it is the ground of the Nous, which wouldn't exist without it. The Nameless is beyond mind, and the Absolute is beyond that.

In contrast, the personal mind, or the realm of personality, is not what actually exists in reality. The content of the personal mind is determined by one's particular history and conditioning, including all kinds of cultural forms and values in addition to concepts formed by one's individual situation. The process of constructing and reifying concepts leads us to perceive the world and even ourselves through—actually *as*—these concepts in the mind. In addition, the personal mind contains evaluations of all this content: Judgments, emotional associations, preferences, and reactions. The personal mind says, "The table is good, the rug is bad," or "The rug is beautiful, the hill is ugly."

The personal mind is based on the Nous; it couldn't exist without it. It is based on the actual differentiations and the objective concepts or forms that appear in the Nous, but distorts these forms, reifies them, and renders them opaque. And the distance between the content of the personal mind and reality is further increased and maintained by judgments, reactions, and preferences, which lead to emotional reactions. "I like this, I hate this. This makes me jealous. This makes me uncomfortable. This makes me comfortable." As we have seen, the origin of these evaluations is the differentiation between pleasure and pain. Then we build on that differentiation: "This is good, this is bad. I like this, I don't like that." This pattern develops into the whole story of the personal mind, and can include enormous elaborations about right and wrong—whole philosophies developing out of our personal perspectives.

The personal mind focuses on certain segments of the Nous and takes these to be the totality of reality. Mostly, it focuses on the physical universe. We have seen how the nature of childhood development tends to lead to this orientation. Because of this physical orientation, the personal mind normally is not grounded in the essential dimensions. It is based on and prejudiced towards the most concrete and localized level of Nous, rather than the dimensions which include more refined awareness. The personal mind perceives mostly from the perspective of the pleasures and pains of the body, even when it is affected by Essence. The self-images that determine ego reactions and feelings, even perceptions, are based on identification with the body. Thus the personal mind doesn't attend to deeper elements at subtler levels of the Nous or Universal Mind, such as Essence and Beingness. We need a lot of education to learn to take those realms into consideration.

The personal mind is based on the Nous, and on the existence of concepts in general, whether they are the universal concepts or noetic forms which actually exist, or concepts that are the constructed in our minds. One example of the relation of personal concepts to universal concepts is the question of beauty and harmony. Personal mental constructs include both subjective historical factors and emotional reactions about what is good and bad, beautiful and ugly. Judgments and reactions about what is beautiful and ugly do not exist in the Nous. It is true that our appreciation of aesthetics involves a response to what moves us closer to the Nous, and in the Nous there is a sense of harmony and beauty. However, this sense of beauty is a response of the soul to the truth.

If you are beyond the personal mind with its preferences, and if you are oriented by the Universal Mind, there is the sense of beauty and harmony. Everything is bright and beautiful. Nothing is ugly. You have to be in the personal mind to differentiate the beautiful from the ugly, and usually what is seen as beautiful is what takes us closer to the Universal Mind.

The personal mind includes our own perceptions and beliefs, evaluations, judgments, preferences, reactions, and philosophizing based on perceptions that originate from the Universal Mind. These beliefs, evaluations, and stories are generally based on our personal history. The personal mind, as we have seen, developed in time with the growth of our organism, and carries the past with it. The Nous does not depend on the past. It does not depend on time because it is a pure perception of what is there. If you see people sitting in a room, you might not call them people, but you definitely know they are there, and you are probably aware that the people and what they are sitting on are not the same thing. So you might not call the different things the same names, but you know there is a difference, unless your senses are flawed in some way. And even if your discrimination accurately reflects the forms of the chair and the person, your personal mind is certain to evaluate—to say, for instance, that the person is more important than the chair. That evaluation is the personal mind. The fact that we can tell the person and the chair apart is a function of the Universal Mind.

We spoke first about the nonconceptual. Then, looking at the conceptual, we divided it into two parts—what is dependent on the personal mind, and what is transcendent to or independent of the personal mind—the Nous or Universal Mind. The Nous contains all the realms of Essence and Being, and all of what we call spiritual experience. All the spiritual levels are part of this Universal Mind.

In this talk I am not making all the possible differentiations and qualifications. There are gradations I have not mentioned; here I am making very rough differentiations between the nonconceptual and the conceptual, with its two parts. The conceptual actually has more dimensions.

S: It seems that there is a kind of evaluation that we talk about here in the Work that seems to fall into the category of the objective, the Universal Mind, which is that something works in an objective sense. There is an efficiency and support for some action, that we can say that something works or doesn't work on some kind of objective level, as opposed to a preference.

AHA: Yes, either something works or it doesn't work. You can say it is independent of the personal mind. Or, we can define what "works" means—to go from here to here. We can see that this path leads from here to here, and this path does not. This is the capacity of the Nous. To say that it is important to go from here to here, that is personal mind.

It is a preference even to say, "I should be alive." No essential aspect says that I should be alive. As we become more in touch with Essence, our values change. The personal mind is transforming, and is more influenced by the Nous. If there is no personal mind at all, there is no evaluation. You just do things from the perspective of the Nous, not because you think one thing is better than another. For example, the tree has a tendency to grow and be healthy. This tendency is not a result of the tree thinking that growing and thriving is the best thing to do. It just does it; it can't help it. That process of manifestation is the operation of the Universal Mind in its dynamic form, what is called the Logos.

So we see that not having a personal mind does not result in chaos. It does not mean, for example, that it won't matter to us if we hurt ourselves or become sick. Like a tree or any other organism, human beings have a tendency to grow and be healthy. It's not that the tree has a personal mind that says, "I prefer life over death," or, "I'm afraid of dying." A tree does not do that. It just naturally lives, grows, and eventually dies.

S: What about the concept of choice?

AHA: Choice comes from the personal mind because choice is dependent on evaluation. Of course, the interaction between personal mind and the Universal Mind is a whole big subject. That is the realm of the Work. We often hear "Well, I've experienced Essence. What should I do now?" We might think, "If I'm free, I should do this or that," or, "If I'm in touch with Essence, I shouldn't have to work." We have such thoughts because we are still looking at reality from the perspective of the personal mind.

S: So your implication is that if we could shut off the mechanism of personal choice and trying to control everything, that Universal Mind would be there to support us. We could flourish that way.

AHA: Right. And that's the tendency of the Universal Mind—its forms have the tendency to flourish and die. It is the usual rhythm of life, the rhythm of nature.

The idea of the Work here is to have what is working be not the personal mind, but the Universal Mind. Only what is natural is what happens. This is not easy to describe, because the picture is quite involved. Let me see whether I can say more . . . The personal mind is part of the Nous, because everything that exists is part of it. One noetic form in the Universal Mind is the human being, the soul of the human being. So one of the concepts or noetic forms of universal mind is soul.

Now that soul, that noetic form of soul, one of the universal concepts that truly exists, is different from all other concepts in the sense that it has the capacity to think and conceptualize and create its reality and determine its own perception of things. A rock cannot do that, but the soul can.

The soul also has the capacity to shut off awareness of the rest of the Universal Mind, and focus on one part of it, like the physical. A whole viewpoint develops based on that orientation towards physical reality. I think that is why it is said that we have free will—we have the capacity to say "no" to some aspects of reality, to live as if our own limited knowledge were all there is. And from that perspective, we make choices. In that sense, we do have free will.

But from the perspective of the Nous, there is no free will. It is all the Nous anyway. At the locations called souls, Nous operates in a certain way: A particular location can cut off its perception such that it believes that it is running the show. Yet the same soul that has the capacity to delude itself also can work to clarify itself and begin to see the Nous, and begin to allow it to function. You can call this process surrendering, allowing the will of God, simply being, or just non-doing.

So through the Work the soul can become free from the personal mind. The work for the soul is to go through the personal mind, which we have been looking at as object relations, images, reactions, patterns, and beliefs, as well as ideas, dreams, and identifications. In our Work the soul can become aware of the specific details of the personal mind, with the prejudices and the beliefs it has adopted, and discover that the soul's reality does not have to be determined by that historical mind. The real concepts—the noetic forms of the essential aspects—correct the distortions.

Thus, the more we experience the realm of Essence and integrate it, the more the personal mind is corrected through being influenced by the perceptions of the Nous, objective knowledge about how reality is and how it actually functions. This process is what I call the clarification and development of the soul. The soul is then governed not by the personal mind, but according to the Nous. We begin to live our lives according to the truth of Essence and the truth we experience in the Work, not according to what we learned from our conditioned existence.

The more we see the Nous and allow it to function, or allow ourselves to see that it operates, the more we experience a sense of harmony, beauty, love, and all the essential qualities. We then experience an expansive sense of release, a lack of constriction. Constriction comes from trying to oppose the Nous, from believing that we are separate and independent from it, and from operating according to beliefs that have nothing to do with what actually exists.

Consider the idea that life is better than death. Who says that? Not the Nous, or the Logos. The Universal Mind in its dynamic form is what is called the Logos; it is the level of the changes and transformations within reality, according to the noetic forms of the Nous. The Logos has both life and death in it; it does not say that one is better than the other. One simply comes after the other, or more accurately, things just change and transform. Ocean becomes rain, and rain becomes ocean. The Logos does not say which one is better. It just does both.

When we come to see and accept this perspective, there is less constriction. Constriction comes from having our own preferences. We want things to go a certain way instead of the way the Logos is functioning. For example, if the Logos is making you sick, that's part of its operation. You might feel, "No, I shouldn't be sick. I shouldn't die. I should worry about it." Well, that's what's happening. You are going to die sometime. Universal Mind is functioning in such a way that you are going to die. And you say, "No, that shouldn't happen. I don't like it. I'll resist it." And you fight it. You become terrified. To accept reality is to accept the operation of the Universal Mind, to accept what happens.

In this context, freedom means that the soul is less influenced by the personal mind, and more in harmony with the Universal Mind. We are increasingly perceiving universal concepts rather than our own constructed concepts and our reactions to them. So what actually exists becomes important. That is why Being is important. Being is what exists, what is now, the ontological field of the Universal Mind.

S: I can understand that someone shouldn't deny the inevitable if they are dying. That seems like an issue around control. But isn't there a danger also of being passive and fatalistic, accepting death when fighting for your life might save it?

AHA: Your question reflects a belief that if the personal mind is not in control, things will not go the way that you think is good. However, the Universal Mind has its functioning; it moves in its natural way. And part of its functioning is that when you are sick, you might do something to take care of it. But to do something about it does not mean to reject it. You do not have to be afraid or angry or reactive in order to act. This is the interaction between the personal mind and Universal Mind, which is very difficult to understand. It is not obvious how to go from one to the other; there is a lot of ambiguity. For instance, allowing nature to function does not mean not having technology. Universal Mind is what creates technology. The more we see the Universal Mind and the more we let go of our constricted beliefs and ideas of how things should be, the more that nature will take care of itself, and our natural beingness will function. And that will bring health. Nature has its own health and well-being.

People get into confusion wondering what is the difference between nature and civilization, nature and culture. It's not necessarily a conflict. Technology and civilization are not necessarily against Universal Mind. If we are not controlled by our personal beliefs and ignorance and preferences, how will things happen? How will we deal with nuclear energy? Will we want it or not? We don't know. Someone might say, "Civilization is no good. I'm going to go live in the jungle." That's not necessarily being natural. Universal Mind includes machines and atom bombs. All these are part of Universal Mind.

As we make a transition to Universal Mind, how will we go about things? How will we live? How will we look at things if we are infused by Universal Mind, by perceiving what actually is happening without our own prejudiced reactions to it? That is a function of the Work.

S: I thought that would lead to passivity, but then I considered the idea of True Will. I see that if you're in touch with Universal Mind, you won't act unless true Will arises. You won't act out of false will.

AHA: Right. But action definitely arises. Or you might not act. Allowing Universal Mind to work does not mean there is no action. It does not mean passivity. The personal mind sees this as passivity. In many traditional spiritual practices, you become more passive or receptive, not to the personal mind, but to the Universal Mind.

If your body needs to be healed, the Universal Mind will manifest in you as Will and Strength and Intelligence, and you can go about healing it in the most efficient way. But if you are using your personal mind, you might block your Will and your Strength by messing with yourself. Or you could go about it in a unnecessary or inefficient way. You might exert too much effort or the wrong effort.

S: When you're shifting your perspective from personal mind it's difficult to understand how to be in accord with a different way. There's a lot of gray area.

AHA: Right. The confusion happens in the realm of functioning. That's when it's difficult to tell. But seeing what exists is much easier to understand. In a sense, when you define yourself with a self-image, you're telling yourself how you exist. That's personal mind. If you let that go, if you are not defining yourself by images from the past, but you just let yourself be, whatever you are right now, without the past, how will you experience yourself? You would experience yourself as Essence, as Being, and you would begin to see that you're not separate from everything else. The apparent separation has to do with the concept in your mind that you are separate from other things, and especially the concept that the body defines you. Taking the concept of the body to define who you are, that's the personal mind.

It might be possible to see this truth, but then it gets more difficult when we get into the realm of functioning. It is more complex, and harder to see the true perspective. So, it's good to start with the questions: "What exists?" and "What is reality?" And then, after we have some understanding, it becomes easier to understand doing and functioning and activity from the perspective of Universal Mind and the Logos.

We have seen that the ego defines reality according to the physical part of the Universal Mind. That's basically what the personal mind is all about. You see yourself and your life and what it means from that perspective. So clearly, the Work is a matter of reeducating the personal mind, disposing of the deluded education from your childhood, and bringing in an education that comes from the Universal Mind. Let the Universal Mind start educating you about how things are.

However, because the ego uses concepts ultimately to define everything, it will hold on to any concept to maintain its existence. It will even hold on to universal concepts to make itself exist. It can take experiences of Essence, and say, "Oh, I am Essence." It is conceptualizing and reifying, and saying, "I am Essence, I am Essence." It is defining itself as Essence instead of experiencing itself as Essence. So you have a memory of an essential experience, and you say, "That's me." But it's a self-image, as opaque as any other self-image. Although the experience comes from the Universal Mind, the personal mind can use it to continue defining itself. This is why we need to go beyond the Universal Mind to the nonconceptual reality where there is nothing for the ego to use to define itself—there is nothing there to define.

So in the Work we need to go from a personal mind to the Universal Mind, which means to go from the realm of the personality to the realm of Essence and its dimensions. But we also need to go beyond that to the realm of the nonconceptual. Otherwise the ego can still use even the objective differentiated perceptions, remembering them and holding onto them in order to define itself.

As we have discussed, when we perceive the physical universe and the essential universe from the perspective of nonconceptual reality, they look like thoughts; this is why we call them "mind." The Nous can be seen like a structure or pattern of ideas, and just as we perceive mental images when we see through the concepts in the personal mind, we see these ideas in the Nous as images. From the perspective of the nonconceptual, the Universal Mind looks like images. The table looks like the image of a table. It's not really a table. It remains real from the perspective of the personal mind, but from the perspective of the nonconceptual, it's not that the table is not real, it's just not as real as the nonconceptual. The nonconceptual is a much more fundamental reality. And the things in the physical world and in the essential realms are laid on it like images. That is why we call it the Universal Mind.

We call it the Universal Mind because when we go beyond it, we see it as mind. But it is not mind as created by me personally. It's the mind that actually exists as the totality of the Universe. Some people call it God's mind.

So from the level of the nonconceptual, the physical universe and Essence and all that exists are mind. They are concepts, like ideas or forms that are filled out with something. What they are filled out by is the nonconceptual, the original consciousness. Until you can perceive and understand things from the perspective of the nonconceptual dimension, you are what both Buddhist and Western philosophers call an "essentialist." You believe that things and essences exist, each with a permanent self-nature. Much confusion in spiritual work and philosophy rests on the fact that people take one dimension or another to be the final or total truth. Having some capacity to perceive from the nonconceptual level brings a lot of clarity to our understanding of the various dimensions and their relationships.

So the nonconceptual is like one big block with nothing differentiable in it. Then this becomes carved. And this carving is what we see as Universal Mind. Remember, it is not a mind like the personal mind. We cannot understand Universal Mind until we differentiate between personal mind and Universal Mind. And in Universal Mind all manifest existence appears as concepts.

When we say that the heart is a concept, for example, what do we mean? It is true, that seen from a certain place, the heart is an idea, an image. But it is not the usual idea or image. It is a noetic form, which when looked at from the normal dimension, looks like reality. It *is* reality.

The nonconceptual has a powerful effect on the ego. The ego continues to believe that the physical and essential realms are the real things, until you get to the nonconceptual. Then you realize that the whole thing is really mind. And then you wonder, "If the whole thing is really mind, why do I believe it so completely?" At that point, your belief in the ultimacy of what exists gets really challenged. If you begin to see that everything is mind, then you wonder, "What does it mean to die?" It's not that death and life don't exist, but they lose their importance. They do not have the same significance that they have in the conventional dimension. So this realization will bring in more possibility of freedom. The challenges that the nonconceptual presents to the fixations and beliefs of the ego are powerful and fundamental. And of course if we go to the Absolute, the challenge is even greater. There, even the consciousness itself doesn't have to be there for me to be myself.

S: Since in the nonconceptual, there was no experience of differentiation, I'm having difficulty seeing how you can look from the nonconceptual and see these other levels as mind. That would be differentiation.

AHA: I distinguished between the nonconceptual experiencing itself as nonconceptual, and the nonconceptual experiencing the conceptual. I can be the Absolute experiencing myself as the Absolute, in which case there is no consciousness of myself nor of anything. But I could be the Absolute experiencing the world. Then I am not purely the Absolute; then the level of the Nous is present with the Absolute, so there is discriminating awareness. Only because there is Nous do I know there is an Absolute. Without discriminating awareness I would never know the Absolute; I would just be the Absolute without knowing that I am the Absolute. So in some sense, in order to know it you have to get out of it. For awareness of the Absolute, another dimension needs to arise, which is the dimension of the nonconceptual, which is pure awareness. As the nonconceptual, you can become aware of the Absolute. You realize that the Absolute is simply a bigger abyss than you have seen.

This is why it is said in the Tibetan tradition that a subtle consciousness is needed to apprehend emptiness. This subtle consciousness is called the clear light. The clear light of the Void is what apprehends the Void. Without the clear light, without consciousness, you don't know whether there is a Void or not.

In the Sufi tradition they say that God existed in the beginning as his own Essence, God's own identity and nature, which is the Absolute. God said, "I am a hidden treasure. I wanted to be known, so I created the Universe in order to be known." How can the Absolute be known if it does not become something else? How, unless it becomes consciousness and then the world? As the Absolute, God does not know Himself. So to know Himself, God created everything. Then, because there is consciousness, He could say, "Ah, here's our mind! Isn't that wonderful!" This is one story to explain what we are talking about today, one way of looking at it. We don't really know whether God did it that way, but it makes sense. This story can explain the creation of all these gradations of reality.

The Absolute is a pure awareness that is not aware of itself, but it is aware of anything that comes out of itself. The moment consciousness arises, the Absolute becomes aware of it as pure light, pure radiance. So you can be the Absolute being aware of the nonconceptual.

Or you can lose the Absolute and become just the non-conceptual. You can be just the nonconceptual experiencing the nonconceptual, which you experience as just pure awareness without anything to know. Or you could be the nonconceptual and be aware of the Absolute. And then you know the Absolute. That is how we can talk about the Absolute and its absence of qualities.

At any level of experience, you can perceive both the more superficial realms and the next deeper realm. Except if you go to the Absolute, there's only one way to go, which is towards the more superficial. If you are in the personal mind, there's also only one way to go, which is towards the deeper. The Absolute is the most fundamental, and the personal mind is the most superficial.

It's amazing, really, when we see how reality exists, how it is multifaceted and multi-layered. We see in contrast how the perspective of the personal mind is very restricted, very constricted, very small, very truncated. This constriction explains a lot of the suffering and negativity of egoic life. You are taking the whole of reality and seeing it as a little thing, and trying to live from that perspective. It's like taking a finger, and tying it off here where it meets the hand, and believing that only that is you. Only this finger is me. Such a belief is bound to be very painful.

Becoming aware of the essential dimensions allows us to experience reality beyond the personal mind. That's why we call it our essence; it is the inner nature of what we are. When we experience ourselves as Essence, we experience ourselves as nowness, not as a continuation of what happened in the past. We are not defining ourselves with images from the past. We experience ourselves simply now. But this capacity develops gradually. You don't get rid of your images all at once. The more you are free of the images, the more there is a sense of presence; the bigger the sense of presence, the more inclusive and the more universal it is.

Ultimately, what happens is freedom from the personal mind. You will fear that, if you go to the Absolute, there will be nothing left. Actually everything will still exist, but it will exist in the Universal Mind. The Universal Mind becomes the content of life and existence. This is why the Sufi tradition says that when a person has been freed, the man changes from being a man to being a universal man. A universal man is a man who is free, who is realized. He is a universal human being.

The whole thing is very mysterious and magical. Just contemplate the implications of what I have said today. I can experience myself as the Absolute, not aware of anything else and not aware of itself. It is possible to be the Absolute completely and feel like there is no world, there is nothing. But then you open your eyes, and the whole world exists.

But what happened when I wasn't experiencing it? Was the world there? When I am the Absolute being the Absolute, it is like deep sleep. You believe that while you are in deep sleep, the world exists. But maybe when you wake up, you discover that world was not there. How can we know? The thing is much more mysterious than that. The fact that I can experience myself as not experiencing anything, and then I experience everything . . . how can that happen?

So it is not a linear kind of thing. It is not that one dimension sits on top of another. You can see them as one layer after another, but it is not really like that. They interpenetrate in a mysterious way, so it's possible to experience all the levels at the same time. Sometimes you experience just one level; sometimes you experience none of it. It is very difficult to explain this part of it. Reality is very mysterious and magical. There is a beauty and miraculousness and wonder in the whole situation.

This is why human beings are said to be special kinds of beings. They are more special than animals, for instance. Why? Because a human being can experience all the realms. We can actually experience, go through all the levels and see one or all of them, while animals stay in the same place.

It is said in some traditions that even angels are not as high as human beings because angels exist at one level. Maybe they exist at one of the love levels, the love angel, for instance. But that angel can only experience love. It cannot experience anything else. It is always loving, always wonderful, but cannot experience other things. A human being can experience all of the realms.

S: Normally, when we consider a continuum of spirituality, it seems that it goes from God down to animals or mineral or something more basic than that. We're in the middle there. But in the way you're talking, it seems the animal and mineral are at the universal concept level.

AHA: The lowest is the personal mind. The unenlightened personal mind is the lowest, lower than animals. That's why it is said in some holy books, for instance, the Koran: "We created you as the best of creation, but we threw you down all the way to the bottom." Something like that. Because the personal mind can become really the lowest. The human being can become so constricted, you would have a much better life if you were a cat.

When I say we have the possibility to be something much freer, much more wonderful, than any other existence, I mean we have the whole range. That is why the human being is said to be "made in the image of God." The human being can experience all of it because God is all of it.

One way of understanding the concept of God is that God is basically the totality of the Universal Mind, all the levels. The human soul can experience all the levels. The only being that exists in the universe as far as we know, that experiences all the levels, is the human soul. So in that sense, we are similar to God. And the human soul can integrate its knowledge to the degree of being aware of itself as all the levels. You can continue being a human being, but have all the levels in you, and you can be aware that you are all the levels, all the variations, in one integration, which is a human being—a miniature God, in some sense. God is the totality of all the levels. A human being can be all the levels in a personal sense. That is what is called the Complete Man, the complete human being.

The Complete Man is also referred to as a Vice-Regent of the Absolute, a representative of God, the son of God. In a sense, he is made in the image of God, made of the same thing. God is the only thing that exists that has all these levels, besides the human being. The human being cannot be the totality of the universe, but can be a human being with all the levels, like a miniaturization of all the dimensions as a human being. If you experience all the dimensions, you are not experiencing you; you are experiencing God Himself. The state of oneness is like the experience of being God; it is God realization.

SEVENTEEN

Selflessness

Today we will explore the central issue of the nonconceptual dimension, using a specific passage from the
Bible. In *The Gospel According to Luke*, Christ says, "If
any man would come after me, let him deny himself and take
up his cross daily and follow me. For whoever would save
his life, would lose it, and whoever loses his life for my sake,
he will save it." Since it is Christmas time, I thought we would
work with something relevant to this holiday. I believe that
this quote describes the spirit of Christmas. Today we want
to explore it and come to an appreciative understanding of
it: ". . . whoever would save his life will lose it," and ". . . whoever loses his life for my sake, he will save it."

This statement cuts to the core of our Work and any work
that is aimed towards realization of the truth. The self is the

main barrier against realization. The self-centered self lives from the self for the self. Why is that a problem? Why is it that if you try to save your life, to have your life, you will lose it? And if you sacrifice it, you will more truly save it?

Even when you are doing the Work, even when you are very deeply into it, you are still doing it for yourself. There is something you want to gain, something you want to happen for you. Even when you think of union with God, you need to wonder, why do you want union with God? You want to feel good. You might feel you can be God's bride.

This perspective is normal; for most people it is how life is. It's how everyone lives. You come from the place of being that self, and you live mostly for that self. You might be serving others, but the self stays at the center. You are the center of your life. It is not only that your self is the center of your life—your life is *your* life. The life you live is for you. It's your life. It's related to you.

From my perspective, when Christ says, "If you follow me," I don't think he meant following him as a person, walking around Jerusalem. To follow Christ means to follow the truth, to follow what is real, with Christ as a representative of truth, of the real. To follow the real is to follow the truth and to recall its essence: God, reality.

So to follow the truth, one must deny oneself and take up the cross daily. This is a very advanced, tricky, and subtle statement because we generally believe that we can have two masters, even when we are committed to the truth. We believe we can live for the truth, and at the same time we can have what the self wants. We can fulfill and gratify the self. A large part of the Work is working out this struggle. What are the demands of the truth? What are the demands of the self? We basically compromise most of the time.

Christ's statement says that if you live your life for the self, or try to compromise and serve two masters, it won't work. You will lose the life that you feel you are saving. You will lose the life that you think you're going to have. To lose your life means that whatever life you are living will not be a real life. It will be a false life, an empty life, a meaningless and unfulfilled life. So it is not a life in any real sense. You might as well be dead.

There is another word for this condition. Rather than "dead," I usually call it "undead." That's how the life of the ego is. It is the life of the undead. It's not really a life, but you are not physically gone. You're still walking around, but you are dead. You are undead.

In the phrase, "let him deny himself," there is an implication that the demands of the self are either contrary to the needs of truth, or in competition with the needs of the truth. If we understand it clearly, deeply, we will see what it means to say, "I want to do this for the self." If you have an understanding of what the self is, you realize it is contrary to the truth. The truth is that the self is not something that exists the way the self believes itself to exist. So it is false even to say, "I am this self that has a life, and this is my life," whether you think you are compromising with the truth or in contradiction to the truth. Most of us believe, "This is me, this is the self that has a personal life. And having a personal life is for the person that is me." Simply having that belief means you are not living for the truth, but for yourself, which you are taking to be something other than the truth. On the level of Christ, the Christ Consciousness, the Logos, or the Universal Mind, the truth is that there is no such thing as a separate self with an independent life. In reality, it is not there. It does not exist. So to live for that self, even a little bit, is worshipping a falsehood, worshipping something that is not there.

It is not easy, of course, to see that what we call the self, that what we think of as our own selfhood, our own personality, does not really exist in the way we believe it does, and that what we call our life is not exactly our life. The concept that we have a life is not exactly accurate.

In his statement, Christ does not simply say the self is a falsehood, is not the truth. He conveys it in a way that is characteristic of Christ, a way that can give us more insight about the resolution of this situation. Do I live for the truth, do I live for God, do I live for Christ, or do I live for myself?

The way he actually says it is, "If any man would come after me, let him deny himself and take up his cross daily and follow me. For whoever will save his life will lose it. Whoever loses his life for my sake, he will save it."

The idea here is to be a follower of the truth, so much so that what I call my life is to be constantly sacrificed to the truth. To be constantly sacrificed to the truth is the meaning of carrying your cross daily. Daily, it is sacrifice: It is given away. It is given away to the truth, to the way of truth.

We find this assertion in many places in religious and spiritual traditions. Today I am introducing it as part of our Work. This Work does not work if you want to save yourself. If your work is self-seeking, if it is for the benefit of what you consider to be yourself, it won't work. It's as simple as that—it simply won't happen. The process of the Work is a way of giving away the self, surrendering the self, giving up the self, sacrificing the self; and sacrificing it to the truth.

This is not a moral idea. It's not that if you do the Work for yourself, you are bad, and God will punish you. Some people think of it that way. I don't. I think of it as a law of nature. If you want to follow the path of truth, how can you do something for the self, when the self is not ultimately something real? It's a contradiction. It just doesn't work that way.

If you do the Work for the self, and you live your life for the self, the way you understand yourself, I don't see you as bad. You don't need to be punished. You are just living your life for the self. And that's what you'll get—the self, and the life of the self. But you will not get a life of truth.

I don't think it's bad, and no one is telling you you shouldn't do it.

In the statement we've been contemplating, Christ does not say you *should* follow him. He says, "If any man *would* come after me." If you want to, if that's your choice, then you need to be clear about what is your choice. You have to be clear about what it means, what needs to happen: that this work is a process of self-sacrifice, constant, daily. You daily carry your cross.

When I say self-sacrifice, I don't mean that you have to be a victim, or that you have to suffer, or have a hard time. That's not the idea here. Self-sacrifice means choosing the truth over the false. You sacrifice what is false to the truth.

Christ is not talking about choosing the truth from a preference for the false in the sense of having an insight or an experience of the truth. He is talking about how to live. Do you live from the perspective of the truth, or from the perspective of the self, which is ultimately false? "Whoever would save his life," meaning 'save it for himself', "will lose it." Then he doesn't simply say, "whoever will lose it," but "Whoever loses his life for my sake," for the sake of the truth, "he will save it." I have not yet given any explanation or interpretation of these statements so far.

What could this statement mean, in practical terms, in terms of how you live every day, every minute? For instance, suppose you finish work, and you go home and have three hours of free time. What are you going to do? Are you going to live your life for yourself, or for the truth? For instance, you might go to a movie, go see friends, watch television, read, make something. In any of these cases, what are you serving? Where are you coming from? What is your center? What is your motivation? What fires your impulse? Are you doing it to satisfy the self, or are you doing it to give away the self, to surrender the self to the truth?

It is not always clear-cut. Christ does not say, "If you are really living your life for the truth, then you never watch television." I don't think it means that, but it gets very tricky. All spiritual traditions say in some way that the self needs to be denied, desires need to be denied, and the self should be sacrificed. This is the root of asceticism, renunciation, and various kinds of disciplines. I think the rationale behind it is that as long as we serve the self that we take ourselves to be, we are automatically engaging in a perspective that eliminates the dimension of truth. We are already operating from the purely physical dimension. In other words, we are operating from the perspective that there is a separate, individual, independent self, that has a life, and has a center, and this self does things and needs things, and needs to live and subsist and develop, and so on. And the general assumption is that it lives and subsists for itself.

Christ is not saying here that the self does not exist. He says that the self should live for the truth. That's an important distinction. He is not saying that the self should not exist. No, he said the self should follow him, live for him. That is a specific understanding, in contrast to the notion that the self should just disappear, and then there will be some kind of spiritual rebirth. Christ is actually presenting an understanding of what this means. What does it mean to die? To die means to die to the self. To die to the self is to die to the concept that there is me as an individual identity, a separate entity, with its own volition, center, and life. In the spiritual perspective, *to die* means not to live from that perspective, not to live from that center. We can live from a center which is actual presence of Essence, the actual presence of God, the actual presence of the truth.

This is a subtle issue because when we say we can live a personal life, but not live it for the self, to do this selflessly, is tricky. How do you do it? To live selflessly cannot mean anything *but* to live for the truth. You cannot have a personal life for you. You cannot have a life that you think of as "my life." Yes, you will be living and doing things. But what is the center? Where is your living coming from, and what is it serving? What is it directed to? Where is it going?

We know ourselves generally as some kind of consciousness or beingness that has a center. We are some kind of self, some particular orientation, some identity. The identity is separate from other people, separate from the universe, separate from the rest of life. And we think of life as the life of that self, for that self. It is very difficult to imagine how we could live, how we could have a life that is not for that self, a life that is not lived to gratify that self.

The orientation tends to remain self-centered even when you are having a wonderful spiritual experience, even when you experience enlightenment. You are in some expanded state, and the ego disappears, and you realize that there is only one thing, one existence. Five minutes later, you are all excited about it. It happened to you. It is very important that it happened to you, not to someone else. Even though you think you lost yourself, you still refer to it as your self. But actually, if you are truly not living for the self, then this experience happening to you is just the same as if it happened to somebody else. It is just as wonderful as if it happened to you. There will not be any difference.

I am not saying that after this meeting, you could go home and live from this perspective. Not living from, and for, the self, is the ideal. It is where we want to go. That is the aim. That is living in reality. Today, we are trying to become clear about this aim, this reality, what it is we're really doing, and the implication of our Work. We need to appreciate the self-sacrifice that is going to be needed. Remember, we are not talking about sacrificing to anyone, to an organization, a teacher, school, or group. It's a matter of sacrificing to the truth, to what is real.

It is difficult for us to understand how self-sacrifice is the right way because in our cultural environment, self-sacrifice is typically understood as a way to be exploited or victimized. If someone engages in self-sacrifice, it is assumed that the person has a martyr complex, or is manipulative. It is not easy to understand how self-sacrifice can be serving the truth.

Self-sacrifice is not only a matter of serving the truth. In some sense, it is the perception of the truth. To truly perceive the truth, there must be some kind of self-sacrifice, because perceiving the truth is realizing that the truth is something bigger than the self, beyond the self, which ultimately abolishes the self. To see the truth is to see that the self does not exist in the way we think that it exists. Then we see also that a true life is not the life we have conceived of.

Self-sacrifice is not a matter of suffering. In fact, if we see self-sacrifice as painful, we are still not seeing the truth completely. It is bound to be painful for a long time. It will become less painful. After a while, self-sacrifice is an impulse that arises out of love for reality. When it becomes truly understood, it is a joyful thing to sacrifice yourself to the truth. To give up your life for the truth means to live life the way it is supposed to be for a human being. In that sense, if you give up your life, you save it.

When thinking in terms of the self, when we have a self-centered point of view, we are dominated by what the spiritual traditions call the animal soul or the carnal self—the part of us based on, and oriented toward, physical reality. Its aim is to satisfy instinctual needs, such as survival, security, pleasure, and social comfort. To satisfy the self, basically, is to satisfy those needs. But even when those needs arise, they are inseparable from the belief in a self that is separate from the rest of reality, that needs to be supported in order to survive. We generally cannot separate the body from our sense of self, of identity.

If we look at it from the perspective of nonconceptual reality, we see that the self is really a concept in the mind—an idea that we have believed for a long time. We have believed it for so long that we are convinced that it is absolute reality. This idea is based on seeing that the body is separate from other physical objects, and concluding, "I exist as a self, as an individual with instinctual needs." We find that many of our needs, if not directly instinctual, are just modifications or elaborations of, or reactions to, those basic needs. Those needs are real, but if they are what you live for, then as Christ says, you will lose your life. You will not have a true life. But if you lose your life for his sake, for the sake of truth, you will regain it.

For most of you, that would feel like the loss of your life. But what is your life? It is basically the life of your instinctual self. That is what you usually think of as your life—being concerned with how to survive in the physical world, how to have pleasure and security, how to have some social comfort and recognition, companionship, and all these things. These things are real concerns, but what Christ is saying is that to live the true life, these concerns should not be primary. They should not be the source of your actions, nor the center of your life.

The center of one's life, then, is the truth. To follow Christ is to follow the truth, and to live according to it and for it. Christ's statement is an indication of what is of value. It is also a statement about depth. If we live to satisfy our usual worldly self, we are living a superficial life, a dead life, a life without true aliveness of spirit. Aliveness of the spirit is something much deeper, more intrinsic, more fundamental, than physical life and its needs. Aliveness has nothing to do with the satisfaction of those needs.

Material needs do need to be satisfied to some extent, because we need to survive, we need to have some kind of comfort in our life *so that* we can discover what true life is.

Life is for realization, not the other way around. We don't have spiritual realization so that we can have better relationships or better jobs. We don't have spiritual realization so that we will have more or better friends, or be more successful in life. Spiritual realization is something deeper, and what Christ is saying is that if we want to follow him, it should be the center of our life. And those things—the instincts, the instinctual self—must follow the truth. To sacrifice one's life, to carry the cross, means that if it happens that your sexual, social, or preservation needs seem to be in conflict with the truth, or in competition with it, the choice should be obvious: You must abandon those needs, not just once in a while, but with consistency, daily, always.

This is what true renunciation means. You do not give up the self so that you will become saintly, or so you will become good, or so that God will reward you. You will probably not be canonized. It's more that you are choosing that the truth is important to you, that reality is important to you, that the essential life is important to you, that God is important for you. You are making a choice and doing the practical things to support that choice. It's as simple as that.

It is good to talk about this subject during the holidays, to remind us of what the Work is about. Sometimes, we tend to forget our purpose and begin to think that the Work is about working on our relationships. We want the Work to make us happier, to help us have better connections with people, to have no more problems with the boss. It is true that in the Diamond Approach, we work on these psychological things, but the aim is not to make relationships better. The aim to see the deeper truth through understanding our issues. We go through the psychological part because by understanding it, we can see the essential part, what has been hidden, because of the misunderstanding.

It is fine that when the issues are resolved, you might have a better marriage, or enjoy your job more. But that is not why we are doing the Work. If that is why you are doing the Work, then you are wanting to do psychotherapy. Psychotherapy has its place, but the Work is not psychotherapy. It is not alleviation of pain. It is not trying to make your life better. It has to do with the relationship to the truth, making truth your center. To really do the Work is to make truth the source and the aim of your life. It is to make truth your Lord, your God, who you pray to, who you sacrifice to, who you're humble to, who you serve, who you live for.

We tend to feel that if we serve the truth, this self within us is going to lose something. "If I meditate for two hours, I won't be with my friends. I'm going to miss the fun of gossiping about everybody." How often do we find ourselves in that conflict? Meditation time comes or group time comes, but there is something else you want to do, some kind of fun possibility, so that you feel you have to choose.

Being involved in work on yourself is a long struggle. That struggle is basically the Work. In time, we can come to choose the truth. Meanwhile, when we are doing the Work, we are struggling with that conflict. Is it for me, or is it for the truth? Part of that, of course, is finding out what is the truth. At the beginning we take our sense of who we are, the life we live, as the truth. We do not see the falsehood of it.

I was reading last night about the life of a Sufi woman in the 13th century, named Rabia. She was a realized woman, a saint. Before she died, three other famous Sufis went to visit her. Each one of them gave her some advice about misfortune. The first one said something like, "To really serve the truth is not to complain about misfortune because it comes from God." She said, "That sounds egoistic to me." The second one said, "To serve the truth is to be happy because that is God's will." She said, "That doesn't do it for me." So the third one said, "To serve the truth is to be grateful to God, that he thought of you and gave you misfortune." She said, "Well, I'm about to die, and that still doesn't do it for me." So they said to her, "Why don't you tell us what you think?" She said, "For me to serve the truth is to see the truth so completely that I won't even know if there is misfortune or not, I will only see the truth." You can see her love here, her expression of love. For Rabia, the truth is significant and valuable.

The more we think about it, the more we discover how difficult it is to actually live in this way, how it goes against the grain of the personality. The Christmas spirit is not a matter of just having fun. It is having fun in a certain way: It is the joy of self-sacrifice because it has to do with the love of truth. And the love of truth *is* for its own sake. We don't love truth because it's going to give us something. We love truth because we love truth. We love it because it is what is there to be loved.

Two factors contribute to our ability to live according to the truth: Perception of the truth, and willingness to sacrifice when we are aware that we do not yet perceive the whole truth. First of all, to see the truth about the self is to recognize that the self as we know it, is not as fundamental, is not as real, is not as important, as we take it to be. The self, the way we think of it, is ultimately a construct. It is a self-image based fundamentally on the body. The self-image is the most superficial part of us, the skin of who we are. When we see the truth, we recognize that our nature, the depth of our reality, is the truth itself. So to live for the truth is in some sense living for the self, but not what we think of as the self, which is the worldly self. If you see the truth, to live for self and for the truth is not two things, but one. My true self is not separate from the nature of the universe and also is not separate from your true self. It is the nature of existence. If I take an action that is real, it will serve me and you at the same time without my thinking about me or you, because the reality is the reality of all of us. So to sacrifice your life means to take real action, to do what is correct and objective. It is to do the right thing at the moment, which has nothing to do with serving you or me. It is to serve the truth that is the nature of you and me and beyond.

To give one's life to Christ means to live according to the truth, which is to live objectively and to act according to what reality is. There is not a sense of self-sacrifice when you recognize that the self you are sacrificing is not you anyway, not the depth of you. It is not your heart. It is not your center. It is not your reality. By sacrificing that self, you are in some sense gaining something much more fundamental, much more real, much more fulfilling.

After a while, you may say, "I don't want to be fulfilled. I only want God to be happy. I don't want to be happy. I just want him to be happy." So you don't pray to God, asking, "God, give me this, make me happy." You're always telling God, "Tell me what to do so I can make you happy. What will make you happy?" But the moment you think you want something for you, that's separation. Then you are living for that external self, which means you are abandoning the deeper truth.

Christ calls following him a sacrifice: taking up the cross. But if we understand the situation from the perspective of the truth, it is not a sacrifice. It is the realization of what reality is. And because it is the realization of what reality is, it is saving your life, your true life. You recognize there is no sacrifice at all because what is given up is not you anyway. The package you come in is not you. We take the package to be who we are. But the package is not important—it's what is inside that is important. The package is to serve what is inside the package. What is inside the package is more important than the package, but it needs a package. We think the package is the true self, and everything—including what's inside the package—is for the package. We believe that package, the surface part, is the self because that's what everyone believes.

Christ understands this. At the same time, He understands that although this is the objective truth, it is still difficult for human beings to act upon this truth. He says it
in a simple way that is understandable to everyone, which
is that you have to sacrifice. He used the word "sacrifice"
because that is how you will feel it, even though it is not
actually a sacrifice. Christ says, "You have to follow me."
When you follow him, you are not following anything but
yourself. But that's how you will experience it. He said, "You
have to lose your life." It is not actually a loss, but you will
experience it as one. This is why we have to be willing to
sacrifice ourselves for the truth.

For instance, you could have an experience when you are
meditating: after two hours of meditation, suddenly you
have a certain perception, and you recognize that the truth
is the center, the nature, and the value of all existence. You
might have that realization, but what does it mean to live
according to it? If you want to live according to that realization, you will be confronted with giving up your life. You
know from what you perceived that you are not giving up
your life, but when you get up from meditation, how can
you do it without giving up your life? The superficial self,
the worldly self, is still there. It is going to assert itself, and
there will be conflict. Although you had that enlightenment, you will still struggle because you are so convinced
that you are the superficial self. It's true that the understanding, the direct experience, is ultimately what is needed. But
a lot of the Work is going to be a kind of sacrifice.

The self we need to give up is not the body; it is a concept
in the mind. It is a psychological belief. But the mind cannot
distinguish that psychological belief from the body. Giving
it up will feel like the death of the body. So to live according
to the truth, we have to accept, we have to be willing to let
go of the body and the life of the body. For example, being
rich or being poor has nothing to do with living for the truth.

But because the worldly self is interested in being rich and in being comfortable and supporting its instinctual needs, you have to be willing to let go of being rich. You have to be willing to accept poverty, if it seems that that is what needs to happen for you to see and live the life of the truth.

Nothing about the truth says that you should not have a family, you should not have a lover, you should not be married. But because the worldly self is so invested in having these things, you need to be willing to sacrifice these things for the life of the truth. The worldly self is so habitually oriented towards these external satisfactions, and so identified with them, even defined by them, that we believe that to live the life of the truth must mean some kind of surrender of all these things in exchange for the truth. Surrender does not mean that you should give your money away to everyone. It means that if it comes down to it, you have to be willing to do that. When I say, "comes down to it," it has to be a genuine thing. Whenever there is the choice, the choice will be made in favor of the truth.

It is difficult to live according to objective truth because the worldly self will tend to distort it. We are partly physical—our external facade, our skin, our wrapping—is physical. But our inside gets less and less physical, more and more spiritual, and more and more the nature of Being.

We do have physical needs, and we have even deeper spiritual needs. So then, we might think there's no conflict! We can do all of that together. I can have those, and I can have these. In practice, it doesn't work that way. In practice, you have to give up the external for the internal because it is very hard to actually know that our nature is the inner reality more fundamentally than the physical. How much attention and effort should I put in the physical, how much in the spiritual? How can you know? In some sense, you can't know until you're completely integrated. There is no way to know, because the worldly self is always asserting its needs, always wanting to survive. It's always operating in your mind and affecting the way you see things. Its nature is that it just wants the instinctual satisfaction, and that's it. It is not concerned with the inner life, the spiritual life, the essential life, the life of truth, serving God or Jesus. It is simply not interested. When it comes down to it, that part doesn't even know what spiritual means. When that survival-oriented self is in charge, and you try to remember your spiritual experiences, isn't it as if they're dream images? "I wonder what that was . . ." Not only do your essential experiences not make sense, they seem irrelevant to your need to make a few bucks in the next day or so, or to look for a good piece of ass.

We need to recognize that all of us have that part, the instinctual, survival-oriented self. It's part of being human. This part functions in the physical world to help us survive. It is needed, but it wants to take over the whole show. It is supposed to be a follower, and it wants to be the master. Until it is educated and developed, its nature is always to try to be the master. But education is the whole of the Work. To understand this issue is to see the Work in a deeper way. We have explored the Work for a long time in terms of see- ing truth, objective reality. Now we are seeing it from Christ's perspective. We need to be willing to sacrifice the self-centered self because, in some sense, we can't see it any other way. For that part, the Work is a sacrifice. For that part, following Christ, the truth, is giving up life. There is no other way that that part of us can feel about it.

So our first point about this process is that we can come to see that, objectively; there is no sacrifice. There is not a giving up of one's life because the self you are sacrificing and its life do not truly exist the way you think of them. So it is not truly a sacrifice. The second factor we referred to, however, deals with the fact that it is almost impossible to live from that perspective, so subordinating our will to the will of the truth will always feel to us like a sacrifice. It will feel like being a servant to reality, like giving up one's life and one's needs and one's desires for the truth. So there will be a sense of giving up one's life, even though we are gaining the true life.

In our Work, each of us will encounter challenges; we will arrive at crossroads where we have to make changes. These challenges and crossroads will help us to develop. They will enable us to realize the life of truth. The more of those challenges we have, the more chances we have to realize the true perspective.

If your life is comfortable, if you are always getting what you want, you might think it's great. You might think, "Everything is going wonderfully. Now I can do my spiritual work." In reality, it doesn't work that way. The more comfortable you are, the less chance you have to make the choice, and the less chances you have for the choice to be clear. If everything is going fine, it will be very hard to tell what is serving the truth, and what is serving your self. It's almost impossible. So, as one Sufi said, "If there is misfortune, you should be grateful for it," because it gives you a chance to face choices between your self and the truth, a chance for you to follow the right course. I think that the Christian perspective emphasizes this understanding. It emphasizes the value of suffering, the idea of sacrifice, the significance of taking up the cross. I do not know what the fathers of the church believe, but from my perspective, following the truth is seen as suffering and sacrifice not because you need to inflict pain on yourself, but the presence of the problem gives you the chance to separate the true from the false.

St. John of the Cross talked about suffering and pain. He invited it all the time. He was happy when there was pain because it gave him a chance to give up his self for the truth. If you really want the truth, you'll be happy when there is misfortune because you will view challenges as help and guidance. In general, however, we do not need to go out of our way to ask for misfortune in our lives. Challenges are there all the time. I don't think we need to generate pain for ourselves. In the Work here, for instance, we do a lot of things that are challenging. We present you with certain challenging situations, which are actually small challenges when compared to real life problems. We might make you stay up all night long and work continuously. Sometimes a meeting goes an hour later than you expected when you have a date for 5:30. That gives you little challenges. I do that once in awhile. But that's nothing compared to the challenges that life can present to you.

When I do these things, it's not because I want to give you a hard time. That is not the idea. If I wanted to give you a hard time, there are more effective ways. The main issue, however, is not what we do in the group. The central question is how you live your own life. What are the choices you make? From which perspective do you do your work? In terms of this Work, from where do you live your life? What is the orientation? What is the aim, the purpose? What is the center? What is the motivation? What is the commitment?

Christ said, if you want to follow him, you have to leave your family, your children, your father and mother. And we have seen in our Work that the mother you need to leave is not the external mother. It is the image of your mother in your mind. Basically, you have to leave all internalized object relations, because these internalized object relations are what define your sense of self.

When it actually comes to doing the Work, however, it will feel sometimes like leaving your actual family, even though you understand that the attachment is not to your present mother. Most people are not attached to their present mothers. Many people don't even talk to their mothers. What you need to leave is your attachment to the inner mother. But the ego cannot separate the mental construct from the actual physical reality. Our mental constructs, we think, *are* physical reality. So the choice to live according to the truth will always seem to the ego to mean loss and sacrifice. I think students experience that a lot. You come to this Work expecting to gain a lot, and year after year, you lose things. There is one loss after another. After a while, people feel, "I don't know what's left."

Christ says, "Give your life to me. Sacrifice for me." We don't do it that way. I don't ask you to give your life to me. I ask you to just recognize the truth, and to give up the false. When you are willing to truly give up the external, it means you have enough love in your heart to say, "I can give up my life, all of it. I can give up my kids, my granddad, my job, my car, my reputation, my success, my future, my beauty, my accomplishments." When you really do that, when there is enough love and dedication for that to happen, what you find is that you are not left in poverty in the sense you expect.

What you find is that a huge burden falls away, and a darkness lifts. It is as if your whole life has been like a dark cloud that is lifting off—all the life that you think you had, the people around you, the houses, the cars, the involvements, the activities, the interests. But before you recognize this truth, you are afraid of losing everything. Your mind expands on the fear, and you imagine: "I am going to be sitting somewhere, sick and decrepit, with no one there to take care of me. I'm old and poor, I don't have any money, I don't have any insurance, no one loves me enough to give me any money, no one wants to talk to me, I have nowhere to go, it's cold and snowing, and I don't have enough clothes, they all have holes in them." That's the fantasy that arises in your mind. And you feel that you can't accept life on those terms.

If you really accept that you could lose everything, after a while, you realize that all the things you have given up do not truly exist in the way you thought. You don't really have a car. Nobody actually has a car. You know why? Because they're all Christ's cars. He's got all of them. If you really let go of all that you've got, that's what you will find out; that all your cars belong to Christ. All your houses belong to Christ. All your parents belong to Christ. All your kids belong to Christ. And all the activities are Christ's activities because there is only one truth. One unified total wholeness. This is what we can come to recognize. If we give up all that we think is real, we will see the truth of oneness

When that happens, it's not that you will no longer see cars. For a while, maybe the car will disappear; maybe everything will disappear. That is the death, the crucifixion. Then there will be the resurrection, when you realize everything is back, but not back the way you thought of it before. The resurrection will come about out of the annihilation, the loss of everything, including your life, including everything you see around you. If you really let go of all that, you recognize that all is gone, all is dissolved in the Absolute. From there, can arise the resurrection, which is the Christ, which is the life of Christ, in which you recognize that everything around you is life itself, is life, harmony, love, gratitude.

You regain your life. You save it, in some sense, that way. Then the body we see, we see as an expression of harmony. It is Christ's body. Everyone is Christ's body, and Christ's body is love and fullness and harmony and beauty.

The perspective of the self is that there is you, and there is me. I have a car and I drive it every day. You've got your car. You have your claim on your car, and I have my claim on my car. Yours is registered in your name, and mine is in my name. If something happens to my car, not only might I lose money, I might not even know who I am. Have you noticed that if you lose something, you get disoriented? If you lose a relationship, or your house catches fire, or your mother dies, you feel, "I don't know who I am." These things define us.

Today we have connected the perspective of letting go of mental concepts with the perspective of Christ. They actually amount to the same thing, looked at in a slightly different way. Christ's teaching is more ordinary, more human, than trying to see pure nonconceptual reality. He speaks in a way that most people can understand.

We think of the Christmas spirit as giving and sharing. What is it we are giving? If you give money or a gift, it's not necessarily a Christ kind of giving. If you are giving of yourself, if you are giving away yourself for the truth, then it is giving. If you are giving just because everybody gives, because that is what you're supposed to do at Christmas, or because giving makes you good, or you have to give because people are giving to you and you should give back, do you think it is in the spirit of Christmas? I'm sure many people do it that way. This is not really celebrating Christmas the way Christ would think of it, according to my understanding.

The Work is to see objectively what reality is, how the physical relates to the spiritual, how the outer self is related to the true self, and what the role of each one is. Practically, it means sacrificing the external to the internal. However, we interpret this giving up of the self as a sacrifice only because of our identification with the external.

About the Diamond Approach

The Diamond Approach is taught by Ridhwan teachers, ordained by the Ridhwan Foundation. Ridhwan teachers are also ministers of the Ridhwan Foundation. They are trained by the DHAT Institute, the educational arm of the Ridhwan Foundation, through an extensive seven-year program, which is in addition to their work and participation as students of the Diamond Approach. The ordination process ensures that each person has a good working understanding of the Diamond Approach and a sufficient capacity to teach it before being ordained and authorized to be a Ridhwan teacher.

The Diamond Approach described in this book is taught in group and private settings in the United States, Canada, Europe, and Australia by Ridhwan teachers. For information about the various contexts for pursuing this work, we invite you to visit www.ridhwan.org.

If you would like to explore starting a group in your area, taught by ordained Ridhwan teachers, write:

> Ridhwan
> P.O. Box 2747
> Berkeley, CA 94702-0747

For more information on the books of A. H. Almaas, go to www.ahalmaas.com. DIAMOND APPROACH and RIDHWAN are trademarks or registered trademarks of the Ridhwan Foundation.